Silvia Vianello

Online Consumer Behavior in Social Media

D1824663

Silvia Vianello

Online Consumer Behavior in Social Media

Successful Strategies to Get Engagement, Loyalty, and Sharing Behavior from Your Customers

LAP LAMBERT Academic Publishing

Impressum/Imprint (nur für Deutschland/ only for Germany)

Bibliografische Information der Deutschen Nationalbibliothek: Die Deutsche Nationalbibliothek verzeichnet diese Publikation in der Deutschen Nationalbibliografie; detaillierte bibliografische Daten sind im Internet über http://dnb.d-nb.de abrufbar.

Alle in diesem Buch genannten Marken und Produktnamen unterliegen warenzeichen-, marken- oder patentrechtlichem Schutz bzw. sind Warenzeichen oder eingetragene Warenzeichen der jeweiligen Inhaber. Die Wiedergabe von Marken, Produktnamen, Gebrauchsnamen, Handelsnamen, Warenbezeichnungen u.s.w. in diesem Werk berechtigt auch ohne besondere Kennzeichnung nicht zu der Annahme, dass solche Namen im Sinne der Warenzeichen- und Markenschutzgesetzgebung als frei zu betrachten wären und daher von jedermann benutzt werden dürften.

Coverbild: www.ingimage.com

Verlag: LAP LAMBERT Academic Publishing AG & Co. KG
Dudweiler Landstr. 99, 66123 Saarbrücken, Deutschland
Telefon +49 681 3720-310, Telefax +49 681 3720-3109
Email: info@lap-publishing.com

Herstellung in Deutschland:
Schaltungsdienst Lange o.H.G., Berlin
Books on Demand GmbH, Norderstedt
Reha GmbH, Saarbrücken
Amazon Distribution GmbH, Leipzig
ISBN: 978-3-8433-5555-1

Imprint (only for USA, GB)

Bibliographic information published by the Deutsche Nationalbibliothek: The Deutsche Nationalbibliothek lists this publication in the Deutsche Nationalbibliografie; detailed bibliographic data are available in the Internet at http://dnb.d-nb.de.

Any brand names and product names mentioned in this book are subject to trademark, brand or patent protection and are trademarks or registered trademarks of their respective holders. The use of brand names, product names, common names, trade names, product descriptions etc. even without a particular marking in this works is in no way to be construed to mean that such names may be regarded as unrestricted in respect of trademark and brand protection legislation and could thus be used by anyone.

Cover image: www.ingimage.com

Publisher: LAP LAMBERT Academic Publishing AG & Co. KG
Dudweiler Landstr. 99, 66123 Saarbrücken, Germany
Phone +49 681 3720-310, Fax +49 681 3720-3109
Email: info@lap-publishing.com

Printed in the U.S.A.
Printed in the U.K. by (see last page)
ISBN: 978-3-8433-5555-1

Table of Contents

2

Chapter 1. Introduction

The explosive diffusion of the Internet in developed countries such as the United States was accompanied by the proliferation of online communities. Today, online community can be used for a variety of social groups interacting via the Internet. Virtual consumer communities represent one of the most interesting phenomenon of the information age, not only from the point of view of social interaction but also as far as marketing management is concerned.

There has been much popular discussion of the economic potential of virtual communities, but little empirical evidence of the motivations and characteristics of their success. Achieving this potential, however, is a challenge. Successful profitable influence must achieve a harmonious interplay between the social and economic motivations of community constituents. For the community organizer, this interplay implies that marketing strategy and approach have to be designed and intended so that economic activity is embedded within, rather than merely coincident with, social interactions.

As can be noticed in figure 1. the potential for online consumer communities spirals onward and upward. In 1989, only newsgroups emerged online through Usenet. During the following years instead, for example, Classmates.com enabled old friends to get back in touch. It appeared online in 1995. IMDb is an internet movie database; started as a hobby, the IMDb gets 35 million visitors per month, attracted by 31,000 independent reviews by fellow movie lovers and a wealth of content. Contrast this with the world's biggest movie franchise, Star Wars, whose official site attracts a quarter of that number. Match.com is a Dating website. As a proven leader in online dating services, Match.com offers millions of profiles for millions of possibilities to meet "the match". The company's online dating sites and affiliated businesses span six continents, operating more than 30 dating sites in 18 local languages and supporting local currencies. BearShare is a Music sharing website. Habbo Hotel is a Graphical chat for teens. Sha-Mail is a website for sending picture and/or email through mobile handsets. This term is made from Sha, which is the front part a Japanese word Shashin meaning photograph, and Mail. Many other online consumer communities are expected to emerge in the future.

Figure 1.

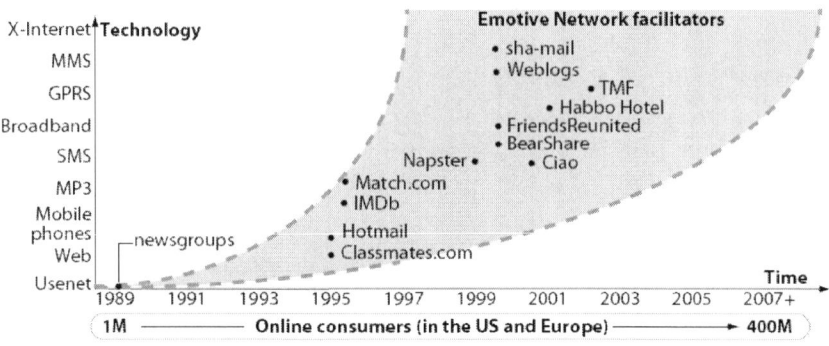

Source: Forrester Research, Inc.

Marketing researchers showed optimism expressed by studying online communities (e.g., Balasubramanian and Mahajan 2001), and suggest that online communities are only likely to grow in importance, magnitude, influence, power, and the range of activities for which they are used, as consumers become more comfortable, at ease, and adapted with these environments. Online communities deserve persistent and increasing attention from both practitioners and marketing researchers.

Additionally, virtual communities, as group of people who interact and share information online based on common interests or affiliations, offer business benefits. Community services are implemented because they attract more people to a website and keep them longer. E*Trade, for example, reported that quarterly membership growth jumped from 14 percent to 55 percent the quarter after it added a chat capability to its site.[1] eBay reported that it could attribute the growth of its 212 million users all over the world (October 2006)[2] base to the addition of chat rooms, discussion areas, and news alerts to its

---

[1] *The Real Value of Online Community*, The Yankee Group, February 2000.

[2] http://news.bbc.co.uk/1/hi/business/6064718.stm

6

site. Some benefits companies can obtain through online communities are: the revenues generation, for example through advertising and eCommerce, building their brands through sponsorships, and monitoring and gathering real-time feedback on customer needs, providing essential customer intelligence that allows them to compete effectively.

Community members may include customers, employees, distributors and resellers, suppliers and vendors, contractors, and service providers.

Online communities are not only business to consumer (B2C) interaction; they include also business-to-employee (B2E) online communities and business to- business (B2B) dealings. In B2C online communities, consumers are motivated to interact based on such factors as a common interest, product passion, hobby, and so on. In B2B and B2E communities, people interact based on a potential or existing business relationship, customer service, support needs, intra-company interaction, or the need to solve a problem or accomplish a task.

This dissertation will focus on the first type: online consumer communities. The factors that enhance member participation in business to business (B2B) virtual communities and business to employee (B2E) may be quite different from those in business to consumer (B2C).

Communities connect consumers and business people alike with broad sources of information, possibility of interaction, and eCommerce opportunities. Trading mechanisms such as eBay auctions allow people to complete transactions and close deals quickly, because consumers do not have to rely on traditional correspondence and means of communication.

Furthermore, consumer community members can save time in the decision-making process by going to other peers or experts to get information.

Sites such as Apple, Adobe, Microsoft include technical support that allow people to get answers to questions about how to use products more effectively or how to solve a specific technical problem. Instead, general advice sites such as about.com and askme.com help people get answers to questions and learn from experts. Community services may include message boards, chat, email, instant messaging. All these services help consumers get the information they need by enabling them to find and interact with other consumers and to support each other.

Communities offer user-new generated content and provide a precious resource for gathering perspectives on products and gaining insight from experts as well as from other customers. Consumers can get input that helps them make informed buying decisions. Examples include product reviews and discussion boards at Amazon, Expedia, product reviews, opinions, and advices at Epinions. Online consumer communities with message boards, email, chat, and IM offer flexible formats for sharing information, in that way facilitating the flow of knowledge among community members. Additionally, consumer communities offer a social experience, drawing people together based on leisure-time interests.

Through online consumer communities, companies can provide more personalized customer service to increase customer satisfaction and loyalty. Community services complement customer relationship management solutions by providing a positive community experience that builds customer loyalty. Community also demonstrates a company's responsiveness to customer wants and needs. Consumers are demanding community services on sites and they buy from sites that provide it.

Online consumer communities meet the need that individuals have to interact. Successful firms are encouraging online interactions, communications and relations by giving their customers, employees, and business associates a vast assortment of community services, such as message boards, newsletters, email discussions, online discussions in public chat, instant messaging as private chat, member profiles and so on. Companies are just beginning to recognize the potential of online consumer community to increase revenues and reduce costs. As this dissertation points out, companies can increase profitability, gain a competitive advantage, and enjoy greater success in the digital economy.

It becomes important and crucial to study and highlight virtual communities for many reasons and explanations. There are many motivations behind this dissertation.

First, the online community could be the new market for a business, thus many companies develop their virtual community for the purpose of commerce (Hagel III and Armstrong, 1997).

Second, the virtual community could be used for enhancing customer loyalty for a specific brand (Reichheld and Schefter, 2000; McWilliam, 2000).

Third, another important reason is the basic human need for personal relationships (Rheingold, 1992). For example, the Yankee Group reports that U.S. companies invested over $300 million in community software, implementation and management in 1999 (Meehan, 2000).

Forth, the emergence of new information and communications technologies has initiated a drastic revolution of customer-producer relationships in many businesses, with important implications for new product development (NAMBIISAN, 2002). Online customer communities could facilitate the deployment of distributed innovation models that involve wide-ranging customer roles in new product development (Holmstrom, 2001; Kambil, Friesen, & Sundaram, 1999; Prahalad & Ramaswamy, 2000). Online customer members can be involved not only in generating ideas for new products, but also in co-creating them with companies, in testing finished products (beta testers), and in providing end user product support. For example, Lego has built its success out of a relatively simple idea (plastic blocks) and recently gained a relevant market success with a robot kit called Mindstorms. So when the time came for an upgrade, they turned to their obsessed fans and rewrote the rules of the innovation game. Their fans signed a NDA, received a username and password, and was ushered to a secure online forum. They thought Lego probably needed beta testers for a Mindstorms update. Lego needed a Mindstorms User Panel, or MUP, to help with the design. "I was surprised they were so early in their development, and I think everyone else was, too," recalls Barnes, an electronics engineer from Holland Patent, New York. "We realized that our input was going to be a lot more important than we had imagined." Over the next 11 months, they were de facto Lego employees. They exchanged numerous emails with Lund (the Lego Mindstorm director) and his team. They gave ideas for new sensors, redesigned input ports, stabilized firmware. They met with Lund at Brickfest in the US, and at Lego's Denmark headquarters to hash out specs for the computer brain of Mindstorms. They had no prototype, way too early for beta testers, Lego got customers involved in the actual design of the product. The one key difference between the four panelists and actual Lego staffers was a paycheck. What did these de facto Lego employees receive for their trouble? A few Lego crane sets, Mindstorms NXT Prototype and the eternal gratitude of Lego managers! (They even paid their own airfares to Denmark). Hassenplug: "They actually want our opinion? It doesn't get much better than that." Barnes: "When I met Søren, he said he wondered why we were all doing this. I told him that if it had been any company other than Lego, I wouldn't be here."[3] This example shows the potential of voluntary sharing in online community where online customer members can be involved not only in generating ideas for new products, but also in co-creating them with companies, and in testing finished products.

Fifth, social interactions in online consumer communities are various and often multifaceted and intricate, as are the communities themselves. The characteristics of the consumers, the range of purposes they pursue, the type of governance policies they develop, and the design of the software supporting a community, vary from community to community. Online communities can vary tremendously in their social and technical structure (De Souza, C., S., Preece, J.; 2004).

Sixth, online consumer communities are dynamic, active, evolving and constantly change. Understanding what makes a community successful is consequently complicated. Technology alone does not guarantee a successful online community. Success is determined also by social factors (i.e., sociability) as well as software functionality and usability. Sometimes, sophisticated software design seems to have little impact (Maloney-Krichmar and Preece 2004).

Seventh, since online consumer communities evolve and change, many design decisions will need revisiting regularly. For example, guidelines, rules, policies and software that sustain a new community may need to be changed as the community becomes established.

Eighth, online communities can involve large groups. "Communities have strong upper limits on size, while audiences can grow arbitrarily large. Put another way, the larger a group held together by communication grows, the more it must become like an audience -- largely disconnected and held together by communication traveling from center to edge -- because increasing the number of people in a group weakens communal connection. The characteristics we associate with mass media are as much a product of the mass as the media. Because growth in group size alone is enough to turn a community into an

---

[3] http://www.wired.com/wired/archive/14.02/lego.html

audience, social software, no matter what its design, will never be able to create a group that is both large and densely interconnected."[4]

Ninth, participants in online communities are often widely distributed and may cross cultural and geographical divides. They are open to a wide variety of people. For this reason, the skills and knowledge of consumers may be very broad in some online communities. Virtual communities are provided in many countries, making them a global phenomenon. Thus, understanding online consumer behavior in communities is managerially important.

Tenth, because online consumer communities form around shared interests, they can serve to launch new products and to market existing products. This enhances the interest of management and marketing scholars in virtual communities.

Additionally, Bressler & Grantham (2000) argue that many of the future B2C commercial transactions will be conducted via virtual on-line communities, since the Internet enables millions of people worldwide to exchange information and conduct business. Internet is a truly global market place characterized by commercial transactions 24 hours a day, 7 days a week. The rate of adoption of the Internet, which has been estimated at 4,000 new users per hour, outpaces all other significant innovations in consumer technology, including the telephone, VCR, and PC. Internet World Stats has adjusted estimates of the current number of Internet users in the world to 1,076 billion people as of November 27, 2006, as can be seen in Figure 2 and 3.[5] This rapid growth has a tremendous commercial impact. Leadpile.com, a centralized online lead marketplace, says 2006 United States E-Commerce sales, defined as B2C sales of goods including auctions and travel, will top $100 Billion. This follows a report by JupiterResearch that predicts online retail sales are expected to grow from $81 Billion in 2005 to $144 Billion in 2010 only in USA.[6] As another example, The Interactive Media in Retail Group (IMRG) also found that October 2006 was the biggest ever month for online sales in the UK, with customers shelling out a record £2.7 billion.[7]

---

[4] **Source**: Clay Shirky, April 6, 2002

[5] http://www.internetworldstats.com/blog.htm
[6] http://www.ecommerce-guide.com/news/news/article.php/3598281
[7]
http://www.directtraffic.org/OnlineNews/Online_sales_to_grow_by_40_per_cent_next_year_17986709.html

Furthermore, through online consumer communities, new study has shown that online advertising is likely to take more and more of the market share from traditional media such as TV over the coming years. The study predicted that a particularly marked increase would take place next year, when budgets for online advertising are expected to rise by an average of 42 per cent compared to 2006. In terms of integrating advertising campaigns with the web, the following companies were thought to have performed the best: Dove, Burger King, Volkswagen, Honda and Nike. Magazines were thought to be the most effective method of driving consumers online. [8]

Figure 2.

WORLD INTERNET USAGE AND POPULATION STATISTICS						
World Regions	Population (2006 Est.)	Population % of World	Internet Usage, Latest Data	% Population (Penetration)	Usage % of World	Usage Growth 2000-2006
Africa	915,210,928	14.1 %	32,765,700	3.6 %	3.0 %	625.8 %
Asia	3,667,774,066	56.4 %	378,593,457	10.3 %	35.2 %	231.2 %
Europe	807,289,020	12.4 %	311,406,751	38.6 %	28.9 %	196.3 %
Middle East	190,084,161	2.9 %	19,028,400	10.0 %	1.8 %	479.3 %
North America	331,473,276	5.1 %	231,001,921	69.7 %	21.5 %	113.7 %
Latin America/Caribbean	553,908,632	8.5 %	85,042,986	15.4 %	7.9 %	370.7 %
Oceania / Australia	33,956,977	0.5 %	18,364,772	54.1 %	1.7 %	141.0 %
WORLD TOTAL	6,499,697,060	100.0 %	1,076,203,987	16.6 %	100.0 %	198.1 %

NOTES: (1) Internet Usage and World Population Statistics were updated for Nov. 27, 2006. (2) Demographic (Population) numbers are based on data contained in the world-gazetteer website. (3) Internet usage information comes from data published by Nielsen//NetRatings, by the International Telecommunications Union, by local NICs, and other other reliable sources.Copyright © 2006, Miniwatts Marketing Group. All rights reserved worldwide.

---

[8] http://www.aaf.org/news/pdf/1

Figure 3.

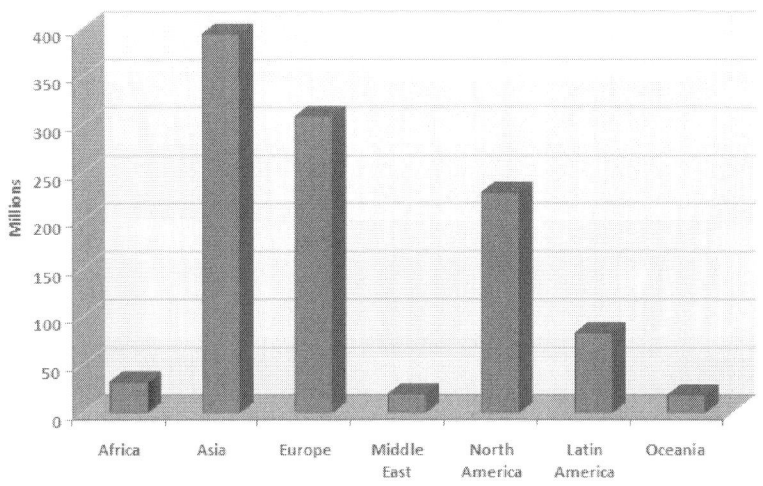

Internet Users by World Region

All these reasons gave us the motivation to study online consumer communities. In particular in the first paper we investigate two key group determinants of participation in online communities, venue interactivity and community engagement, and consider their consequences on online and offline consumer behavior. Participation should be enhanced for the community to become more successful. Since online social interactions may occur in many different internet venues in my study, involving 545 participants, we consider seven types of online venues: Email Lists, Website Bulletin Boards, Usenet Newsgroups, Instant Messaging, Web-Based Chat Rooms, Multiplayer Games, and Multi-User Domains (MUD). Interactivity is proposed as the first central variable to distinguish them and it is intended as a condition in which simultaneous and continuous communication takes place between participants. Many measures are studied by comparing statistical differences between members of high- and low-interactivity groups. As second determinant, we describe how different levels of group engagement lead to different participants' online and offline behaviors. Sets of hypotheses are theorized considering the potential similarities and differences between these two groups. The success of the manipulation is

13

determined by running an ANOVA. Our survey-based study, which was conducted across a broad range of virtual communities, highlights many significant and not obvious differences between the groups: high-and low-interactivity venues and high-and low-community engagement. Additionally, many interesting key interactions emerge and are discussed.

During the first study, we noticed that an issue deserves further investigation. In particular that a key ingredient for customer community success is active and enthusiastic contribution and participation by customers. The purpose of the second study was to find the factors that enhance member participation and sharing in business-to-customer virtual communities. In the second paper of the dissertation, we seek to better understand why consumers contribute content, and share their resources in customer communities. We make the distinction between sharing behaviors that are intrinsically motivated, and those that are spurious. We then propose a causal model detailing the antecedents of these different sharing behaviors. In the model, motivated sharing is influenced positively by identification with other members, customers' sense of personal responsibility, their overall engagement in the community, their sense of reciprocity, their belief in the sponsoring organization's principles, and beliefs that they will gain personally from sharing, and it is influenced negatively by perceptions of costs associated with making contributions to the community. Spurious sharing is influenced by economic benefits, increase in social stature and reputation enhancement. A manager of a community has to emphasize the sense of community, membership in particular, in order to enhance participation. Managerial implications include free-riding-mitigating mechanisms that can be employed in consumer communities to increase sharing behavior.

After the first study, we discovered another topic deserves further investigation and understanding: online brand communities. It is analyzed in the third paper of the dissertation, where we study firm-managed and customer-managed brand communities of many large firms such as National Instruments and Microsoft. Marketers have become more and more interested in organizing, nurturing, and monitoring such brand communities where their customers can interact with one another. Little research has examined differences between firm-managed and customer-managed brand communities. Some unanswered questions that we focus on are: do customers favor a particular type of community and are they entrenched within it? Does company involvement reduce the enthusiasm of customers? Which communities have a greater number of social interactions and are more effective in disseminating knowledge? Do these communities favor different sorts of interactions? Results, derived using Netnographic methodology, in-depth interviews and an internet-based survey, reveal among other results, considerable overlap in membership across the firm- and the customer-managed communities. They also show that firm-managed communities are employed primarily for focused, instrumental purposes whereas customer-managed communities allow more for broader "off-topic" social interactions among consumers not necessarily involving the firm's products and brands. Additionally, firms can play a meaningful role in customer-managed communities and firm-managed communities are more organized and comprehensive than customer managed communities. About technical issues or brand information people trust more the firm-managed communities, but they trust more the consumer-managed communities for people they interact with and about product reviews and for honesty of participants. There is more honest conversation in consumer-managed communities when compared to firm-managed communities. In the paper, we discuss the theoretical bases, the practical implications of results, and future research.

References

Balasubramanian, S., & Mahajan, V. (2001). The economic leverage of the virtual community. International Journal of Electronic Commerce, 5(3), 103–138.

Bressler, S. E., & Grantham, C. E. (2000). Communities of commerce. New York: McGraw-Hill.

De Souza, C., S., Preece, J. (2004). A framework for analyzing and understanding online communities. Interacting with Computers, The Interdisciplinary Journal of Human-Computer Interaction.

Hagel, J. I., & Armstrong, A. G. (1997). NetGain: Expanding markets through virtual communities. Boston: MA: Harvard Business School Press.

Holmstrom, H. (2001). Virtual communities as platforms for product development; An interpretive case study of customer involvement in online game development. Paper presented at the International Conference on Information Systems, New Orleans.

Kambil, A., Friesen, G., & Sundaram, A. (1999). Co-creation: A new source of value. Outloot Magazine, June: 23-29.

Maloney-Krichmar, D. and Preece, J. (in press) Which factors facilitate effective and meaningful support of members of an online health community? A multilevel analysis of sociability, usability and community dynamics.

Meehan, Emily. (2000). Using Online Community as a Crucial Market Intelligence Resource, Internet Market Strategies (6:13), pp 1-12.

McWilliam, Gil (2000). Building stronger brands through online communities, Sloan Management Review (41:3), pp. 43-55

NAMBIISAN S. (2002) Designing Virtual Customer Environments For New Product Development: Toward a theory, Academy of Management Review, Vol. 27, No. 3, 392-413.

Prahalad, C. K., & Ramaswamy, V. (2000). Co-opting customer competence. Harvard Business Review, 78(1): 79-87.

Rheingold, H. (1992). A slice of life in my Virtual Community, http://www.communities. com/paper/ settlmnt.html.

Reichheld, Frederick F. and Schefter, Phil (2000). E-Loyalty: Your Secret Weapon on the Web, Harvard Business Review (79:4), pp. 105-113.

Chapter 2. The Impact of Venue Interactivity and Community Engagement on Online and Offline Consumer Behavior

Abstract

In this paper we investigate two key group determinants of participation in online communities, venue interactivity and community engagement, and consider their consequences on online and offline consumer behavior. Online social interactions may occur in many different internet venues. In this empirical study involving 545 participants, we consider seven types of online venues: Email Lists, Website Bulletin Boards, Usenet Newsgroups, Instant Messaging, Web-Based Chat Rooms, Multiplayer Games, and Multi-User Domains (MUD). Interactivity is proposed as the first central variable to distinguish them and it is intended as a condition in which simultaneous and continuous communication takes place between participants. Many measures are studied by comparing statistical differences between members of high- and low-interactivity groups. As second determinant, we describe how different levels of group engagement lead to different participants' online and offline behaviors. Sets of hypotheses are theorized considering the potential similarities and differences between these two groups. The success of the manipulation was determined by running an ANOVA. Our survey-based study, which was conducted across a broad range of virtual communities, highlights many significant and not obvious differences between the groups: high-and low-interactivity venues and high-and low- community engagement. Additionally, many interesting key interactions emerge and are discussed. Paper conclusions include managerial implications and opportunities for future research.

KEY WORDS: effects of internet use, venue interactivity, community engagement, social influence, online groups

1. Introduction

Marketing researchers have always been more and more involved in many different subjects about internet interaction such as studying, learning, organizing and managing virtual communities based on virtual group of friends, unknown people or both (Bagozzi, Dholakia, & Pearo, 2004; Bagozzi & Dholakia, 2002; Balasubramanian & Mahajan, 2001; Wellman, 1999; Wellman, & Gulia 1999; Wellman, Salaff, Dimitrova, Garton, Gulia, & Haythornthwaite, 1996).

Researchers' efforts are concentrated on both online and offline internet social functions and influences (Flanagin & Metzger, 2001; Spears et al., 2002; Shah, McLeod, & Yoon, 2001). Through the Web, social interaction is encouraged in many different venues such as Email Lists, Website Bulletin Boards, Usenet newsgroups, Instant Messaging, Web-Based Chat Rooms, Multiplayer Games, and Multi-User Domains (MUD) (Bagozzi, Dholakia, & Pearo 2006; Catterall & Maclaran, 2001; for different ways to run online communities see e.g. Williams, & Cothrel, 2000). People socialize online for many different purposes, reasons, or uses, for example to discuss about ideas or generate new ideas, with many different motivations and intentions, to get information, to learn, to work, to be entertained and so on. Many authors are interested in causes and consequences of this social interaction on the Internet (i.e. Bagozzi, Dholakia, & Pearo, 2006; McKenna & Bargh, 1999) and in motivational antecedents, constituents and consequences of virtual community identity (i.e. Dholakia & Bagozzi, 2004; Sassenberg, 2002). Online group interactions influence participants in many ways; researchers are beginning to understand how participants' ideas, judgments, attitudes, and decisions might change interacting in a group online. It could influence their decisions and relationships and, on a regular basis, it could be a high time-consuming activity (McKenna, Green, & Gleason, 2002). Marketing and social scientists are fascinated in understanding how this time consuming group interaction influence other offline activities, such as using other communication media, visiting, talking and going out with family and friends, activities with neighbors and hobby groups, reading fictions and not fiction books, and renting videos and DVDs (e.g., Bagozzi, Dholakia, & Pearo, 2006; Dholakia & Bagozzi, 2004; Kraut et al., 1998; 2002; The UCLA Internet Report, 2003).

The goal of this research is to contribute to the growing curiosity and comprehension concerning online group interactions (e.g., Bagozzi, Dholakia, & Pearo, 2006; Dholakia & Bagozzi, 2004; McKenna & Bargh, 1999; Spears et al., 2002; Kraut et al., 2002; Burnett 2000) in many ways. First, we seek to better understand how involving in online social interactions relates to the member's online and offline social behavior. Second, we point out similarities and differences in participants online and offline social behavior if interactions occur in high or low interactivity venues. Third, we identify similarities and differences in users' online and offline social behavior if there is high engagement with the group or if the engagement is not so high. Our contribution is to the promising literature on the effects of Internet use for group interactions (e.g., Bagozzi, Dholakia, & Pearo, 2006; Dholakia & Bagozzi, 2004; Flanagin & Metzger, 2001; Kraut et al., 2002; Shah et al., 2001; The UCLA Internet Report, 2003) through the study of specific differences between online group participants.

Set of hypotheses were developed adapting a previous model (Figure 1. See appendix) (Bagozzi, Dholakia, Pearo, 2005) derived from earlier theoretical frameworks, a social psychological model (Bagozzi & Lee, 2002), which introduces critical social influence variables that communication researchers (e.g., Postmes, et al., 2000) and social psychologists (e.g., Kelman, 1974; Tajfel, 1981) have identified as important in explaining intentional behaviors; the Theory of Planned Behavior (TPB, Ajzen 1991; see Hunter & Allen, 1992, for an application), and the Model of Goal-directed Behavior (MGB, Perugini & Bagozzi, 2001), both focus on individual-level constructs, to study online social interactions in 7 different venues.

2. Paper structure

The structure of the paper is the following. Studying the impact of group participation on consumer behavior within virtual venues, sets of hypotheses are divided in two sets. In the first set the differences between high- and low-interactive groups are considering to test a number of its key behavioral online and offline outcome consequences (see next section for discussion about interactivity in virtual communities). In the second set, the differences between high- and low-engagement with the group of friends on Internet are examined (see section "second set of hypotheses" for further discussion about engagement in virtual communities).

Statistical analysis of a data set normally involves testing not only a single hypothesis, but rather many. For any particular test, we assign a pre-set probability $\alpha=0.05$ of a type-1 error (i.e., a false positive, rejecting the null hypothesis when in fact it is true). This means that roughly one out of every twenty such tests will show a false positive. This is the problem of multiple comparisons. We would like to control the false positive, for this reason we considered two similar sets of hypotheses with two different but analogous independent variables, venue interactivity and community engagement. Both the independent variables are key group determinants of participation in online communities.

Subsequently, the used method to study hypotheses is explained: subjects and procedure, measures and type of analyses. Next, results are reported to verify if hypotheses are supported. Additionally, many interesting key interactions are discussed. In conclusion, implications for marketing and future research opportunities are discussed.

3. Interactivity of online venues

Online social interactions may occur in many different Internet venues. In our empirical study as suggested by many authors (Bagozzi, Dholakia, & Pearo 2006; Catterall & Maclaran, 2001), we consider seven different types of online venues: Email Lists, Website Bulletin Boards, Usenet newsgroup, Instant Messaging, Web-Based Chat Rooms, Multiplayer Virtual, Multi-User Domains (MUD).

Interactivity is proposed as the central variable to distinguish them and it is intended as a condition in which simultaneous and continuous communication take place between participants. Successive messages consider both preceding messages and the manner in which previous messages were reactive (Burgoon, et al., 2002; Rafaeli & Sudweeks, 1996).

Many differences in these seven online venues establish the degree of interactivity. First, the synchronicity of communication defined as the capability of a venue to enable a response to be formulated and delivered in real time, and for a real-time dialogue to occur

(Burgoon et al., 2002). Instant Messaging, Web-Based Chat-Rooms, Networked Video Games, and MUDs enable synchronous communications; the others such as Email lists, Website Bulletin Boards, and Usenet Newsgroups, only permit asynchronous communication. Other two important attributes of interactivity are contingent communication and mutuality (Burgoon et al., 2000; Burgoon et al., 2002), both characteristics are present in the four venues allowing synchronize communication.

Contingent communication begins when a person sends a signal to another person: these signals are usually both verbal and non-verbal signals (facial expressions, body movements and gestures, tone of voice, timing and intensity of response, etc.). The second person needs to recognize the signal, interpret it correctly, and send back a signal to the first one. The second person' intervention is dependent on previous ones. The non-verbal messages are the most important for contingent communication. It can be implemented using a web cam, for example in Instant Messaging and Web-Based Chat Room. This phenomenon is increasing, in facts in a recent survey (December 2005), "Pew Internet and American Life Project" shows that 19% of online men and 13% of online women use a web cam.

Mutuality is instead used to describe a reciprocal relationship in which users perceive and create a sense of harmonization, connection, union, interdependence, coordination, and understanding each other. The four synchronous communication venues allow higher levels of contingent communications and mutuality.

Second, Lombard (2001) describes three characteristics regarding the possibilities that users have in modifying the environment: the number of inputs the venue accepts, the number of environmental attributes that can be modified by the participant, and the range of responses possible for each of these attributes. Considering these criteria, Email Lists, Bulletin Boards, and Usenet Newsgroups, where participants may only input text, are the least interactive. Within Instant Messaging and Web-Based Chat-Rooms, participants have control over the text input, over the target of their response, its timing (Lombard, 2001; Trevino & Webster, 1992), and, dependently upon their willingness, they can see each other using a web cam, indicating much more interactivity. Within networked video games and MUDs, participants also have control over the representations of their characters and their movements.

According to all the above considerations, the first three venues -- Email lists, Website Bulletin Boards, and Usenet Newsgroups -are classified as low-interactivity venues, while the remaining four - Instant Messaging, Web-Based Chat-Rooms, Networked Video Games, and MUDs - are considered high-interactivity venues. This classification is used to study differences in online social interactions and their consequences. The degree of interactivity significantly and systematically influences both processes and outcomes of communication within the venue (Burgoon et al., 2002).

4. Internet venues

The first type, Email Lists are focused mailing lists to exchange messages on a predetermined particular topic of interest. Messages posted can come to members individually or in groups called digests. If the Email List is open anyone can join; otherwise only with invitation. Messages may or may not be edited by a list moderator in advance. It is often used to distribute widespread announcements to a large group of people, for example by firms to maintain customer relationship. When a message is posted, each member receives a copy and may choose to read, respond, or ignore that message (For a further discussion of internet venues: Dholakia et al, 2004; Catterall & Maclaran, 2001).

The second type is Website Bulletin Boards, or BBS, Bulletin Board Systems. The term BBS is used to refer to any online forum or message board. BBS are also commonly referred to as Internet Forums, Web Forums, Message Boards, Discussion Boards, and Discussion Groups. They are usually company-sponsored venues that host on-going discussions regarding a particular subject or a variety of issues. Upon registering, participants can post, read, and respond to messages within the Bulletin-Board as well as for publishing articles, downloading software, playing games and many more things using a single application. Common areas for Forum themes are for example: technology, computer games, and politics but there are forums for a huge amount of different topics.

The third type is <u>Usenet Newsgroups</u>. There are currently well over 100,000 Usenet newsgroups, but only 28,000 or so are still active to which subscription is free. [9] A Newsgroup is usually a discussion group for messages posted from many users at different locations. Newsgroups are technically distinct from, but functionally similar to, discussion Forums. Newsreader software is used to read newsgroups. <u>Weblogs</u> have replaced some of the uses of newsgroups. These Usenet Newsgroups have different arguments including: computer-related topics, Usenet, scientific subjects, recreational activities, socializing and discussion of social issues, religion and politics, miscellaneous discussion, and "alternative" topics or "Anarchists, Lunatics and Terrorists" as a major class of newsgroups in Usenet.

The fourth type of online venue included is <u>Instant Messaging</u> computer program such as ICQ, AIM (AOL instant messaging), MSN, Yahoo, Skype. It is a global Internet service which allows subscribers to see when people on their contact "buddy list" are on the Internet at the same time as themselves, then calls them up and "chat" with them by typing real-time, two-way messages on their computer, or even by voice over the Net (VoIP). Whereas chat rooms can have many people chat all at once, instant messenger allow chatting one to one with another person or creating a conference with many contacts.

The fifth type of venue are <u>Web-Based Chat Rooms</u>, such as IRC, AOL, Excite, MSN, and many P2P programs, where interactions about a common interest between participants occur in real-time on a website. People can talk by broadcasting messages to people on the same Forum. Participants never know who is going to be reading their messages or responding to them. Sometimes they are moderated either by limiting who is allowed to speak, blocking access to someone, or by having moderation volunteers controlling the venue watching for troublemaking or undesirable behavior. Some visual chat rooms also incorporate audio and video communications, so that users may see and hear each other.

The sixth type of venue we considered is <u>Multiplayer Virtual Games</u>, they are real time computer role-playing game <u>(CPRS)</u> wherein players can play by simultaneously

---

[9] Data provided by (http://www.rtnda.org/resources/wiredweb/appendixd.html) and by http://en.wikipedia.org/wiki/Newsgroup or for a good list of newsgroups ftp://ftp.isc.org/pub/usenet/CONFIG/newsgroups It is impossible to get a list of all groups because some have been created on only one server. Usenet is too decentralized for that.

logging online together. People can play the same game at the same time. During game-play, players normally engage in lively conversations regarding the game as well as other topics. Examples included Dungeon Siege, Guild Wars, Star Wars and Neverwinter Nights.

Finally, the seventh online social interaction venue in our study is <u>Multi-User Dungeon</u> or sometimes <u>Domain (MUDs)</u>, where participants adopt identities and role play in games, or engage in work-related communal interactions in real time. MUD is a multi-player computer game that combines elements of role-playing games, hack and slash style computer games, and instant messaging. Typically running on a Bulletin Board System or Internet Server, the game is usually text driven, where players read descriptions of rooms, objects, events, other characters, and computer-controlled creatures or non-player characters (NPCs) in a virtual world. Most MUDs are run as hobbies and are free to players; some may accept donations or allow players to "purchase" in-game items. Examples included Avatar, Wheel of Time, and Xyllomer (For further discussion about MUD see: Dholakia et al, 2004; Wellman et al., 1996).

5. First set of hypotheses: high- and low-interactivity venues

After developing a theory of consumer participation in virtual communities to explain why consumers participate in them (Dholakia et al., 2004), we assume that community participation should exert influence on its members both in external activities and in online behavior.

For this purpose, we split our dataset in two groups to compare differences and analogies. In the first group, we included low-interactivity venues participants: E-mail List, Web Site Bulletin Board or Usenet Newsgroups users. In the second group participants belong to high-interactivity venues: Instant Messaging, Web-Based Chat-Rooms, Networked Video Games, or MUDs. We conducted these analyses to verify and to better understand specific effects and differences across low and high interactivity groups. Many measures were studying by comparing statistical differences between members of high- and low-interactivity groups (See Table 1. in Appendix).

5.1 We intentions to participate in online social interactions: past behavior and participation behavior

An expected emerging difference in the high- and low-interactivity groups is "we-intentions", defined as a "commitment of an individual to engage in joint action and involves an implicit or explicit agreement between the participants to engage in that joint action" (Tuomela, 1995, p. 9; see Bagozzi & Dholakia, 2002 and Bagozzi, Dholakia & Pearo for detailed discussions). Since the study is about consequences of online social groups' interaction, the focus is a conjoint intention rather than one's self. Intention synchronization is not required; participants might perform their respective intentions at a different point of time, but they should be involved in coordinated activities. We-intentions, also called collective intentions or shared intentions (e.g., Bratman, 1993; 1997; Searle, 1990; Tuomela, 1995, 2000), are distinct from personal intentions, defined as the "person's motivation in the sense of his or her conscious plan to exert effort to carry out a behavior" by him or herself alone (Eagly & Chaiken, 1993, p. 168). Instead, we-intentions are intended as an engagement participation in mutually endeavors with other people and intentions are formed with reference to the group of friends. The shared awareness to "belong" to the group provides the motivation to interact. We expect that the degree of we-intention is different for high- and low-interactivity venues, because of a stronger sense of belongingness typical of high interactivity activities in groups, where participants are more inclined to refer themselves as "us" instead of "I". Based on the above considerations:

Hypothesis 1a: Greater levels of interactivity lead to stronger We-Intentions to interact with on the Internet as a group.

Recent researches showed a strong impact of frequency of past behavior on both intentions and future behavior (Oullette & Wood, 1998), and proposed a partition of the effects of past behavior into frequency and regency effects (Bagozzi & Warshaw, 1990; Bagozzi & Dholakia, 2002). High interactivity venues are expected to show higher levels of online participation since, as discussed above, the degree of involvement is stronger. Our prediction regards both higher level of past and present behavior participation as well as the average duration of each interaction.

Hypothesis 1b: Higher levels of interactivity lead to stronger currently and past online participation behavior both for average number of interactions and average time spent each interaction with the group of friends.

5.2 Group norms and mutual behaviors

Another predictable significant difference between high- and low- interactivity venues is for the social influence variable "group norms", intended as a process of internationalization (Kelman, 1974). This internationalization could take place ex-ante or ex-post. Ex-ante when a member enthusiastically explore online venues to find out which group fits personal moral values, principles, interests, goals, dreams, ideas, attitudes, and so on (McKenna at al, 2002). Ex-post when internationalization occurs through ongoing interactions, participants adapt to previous existing or recently formed group norms (e.g., see Postmes, et al., 2000; Spears, et al., 2002 for a review). We expect that a different degree of group norms is present between the two groups and, based on the definition of group norms and levels of interactivity, we hypothesize:

Hypothesis 2a: Higher levels of interactivity lead to stronger group norms.

Assuming stronger group norms for the high interactivity group, as a direct consequence another difference might emerge among members' consensus concerning if, when and how to engage in online social interactions. Group norms should promote mutual behaviors such as mutual agreement, commitment, accommodation, support and liking. Mutual agreement refers to specific details of interaction with on the internet as a group. Mutual commitment to a group-interaction promise. Mutual accommodation to a members' inclination to organize own schedule, time and place preferences in order to facilitate interaction. Mutual support to willingness to help behavior to do whatever it takes to make an interaction possible. Mutual liking to how much each member likes other members and the group as a whole. Based on previous hypotheses and this discussion:

Hypothesis 2b: Higher levels of interactivity lead to stronger mutual behaviors. In particular higher level of:

i. Mutual agreement among each of the members of the group to interact with on the internet as a group and stronger agreement of the whole group.

ii. Mutual commitment of members to interact with on the internet as a group and stronger commitment of the whole group.

iii. Mutual support or help other members to do whatever it takes to facilitate interacting together on the internet as a group and stronger inclination of the whole group to help others.

iv. Mutual liking between participants.

Mutual behaviors may lead to social, cognitive, and affective social identity.

Social identity is a primary component of group attachment, composed by three different but inter-correlated dimensions: cognitive awareness of group members, affective commitment to the group and evaluative significance of group membership (Bergami & Bagozzi, 2000; Ellemers, Kortekaas, & Ouwerkerk, 1999; Hogg & Abrams, 1988).

Cognitive component concerns evaluations about similarities to in-group members and dissimilarities to out-group members (see Bagozzi, Dholakia, Pearo, 2005, for a discussion). When a person is actually part of the group and engages in group activities, group membership may or may not produce overlap between personal identity and group identity.

Affective social identity to the group is the effect of two senses of emotionality: the attachment to the group intended as positive feelings toward the group, and feeling of belongingness to the group (Bagozzi & Lee, 2002).

Evaluative significance of group membership is the result of group-based self-esteem (Bergami & Bagozzi, 2000) or collective self-esteem (Luhtanen & Crocker, 1992). It is formed by: valuable membership and importance of membership (Bagozzi & Lee, 2002).

As a result we expect that:

Hypothesis 2c: Higher levels of interactivity lead to stronger

i. Cognitive social identity

ii. Affective social identity

iii. Evaluative social identity

5.3 Anticipated emotions

Anticipated emotions are defined as "pre-factual" (Gleicher et al. 1995, p.284) appraisal, when the individual imagines the emotional consequences of both achieving and not achieving a goal, or enacting and not enacting a behavior (Bagozzi, Dholakia, & Pearo, 2005; Bagozzi, Baumgartener, & Pieters, 1998). We predict a significant difference in anticipated emotions for high- and low-interactivity venues. We expect that stronger forward-looking positive emotions will result when a person is participating in a high interactivity venue, where high interaction may lead to stronger emotional reactions if a successful interaction happens. Specifically, we hypothesize:

Hypothesis 3a: Higher levels of interactivity lead to stronger positive anticipated emotions such as to feel relief, contentment, excited, delighted, happy, glad, satisfied, proud, and self-assured if a person is able to interact with on the internet as a group.

Hypothesis 3b: Higher levels of interactivity lead to stronger negative anticipated emotions such as angry, frustrated, guilty, ashamed, sad, disappointed, depressed, worried, uncomfortable, anxious, agitated, and nervous if a person is unable to interact with on the Internet as a group.

5.4 Offline behavioral outcomes of online social interactions

Another interesting opportunity is to seek out how online participations influence other offline activities. We are interested in discover how mass-media use changes after enrolling in social online group interactions. Activities as watching TV, listen to the radio, read print publications as newspapers and magazines, read books, talk at the phone, use of email and web were included in our study. As a general topic, it has been explored by many authors (e.g. Flanagin & Metzger, 2001; Kraut et al., 2002; Shah et al., 2001; The UCLA Internet Report, 2003), and our contribution is devoted to the study of specific functional changes and consequences of mass media use, especially if a person is involved in a high interactivity venue. By pointing out with an ANOVA analysis differences between high- and low- interactivity venues, we intend to discover how different type of internet involvements might effectively impact group members' offline personal lives.

Hypothesis 4a: Higher levels of interactivity imply a lower use of other communication media such as television, radio, newspapers, magazines, books, telephone.

Hypothesis 4b: Higher levels of interactivity imply a higher use of email and web.

Hypothesis 4c: Higher levels of engagement lead to low activities with family and friends.

5.5 Value perception measures: Purposive value-Self discovery value-Maintaining interpersonal interconnectivity-Social enhancement value-Entertainment value

Purposive value is defined as "the value derived from accomplishing some pre-determined instrumental purpose (including giving or receiving information) through virtual community participation" (Bagozzi, Dholakia, & Pearo, 2004, p. 244). Purposive value concerns on connecting one's self to external objects or issues.

Self discovery value entails understanding and deepening relevant attributes, aspects, preferences, and qualities of one's self through social interaction with the group of friend. Self discovery value concerns to intrinsic values.

Maintaining interpersonal interconnectivity is a value perception regarding social benefits derived from establishing relationships and keeping in touch with other people, such as social support, friendship, familiarity, understanding, closeness and intimacy.

Social enhancement value involves benefits gained from acceptance, recognition, and approval of other members, and the enhancement of one's social status within the group on account of one's contributions to it (Baumeister, 1998). It is a result from the need of recognition by other group members (Hars & Ou, 2002).

Entertainment value is the reward obtained from fun and relaxation through interaction with the group of friends playing, talking, relaxing, gossiping, and passing time when bored.

Hypothesis 5: Higher levels of interactivity lead to stronger use of online group of friend and/or the Internet for satisfying needs such as:

5a. Purposive value

5b. Self discovery value

5c. Maintaining interpersonal interconnectivity

5d. Social enhancement value

5e. Entertainment value

5.6 Attitudes and Perceived behavioral control

Even if they are usually considered to be a function of individual, in our study for attitudes we refer to "attitudes in social action" and not as "an individual action", since we are considering group interactions (see Bagozzi & Lee, 2002, for further discussion). In this context attitudes refer to present and future willingness to interact together on the Internet with the group of friends and they are measured by 7-point semantic differential scales such as foolish-wise, harmful-beneficial, bad-good, punishing-rewarding (see Table 1. for measures discussion).

We hypothesize the following:

Hypothesis 6a: Higher levels of interactivity lead to stronger positive attitude toward interacting together on the internet with the group.

Furthermore, interactivity should be a crucial variable to differentiate groups through expected perceived behavior control, since the control over interaction is expected to be higher if group connections and relations are stronger. By default, highly involved group members should consider easier and unproblematic online interaction opportunities with the group of friends. In the theory of planned behavior (TPB), person's perception of behavioral control is how easy or difficult performing a behavior is considered to be (Ajazen, 1991). In our study, we consider interactivity on the internet with the group of friends the target behavior. High interactivities are characterized by stronger desires to interact for both self's desire and group's desire. As a straightforward consequence, perceived behavioral control should be stronger for this group.

Hypothesis 6b: Higher levels of interactivity lead to stronger perceived behavioral control over interacting together on the internet with the group.

5.7 Subjective norms

The subjective-norms concept derives from the Theory of Planned Behavior (TPB), where it is theorized as a reflection of others' expectations (Ajzen, 1991). It could be seen as a need of others' support, approval and consent, a concept called "compliance" in Kelman (1974). People search for external and explicit confirmations of permission in own activities such as online group interactions. The expectation of significant others may concern family members, relatives or friends and they might or might be not part of the online group.

Hypothesis 7: Higher levels of interactivity lead to stronger subjective norms.

6. Second set of hypotheses: High- and Low-Engagement in online venues

Venues online engagement may be defined as a mutual agreement, promise or commitment made in advance among each member of the group to help and share interests, values, and principles in venues' activities through group identification. It is an intrinsic motivation to interact, team up and cooperate with group members. As a fundamental result, group engagement will lead overlap between own self-identity and group-based identity (Algesheimer, Dholakia, & Herrmann, 2005). Furthermore, stronger engagement is likely with greater degrees of conspicuous participation within the community (e.g., Langerak et al. 2003).

An individual show group-online engagement if affective, evaluative and cognitive social identities are strong and if group we-intentions and personal desires to interact are strong.

We describe how different levels of group engagement lead to different participants' values and characteristics. To understand virtual community participants' motivations, purposes and intentions, we study similarities and the differences between the following two groups. In the first group, we consider people highly engaged in their online group. Instead, in the second group people not engaged.

Sets of hypotheses were theorized considering the potential differences and were tested with a survey created for the study. The success of the manipulation was determined by running an ANOVA.

A median split was used to separate participants into high and low engagement with the group based on summed measure as explained above, including we-intentions and desires to interact (Mantel & Kardes, 1999).

6.1 Mutual behaviors and Cognitive-Affective-Evaluative Social identity

Similarly to the other set of hypotheses, engagement-level through group norms is hypothesized to show significant differences in mutual behaviors. Based on previous discussion, we theorize the following:

Hypothesis 1a: Higher levels of engagement lead to:

i. Mutual agreement among each of the members of the group to interact with on the internet as a group and stronger agreement of the whole group.

ii. Mutual commitment of members to interact with on the internet as a group and stronger commitment of the whole group.

iii. Mutual accommodation to accommodate or adjust to the needs of the others in the group so as to choose a time and place to interact together on the internet and stronger accommodation of the whole group.

iv. Mutual support or help other members to do whatever it takes to facilitate interacting together on the internet as a group and stronger inclination of the whole group to help others.

v. Mutual liking between participants.

As in the first set of hypotheses, mutual behaviors may lead to social, cognitive, and affective social identity. In particular we hypothesize the following:

Hypothesis 1b: Higher levels of engagement lead to stronger

i. Cognitive social identity

ii. Affective social identity

iii. Evaluative social identity

6.2 Past behavior, participation behavior and value perception measures

As discussed for the other set of hypotheses, we expect a significantly difference effect for each level of engagement both for past behavior and participation behavior. Specifically, we hypothesize that:

Hypothesis 2a: Higher levels of engagement lead to stronger online participation both for number of interactions and average time spent each interaction.

We also expect a significantly different use of groups and Internet in general for personal need satisfaction (see Table 1. for detailed discussions of needs included in the study). We hypothesize:

Hypothesis 2b: Higher levels of engagement lead to stronger use of online group and the Internet in general for satisfying needs: Purposive value-Self discovery value-Maintaining interpersonal interconnectivity-Social enhancement value-Entertainment value.

6.3 Anticipated emotions

Since we assume the desire to interact is stronger and the regret in case of no interaction could be greater, different levels of engagement may influence positive and negative anticipated emotions:

Hypothesis 3a: Higher levels of engagement lead to stronger positive anticipated emotions such as to feel Relief, Contentment, Excited, Delighted, Happy, Glad, Satisfied, Proud, Self-assured.

Hypothesis 3b. Higher levels of interactivity lead to stronger negative anticipated emotions such as Angry, Frustrated, Guilty, Ashamed, Sad, Disappointed, Depressed, Worried, Uncomfortable, Anxious, Agitated, and Nervous if a person is unable to interact with on the internet as a group.

6.4 Attitudes and Perceived behavioral control

Similarly to the first set of hypotheses, we hypothesize the following:

Hypothesis 4a: Higher levels of engagement lead to stronger positive attitude toward interacting together on the internet with the group.

Furthermore, engagement should be a crucial variable to differentiate groups through expected perceived behavior control, since the control over interaction is expected to be higher if group connections and relations are stronger. We assume that:

Hypothesis 4b: Higher levels of engagement lead to stronger perceived behavioral control over interacting together on the internet with the group.

6.5 Subjective norms

Also in this set of hypotheses, we assume that:

Hypothesis 5: Higher levels of engagement lead to stronger subjective norms.

6.6 Offline behavioral outcomes of online social interactions

As already discussed for the other set of hypotheses, another interesting possibility is to point out how online participations influence other offline activities. We are interested in discovering how mass-media use changes if the level of engagement in online group is high. Activities as watching TV, listen to the radio, read print publications as newspapers and magazines, read books, talk at the phone, use of email and web for not email purpose were included also in this part of the study. By pointing out differences between high and low engagement, we intend to determine how different types of internet involvements might effectively impact group members' offline personal lives. Based on this discussion:

Hypothesis 6a: Higher levels of engagement imply a lower use of other media such as television, radio, newspapers, magazines, books, and telephone.

Hypothesis 6b: Higher levels of engagement imply a higher use of email and web.

Hypothesis 6c: Higher levels of engagement lead to low activities with family and friends.

7. Method

Participants and Procedure

A total of 545 active virtual community members participated in this research. For "active", we consider currently direct participation on a regular basis in one of the 7 venues. We used the screening condition that respondents had to engage in participation in an internet- based group such as an interactive group or non-interactive group.

Data were collected by conducting an internet-based survey, which was publicized by contacting approximately 75 organizers and administrators of popular online venues for each of the 7 categories. The organizers or administrators informed their membership about the survey, and encouraged them to participate by visiting a website where we had placed the survey. We need to point out that the use of this internet-based survey does not permit us to assess response rates, since we cannot determine how many potential respondents were reached through our website. Thus the nature and extent of response bias are unknown. Nevertheless, as the number of specific instances of groups from each venue and the total sample are large, we think that the convenience sample is relevant for testing hypotheses, although we cannot make any conclusions as to generalizability.

The study was introduced as an "Opinion Survey-Group Interactions on the Internet". First, participants selected the Internet-based group interactions that they most frequently engage in. Second, where they interact the most with the same group of people, such as real-life friends, family members, co-workers, or internet-only friends. In the rest of the survey, they were asked questions pertaining to the one type of group interaction that they chose. We also provided a space to describe the group interaction that they chose in more detail. The most frequently mentioned chat room and mailing was Yahoo, followed by Hotmail (MSN). Participants were then asked to imagine that they were logging on to the Internet to engage in the group that they described where they have a number of friends within that group that they regularly interact with. They were asked to picture briefly in their mind the name and image of each online friend then to write their first name and friends' first names. They might include up to, but not necessarily, 5 group members.

Details of the measures are provided in Table 1 (see appendix).

Measures of participation behavior were collected by emailing respondents approximately two weeks later, as described below. As an incentive for participating in the study, two randomly selected participants got the opportunity to donate $250 each to their favorite charity. At time 2, the sample was 465.

Sample Characteristics

Table 2 provides details of the sample for each of the online venues. Since we realized that only six individuals had responded for the networked video-games venue, these responses were therefore combined with the MUDs sub-sample and are reported in that category in Table 1. Respondents ranged in age from 18 to 79 years, with a mean age of 33.1 years (median = 30, SD=13.43). While 387 (71%) were US residents, the other 29% belonged to a total of 27 other countries. Canada (n = 42, 7.7%), Australia (n = 23, 4.2%), and Germany (n = 21, 3.9%) were the three next largest sub-groups, by nationality, represented in the sample.

These are some examples of the online venues represented in the sample. Among email lists participants, the Michelle Kwan fan-club, the ASCFG-L list for professionals in the specialty cut-flower business, the ACCESS-L list discussing issues pertaining to the Microsoft Access computer software, the Internet Bonsai Club, and the Texas Archaeological Society's mailing list, were all represented. The website bulletin-boards represented in our survey included the Ultimate Rollercoasters web-forum, the Salon table-talk, X-files fan forum, and the Cultural Diffusion Board. Members of the rec.arts.bodyart, rec.art.dance, alt.religion.christian.episcopal, rec.arts.disney-parks, and alt.guitar.amps Usenet newsgroups also all participated in our survey. For high-interactivity venues, the IRC (Internet Relay Chat), AOL Instant Messenger, Microsoft Messenger, Yahoo Messenger, and ICQ were all represented within the real-time online-chat system sub-sample. Members of the Barliman's chat-room at TheOneRing.net, the Park teens lobby, "The Pork" community and chat-rooms at Yahoo.com and Excite.com all participated in the study within the <u>web-based real-time chat-rooms</u> sub-sample. Finally, the <u>MUDs</u> represented in this sample included Porta Unica, Another World, Mozart, Aurealan Realms, Nexus Kingdom of the Winds, Xyllomer, Alexandria, and Avatar.

Table 2. <u>Descriptive statistics for samples from the six internet venues</u>

Internet Venue	Sample Size	% Female Respondents	% Male Respondents	Average Age	Average Years of Internet Use
Email lists	158	57.0%	40.5%	43.9 (13.24)*	7.8 (4.00)
Bulletin-boards	68	32.4%	63.2%	31.5 (12.7)	6.3 (3.9)
Usenet newsgroups	39	28.2%	66.7%	37.9 (13.4)	8.7 (4.7)
Real-time online-chat systems	51	62.7%	35.3%	27.7 (8.4)	7.4 (3.1)
Web-based chat-rooms	35	57.1%	40.0%	28.7 (10.1)	7.00 (3.1)
Multi-user domains (MUDs)[1]	192	27.6%	67.7%	25.8 (8.3)	7.6 (3.1)
Total	545	41.8%	54.3%	33.1 (13.4)	7.5 (3.6)

ANOVA analyses

We conducted One-way Analysis of Variance (ANOVA) on our dependent variables as described by measures to test our hypotheses.

One-way ANOVA tests allow a researcher to determine if one given independent variable, such as interactivity and engagement, has a significant effect on user offline and online behavior across *any* of the groups under study. A significant p-value resulting from a one-way ANOVA test would indicate that a dependent variable (see Table 1. for a complete list) is differentially expressed in at least one of the groups analyzed. ANOVA analysis test main effects.

There are two assumptions underlying the ANOVA technique. First, it is assumed that within each group to be compared the data follow a Normal distribution. Second, it is assumed that these Normal distributions share a common standard deviation (SD). Nevertheless, ANOVA is robust against violations of these assumptions, at least where all groups are of roughly equal size as in our study (Tabachnick et al., 1983). ANOVA is performed in two stages. First stage is an analysis to see if any differences exist. If it seems there may be differences, the second stage is to identify the nature of the differences. The null hypothesis tested by ANOVA is that the group means are equal:

Null hypothesis H0: $\mu_1 = \mu_2 = ... = \mu_N$

A t-test is also appropriate to test differences in means with only two groups.

8. First set of hypotheses: results

We consider venue interactivity in-depth and point out similarities and differences between high- and low-interactivity venues. We conducted these analyses to verify and to better understand specific effects and differences across interactivity based groups. We analyzed these measures by comparing statistical differences between members of high- and low-interactivity groups. These analyses were done by running a one way (high, low) interactivity-level ANOVA with the reported change in level of the *We-intentions, Past behavior and participation behavior, Group norms, Mutual agreement, commitment,*

accommodation, and support, Anticipated Emotions, Offline Behaviors and Value
perception measures (Purposive value-Self discovery value-Maintaining interpersonal
interconnectivity-Social enhancement value-Entertainment value), Social Norms,
Perceived behavioral control, Attitude as dependent variables. ANOVA analyses were
used to compare the low- and high-interactive venues on effects of online social
interactions, as well as to uncover offline behavior related differences. Table 5 provides a
summary of results of any hypothesis test. The analysis generally supports the research
hypotheses.

As expected from hypothesis 1a, one-way ANOVA results indicate that the high
and low interactivity venues participants varied in their "we-intentions" responses (refer to
Table 3. for results). We used three different measures to test this hypothesis: strength of
self's intention, average of the strength of group members' intentions, whole group's
intentions (see table 1 for measure explanation). The average of the strength of group
member's intentions is higher for the high interactivity group. This result is supported by
strength of self's agreement and for the whole group, since differences in means for high
and low interactivity groups are significant. Therefore, Hypothesis 1a is supported.

Hypothesis 1b assumed stronger online participation behavior with the group of
friends both for average number of interactions and average time spent each interaction. A
significant effect is revealed, users belong to the low-interactivity group self reported they
interacted together in a two-week period on the internet with the group 30 times instead the
high interactivity group 15 times. Furthermore there is a significant result for past
behavior, considering the previous 6 months as time period. Hypothesis 1b is supported
because there is also a significant effect for average time spent each interaction .747 for
low interactivity group versus .2.242 for high interactivity group. Additionally there is a
significant result for total behavior defined as the number of times multiplies by hours each
time, 24.87 for low interactivity group and 41.24 for high interactivity group.

According to Hypothesis 2a higher levels of interactivity lead to stronger group
norms as the strength to which friends hold the goal to interact each others. This result is
reversed by our data. Surprising, Hypothesis 2a is in the opposite expected direction.

An ANOVA of mutual behaviors- agreement, commitment, accommodation,
support, and liking- revealed many significant effects for averages of the strengths of group

members' mutual behaviors, supporting hypothesis 2b. High- interactivity venues' users promote mutual behaviors: they agree about details of interactions such as if, when and how to interact; they promise each other to be part of the group; members are inclined to organize own schedule, time and place to facilitate interaction and help to do whatever it takes to make an interaction possible. For this group mutual liking is probably a strong motivation to interaction. Consequently, Hypothesis 2b is supported. Hypothesis 2c stated that higher levels of interactivity lead to stronger social identity: Cognitive, Affective, and Evaluative. Hypothesis 2c is only partially supported since results for cognitive social identity are not significant. Instead, results are significant for evaluative and affective social identity.

Hypothesis 3 posited that higher levels of interactivity lead to stronger positive anticipated emotions and stronger negative anticipated emotions. As can be seen from Table 2, both positive and negative anticipated emotions show significant results. If high-interactivity group members are able to interact together on the internet with the group of friends they feel Relief, Content, Excited and Delighted and if they are unable they feel Depressed, Worried, Uncomfortable, Anxious, Agitated, and Nervous. As a result, Hypothesis 3 is supported.

Hypothesis 4 suggested that higher levels of interactivity imply lower use of media and higher use of email and web (not email). Interactivity-level had a significant effect on using other media. Low-interactivity venues' participants show to use media such as television, radio, newspaper, magazines, telephone much more than high-interactivity group. As can be noticed from Table 2, days of Tv use, radio use, magazine and email use are all in the same direction. Instead web use is in the opposite direction, people belong to high interactivity venues use more the web and less the other media.

In particular, use of TV is higher for low interactivity group; they watch TV at least 5 times per week vs. 4 times for the high-interactivity group. High interactivity group also decrease behavior in visiting family, friends and neighbors, and in doing activities and telephone conversations with them. Surprising, they watch movies in movie theatres more than the other group. The ANOVA analyses support that participation in online social interactions negatively affects the overall use of all mass media considered: television, radio, telephone, magazines, and newspapers, across the entire sample.

Our Hypothesis 5 stated that higher level of interactivity would lead to higher use of online group of friend and/or the Internet to satisfy needs such as purposive value, self discovery value, maintaining interpersonal interconnectivity, social enhancement value and entertainment value. As can be seen comparing Table 3 and Table 1, measures were supported by statistically significant results. For *purposive value*, high interactivity group use more the group and the web to get information, to contribute to a pool of information, to generate ideas, to negotiate or bargain, to learn how to do things, to provide others with information, to get someone to do something for them, and to solve problems than low interactivity group and use more the web to make decisions. For *self-discovery value*, high interactivity group members use more the web and the group to learn about themselves and others and to gain insight into themselves then the other group. For *maintaining interpersonal interconnectivity value* high interactivity group members use more the web and the group to have something to do with others, to stay in touch, to get to know others. For *social enhancement value*, high interactivity group use more group and web to impress and to feel important. For *entertainment value* to satisfy the following needs: to be entertained, to play, to relax, to pass the time away when bored, to feel less lonely. Therefore, hypothesis 5 is supported.

Hypothesis 6a stated that higher levels of interactivity lead to stronger positive attitude toward interacting together on the internet with the group. This result is supported only for the first two measures. Hypothesis 6b affirmed that higher levels of interactivity lead to stronger perceived behavioral control over interacting together on the internet with the group. This result is supported, confirmed hypothesis 6b.

The last hypothesis is that higher levels of interactivity lead to stronger subjective norms.

This result is supported by our data.

There is a statistically significant result about age (M_L=39, M_H=26; F (1, 523) =174, p<.001) where in the low interactivity group there are older participants and in the high interactivity group members are younger.

Results also show a statistically significant result for gender (M_L=1.51, M_H=1.60; F (1, 521) =4.058, p<.05) where in the low interactivity group there are most females and in the high interactivity group there are most males.

Combining these two results, we get a profiling of high and low interactivity venues participants. Low interactivity participants are most young female, teenagers. Young women are more likely to participate online than young men in E-mail List, Web Site Bulletin Board or Usenet Newsgroups. For example, compared to men, online women are more likely to send and receive email, to use it in a richer and more engaging way such as write to friends and family, sharing news, worries, and advices, sending pictures, forward jokes and funny stories (as explained in Pew internet and American life project, December 2005). Instead, high interactivity members are most males, older than 19 years old. Older men are more likely to participate online than young women in Instant Messaging, Web-Based Chat Rooms, Multiplayer Virtual, Multi-User Domains (MUD).

9. Second set of hypotheses: results

We consider engagement as independent variable and point out similarities and differences between high- and low-engagement groups. We conducted these analyses to verify and better understand specific effects and differences across different engagement based groups. We analyzed these measures by comparing statistical differences between members of high- and low-engagement groups. A median split was used to separate participants into high and low engagement group (Mantel & Kardes, 1999).

These analyses were done by running a one way (high, low) interactivity-level ANOVA with the reported change in level of the *Mutual agreement, commitment, accommodation, support, Cognitive-affective-evaluative Social identity, Past behavior and participation behavior, Value perception measures: Purposive value-Self discovery value-Maintaining interpersonal interconnectivity-Social enhancement value-Entertainment value, positive and negative Anticipated emotions, Perceived behavioral control, Attitudes, Subjective norms, offline behaviors* as dependent variables. Analyses were used to compare the low engagement group and high engagement group on effects of online social interactions, as well as to uncover offline behavior related differences. The table 6 gives a summary of results of any hypothesis tested. The results generally support the research hypotheses.

As expected from Hypothesis 1a, one-way ANOVA results indicate that individuals with different engagement level varied in their mutual behaviors responses (Table 4. for results). We used three different measures to test this hypothesis: strength of self's behavior, average of the strength of group members' behavior, whole group's behavior (see Table 1 for measures explanation). Hypothesis 1a is supported in the expected direction for mutual agreement, accommodation, commitment, support and mutual liking. A higher engagement implies stronger mutual agreement, accommodation, commitment, support and liking. Therefore, Hypothesis 1a is supported. High- engagement users promote mutual behaviors: they agree about details of interactions such as if, when and how to interact; members are inclined to organize their own schedule, time and place to facilitate interaction. For this group mutual liking is probably a strong motivation to interaction.

Hypothesis 1b assumed stronger cognitive, affective and evaluative social identity if higher engagement level. First, results showed that high engagement implies a cognitive awareness of group members. Participants affirmed their self-images overlap very much with the identity of the group of friends when they are part of the group and they engage in group activities. They consider group members very similar to themselves, supporting cognitive social identity. Second, high engagement members are very attached to their group and have strong feeling of belongingness toward the group, confirming affective social identity. Third, they are valuable and important members of the group, supporting evaluative identity. Consequently, Hypothesis 1b is totally supported.

Hypothesis 2a stated high engagement should lead to stronger online participation behavior with the group of friends both for average number of interactions and average time spent each interaction. A significant effect is revealed, users belong to the low-engagement group self reported they interacted together in the previous two weeks on the internet with the group 13 times instead the high interactivity group 32 times as well as on average in a two week period during the previous 6 months. Hypothesis 2a is only partially supported because there is not a significant effect on average time spent each interaction as in the case of high- and low-interactivity set of hypotheses but there is a significant result for total behavior defined as number of times*hours each time, 22 for low-engaged group and 45 for high-engaged.

According to hypothesis 2b, higher levels of engagement lead to stronger use of online group and the internet in general for satisfying needs such as purposive value, self discovery value, maintaining interpersonal interconnectivity, social enhancement value and entertainment value. As can be seen comparing table 4 and table 1, many measures were supported by statistically significant results. For purposive value, high-engaged members use more the web to provide others with information than low-engaged group, reversing the result found for the other set of hypotheses. For self-discovery value, high engagement group members use more the web to learn about themselves and others than the other group. For entertainment value, engaged participants use more both the group and Internet to be entertained and to relax. For maintaining interpersonal interconnectivity, engaged group uses more the web to stay in touch with people. Results are also significant for social enhancement value. Hypothesis 2b is totally supported. Additionally, in the informational value measure we included that people use the venue to learn how to do things, to get information, to provide others with information, to contribute to a pool of information. In the informational value measure we consider that people use the venue to generate ideas, to negotiate or bargain, to solve problems, to get someone to do something for them, and to make decisions. Measures included in purposive value were the use of the venue to get information, to generate ideas, to negotiate or bargain, to learn how to do things, to provide others with information, to get someone to do something for me, to solve problems, to make decisions, to contribute to a pool of information. Measures included in the entertainment value were the use of the venue to be entertained, to play, to relax, to pass the time away when bored, and to feel less lonely. These measures also showed significant results.

Hypothesis 3 posited that high level of engagement lead to stronger positive and negative anticipated emotions. As can be seen from Table 4, for positive anticipated emotions contentment, delight, happiness, glad, relief, excited, glad, satisfied, proud, self-assured were statistically significant and in the hypothesized direction. For negative anticipated emotion, sadness, disappointing, angry, frustration, guilty, ashamed, sad, disappointed, depressed, worried, uncomfortable, anxious, agitated, nervous were all statistically significant. Therefore, hypothesis 3 is supported both for positive and negative anticipated emotions.

Hypothesis 4a suggested that higher levels of engagement lead to stronger positive attitudes toward interacting together on the internet with the group of friends: high-engaged members consider the interaction wise, good, beneficial and rewarding. Therefore, Hypothesis 4a is supported.

Hypothesis 4b suggested that higher engagement should lead to stronger perceived behavioral control over interactive together on the internet with the group of friends. Results showed high-engaged people consider easy and unproblematic to interact if they chose to, and for their groups is easy to interact if they want to, thus supporting hypothesis 4b.

Hypothesis 5 suggested that higher levels of engagement lead to stronger subjective norms. If the engagement is low most people who are important to them would disapprove of them interacting together on the internet with the group of friends, instead if the engagement is high most important people in their lives would approve of them interacting with the group. Additionally if the engagement is low most people who are important in their life think they should not interact together on the Internet with friends providing statistical support to hypothesis 5.

Hypothesis 6 assumed that higher levels of engagement in the online group should lead to lower use of other media and less offline activities. Surprising, high engaged people go out with friends more and they visit with family members more. Again surprising, engagement-level had a positive significant effect on using other media such as listen to the radio. It might be that they listen to the radio when they are actually using the community. Additionally, as expected, they use more email and web. On the other hand, they read magazines and they watch movies in movie theaters less than not engaged people. Therefore, on one side high-engaged members are involved in more offline activities such as go out with friends, and visit with family members. On the other side they use more email and web, supporting hypothesis 6b and partially reserving hypotheses 6a and 6c.

Also in this set, gender related differences emerge but no statistically significance differences in age were found. In the low engagement group, there are most males and in the high engagement group there are most females. (M_L=1.62, M_H=1.49; F (1, 521)=4.058, p<.05), reversing previous results.

10. Interactions

In this section, we provide a discussion about some emerging key interactions. In particular, we discuss next:

1. The moderating impact of engagement on the relationship between venues interactivity and use of the venues for informational value.
2. For instrumental value.
3. For purposive value.
4. For entertainment value.
5. The moderating impact of community engagement on the relationship between venues interactivity group norms and social identity: cognitive social identity, affective social identity, and evaluative social identity.
6. The moderating impact of gender (1=female, 2=male) on the relationship between venues interactivity and engagement.
7. The moderating impact of community engagement on the relationship between venues interactivity and participation behavior.

10.1 The moderating impact of community engagement on the relationship between venues interactivity and use of the venues for informational value

Of special relevance from a marketing perspective, informational value is one that the participant derives from getting and sharing information in the virtual community, and from knowing what others think, and using this information to make decisions.

As an example, before buying a new car, a consumer may visit different bulletin-boards to learn about the prevailing tenor of opinions regarding the brand's quality (Bickart & Schindler, 2001).

In the informational value measure we include: people use the venue to learn how to do things, to get information, to provide others with information, to contribute to a pool of information.

Results (see descriptive statistics, tests of between-subjects effects, and the plot) indicate that consumer behavior online is clearly influenced by engagement. The influence of engagement on the use of the venues for informational value would be greater for individuals with high engagement using low interactivity venues. It would be lower for consumer with low engagement using low interactivity venues. As we can see, individuals with low engagement are heavily affected by the level of venues interactivity because their use of the venues for informational purpose is clearly higher when the venues are not interactive in real time. If there is high engagement the use of venues for informational purpose will be higher for low interactivity group and slightly lower for high interactivity venues.

These results have many immediate implications for companies. For example, they have to learn how to use not interactive venues to provide their customers with information since they search for information mostly in not interactive venues.

However, they have to be careful, since for example it is now very common for consumers to receive hundreds of e-mails per day. A person may spend hours each day just answering e-mails. It seems that the ease and lower cost of communicating electronically has led to more messages being transmitted, many of which are SPAM. The growth of SPAM bothers people and also increases the amount of time needed to manage emails. With millions of messages, many with multimedia components, needing to be held on personal servers the hardware resources needed have also increased.

Companies have to learn how to contact consumers in low interactivity venues without SPAM, since nowadays there are many SPAM filters and pop-up blockers. The risk is to spend time and money without providing any information to consumers or, even worse, without even contacting them at all.

From our results, consumer search for information in low interactivity venues, thus it is very important the company has search engine optimization tools to get more traffic in their website and to gain visibility.

Peter Daboll, president and chief executive of ComScore Media Metrix, said one notable recent traffic trend is increased popularity of sites helping people find local information: "Things having to do with local search are really gaining momentum". Greg Sterling, an independent analyst, said local Internet services lagged behind their national counterparts for years but are finally coming on strong because they are much better today and people are more aware of their utility. "This is stuff people need and want in their everyday lives," Sterling said, "and to the extent they can find it online, they are starting to use these tools."[10]

Furthermore, a new important tool available for marketers to understand what customers are searching for and the popularity of their brand is Google trends[11]. They can use these data to improve their business and to change their way to contact customers. They could also mimic competitors if they perform better.

Companies also have to find a way to provide information to old people with easy to use tools and applications to facilitate information spreading[12].

Again, since consumer search for information in low interactivity venues, it is crucial for companies to rank high with the major search engines; effective search engine optimizations are now enormous. Companies have to provide consumers with information they want and they are searching for: they require the most relevant and up-to-date information to match the search term that was used and quickly find relevant websites by searching for a word or a phrase. Information is useless to consumers if it does not relate to the search term, or if they are old. Users expect the most up-to-date and fresh information that is useful to them.

First, a strategic implication of our results is that companies should update their website everyday adding some materials. This will help them to get noticed by the search engines.

Second, if they are going to sell any type of product or service online, companies have to optimize their website for the search engines, in order to boost traffic and sales.

Third, if they want to have the greatest deals in the entire world, they have to be conscious that over 90% of their business will likely come directly from search engine results that people get when they search for information in low interactivity venues. Therefore, better understanding the fundamental elements of search engine optimization is vital for an online business' success.

---

[10] http://www.washingtonpost.com/wp-dyn/content/article/2006/04/03/AR2006040301692.html
[11] http://www.nytimes.com/2006/07/05/business/05leonhardt.html?ex=1152244800&en=379ad605f5d24c76&ei=5087%0A
[12] http://networks.silicon.com/webwatch/0,39024667,39160110,00.htm

Forth, companies should consider different techniques to increase page rank. For example, the most effective method is to provide high quality content consistently. Many websites fail to provide content that consumers find interesting. Companies which provide website content that are interesting, well-written and regularly updated create highly engaged users. As can be seen from our result, if the level of engagement is higher, consumers are more likely to return to the website in the coming days for informational value. A consequence is that companies should avoid having a boring, lifeless site.

Fifth, companies should include keywords and phrases within their content. In fact, to be sure that they are properly targeting their market, keywords and phrases they have on the website have to be the keywords and phrases that their website is actually optimized for. The more keywords companies use in their content, the more likely it is that online consumers will find the website when they do some research with those words. When visitors come to the home page, they should easily find the name of the company, what it does, and what products or services it provides.

Sixth, companies should also have to develop a linking strategy as a part of their techniques to provide people with information they need. Links provide free advertising, and it gives the impression that their site is imperative because of its affiliated links. For each link that companies have pointing back to them, that is another chance for their potential customer to find them. The more inbound links that they have pointing to their site, the higher they will be ranked in the search engines.

Seventh, companies have to develop a content trick. People who get to search from the internet are looking for information. The more information companies provide for them and the more helpful it is, the more likely companies will make the sale. A successful way to build up online content is writing articles, arranging properly their content for example by adding a new page to the website to allow room for extra articles to be added and an to build up an archive of articles which will maintain to draw online consumers.

Eighth, since consumers like to provide information and to contribute to a pool of information, such as product reviews and so on, companies should create a space in the website for consumers' discussion such as a message board.

Ninth, people often search at the search engines for brand shows and events they are going to attend. By including separate web pages about each trade show or brand fests the company is going to attend or exhibit at, there is a good chance that people searching for that show or event in the search engines will see the page on the corporate website mentioning the fact that the company is attending. This mechanism can lead to company and brand consciousness and perception as well as potential sales and new potential customers. If someone is searching for the trade show or brand event, then they are interested in that particular industry or brand or product category; so those types of website guests are extremely targeted and valuable. This topic will be deeply studied in paper number 3 of this dissertation.

Summarizing, companies should provide high-quality, keyword rich content and link website to and from a deliberate family of other sites. These will help improve site's popularity and coerce increased business through their online business.

Descriptive Statistics

Dependent Variable: Average of the informational value measures

Whether DSI is interactive in real time	median split engagment2	Mean	Std. Deviation	N
No, not interactive in real time	1,00	3,4841	,73263	126
	2,00	3,6600	,72150	125
	Total	3,5717	,73098	251
Yes, it is interactive in real time	1,00	2,8305	,93354	146
	2,00	3,3678	,87564	121
	Total	3,0740	,94486	267
Total	1,00	3,1333	,90582	272
	2,00	3,5163	,81268	246
	Total	3,3152	,88302	518

Tests of Between-Subjects Effects

Dependent Variable: Average of the informational value measures

Source	Type III Sum of Squares	df	Mean Square	F	Sig.
Corrected Model	53,094(a)	3	17,698	25,989	,000
Intercept	5733,247	1	5733,247	8419,216	,000
interact	28,814	1	28,814	42,313	,000
rengagment2	16,380	1	16,380	24,054	,000
interact * rengagment2	4,207	1	4,207	6,178	,013
Error	350,019	514	,681		
Total	6096,063	518			
Corrected Total	403,114	517			

a R Squared = ,132 (Adjusted R Squared = ,127)

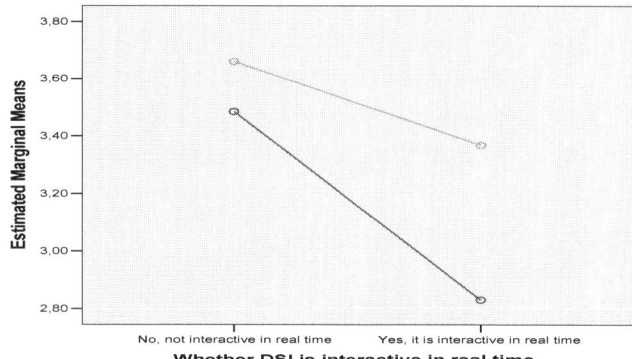

Estimated Marginal Means of Average of the informational value measures

10.2 The moderating impact of community engagement on the relationship between venues interactivity and use of venues for instrumental value

We included instrumental value, that a participant derives from accomplishing specific tasks, such as solving a problem, generating an idea, influencing others regarding an issue or product, validating a decision already reached, or buying a product, through online social interactions (e.g., Hars & Ou, 2002; McKenna & Bargh, 1999). These objectives are all instrumental because they are usually defined prior to participation and facilitate achievement of specific end-state goals (Bagozzi & Dholakia, 1999).

In the instrumental value measure, we consider that people use the venue to generate ideas, to negotiate or bargain, to solve problems, to get someone to do something for them, and to make decisions.

Results (see descriptive statistics, tests of between-subjects effects, and the plot) indicate that online consumer behavior is clearly influenced by engagement also in this case. The influence of engagement on the use of the venues for instrumental value would be definitely greater for individuals with high engagement using high interactivity venues. It would be lower for consumer with low engagement using high interactivity venues. Individuals with low engagement are affected by the level of venues interactivity, because their use of the venues for instrumental purpose is higher when the venues are not interactive in real time.

Instead, individuals with high engagement are affected by the level of venues interactivity, because their use of the venues for instrumental purpose is higher when the venues are interactive in real time. If there is high engagement the use of venues for instrumental purpose will be higher for high interactivity group and much lower for low interactivity venues.

Consumer behavior for instrumental purposes in the use of venues is highly influenced by the level of engagement. Such influence is especially important for consumer with high engagement and high interactivity.

The internet allows interaction in real time, which is online true interactivity, this is crucial since many business activities consist of interactions. A marketing implication is that interactivity enhances the fortune of customer relationships and creates new paradigms of product design and customer service (for example, the customer can customize the product/service and the supplier can learn from the customer). Moreover, venues are open, global network communities that everyone can easily get connected with. The increased connectivity enables new communication and coordination mechanisms both across organizations and customers as well as within groups of customers, while as the number of connections increases the value of the venues grows exponentially.

Another interesting marketing implication is that companies should try to increase with different tools their costumers engagement in the community since higher level of engagement increase a lot the use of the venues to make decisions (e.g. purchase decisions) and to solve problems (e.g.. product technical problem, purchase logistic problems and so on).

If a consumer wants to solve problem (for example a technical problem) using the online venues, he or she needs a supportive technician available to help.

On the other side, high engagement and interactivity in real time may imply not only that consumers use the online community to help, but also that they are available and cooperative to share their knowledge with others. To improve venues efficiency, online community managers should generate and employ some mechanisms to force people to reciprocate or to motivate people to share. This topic will be studied and discussed deeply in the second paper of the dissertation.

An interesting solution for companies is the use of blogs, in particular now that brand blogs and brand portals are storming the web. This is a good way to generate ideas, solve problems, and to make decisions. The current trend is to set up a special brand portal that grants space to bloggers to enrich the website with "logs" of their thoughts and emotions, often resulting in conversations between dozens of different people. Typically, it takes very little time for bloggers to form groups of common interests. Venues interactivity and a focus on communities due to consumer engagement, is changing the way people view and know websites. For example, Sunsilk, Nokia and Axe are just some of the brands that are trying to create online communities. This topic will be discussed on the third paper of the dissertation. Each brand has a subject that helps reinforce the community.

Companies should consider that while old interaction techniques could get over easily, an online experience can last longer and help cultivate a better bond with the customer, if they are able to provide them with the instrumental value they want. For example, for brands addressing specialized needs, internet makes exceptional sense. Take ItchGuard, an itch-relief cream. Its website, created by Tribal DDB India, has been an award-winner. It centers round the ailment that the ointment soothes, the itch, and it is done in a manner that would not be possible offline. Company role is to ensure that brands have a unique presence online. Indeed, online campaigns work best where offline media are inadequate.

Descriptive Statistics Dependent Variable: Average of the instrumental value measures

Whether DSI is interactive in real time	median split engagment2	Mean	Std. Deviation	N
No, not interactive in real time	1,00	2,4643	,67614	126
	2,00	2,7120	,70142	125
	Total	2,5876	,69858	251
Yes, it is interactive in real time	1,00	2,4098	,85122	146
	2,00	2,9118	,77998	121
	Total	2,6373	,85564	267
Total	1,00	2,4350	,77414	272
	2,00	2,8103	,74633	246
	Total	2,6133	,78312	518

Tests of Between-Subjects Effects

Dependent Variable: Average of the instrumental value measures

Source	Type III Sum of Squares	df	Mean Square	F	Sig.
Corrected Model	20,845(a)	3	6,948	12,057	,000
Intercept	3549,305	1	3549,305	6158,772	,000
Interact	,681	1	,681	1,181	,278
rengagment2	18,103	1	18,103	31,413	,000
Interact * rengagment2	2,083	1	2,083	3,614	,058
Error	296,219	514	,576		
Total	3854,542	518			
Corrected Total	317,064	517			

a R Squared = ,066 (Adjusted R Squared = ,060)

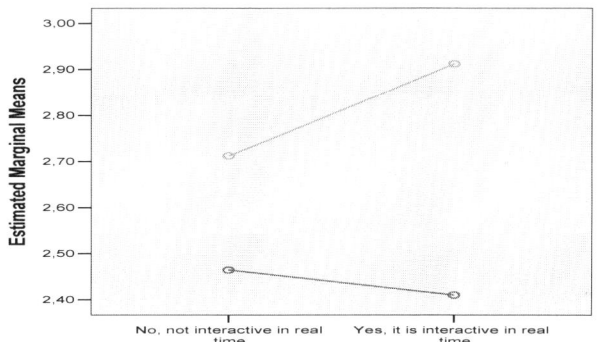

Estimated Marginal Means of Average of the instrumental value measures

10.3 The moderating impact of community engagement on the relationship between venues interactivity and use of venues for purposive value

Although informational and instrumental values tend to be viewed as distinct by communication researchers (e.g., Flanagin & Metzger, 2001), it is perhaps more appropriate to view them as constituents of a single purposive value construct from a marketing perspective, which we define as the value derived from accomplishing some pre-determined instrumental purpose (including giving or receiving information) through virtual community participation.

Considering the sum of all the previous measures results are still significant (see descriptive statistics, tests of between-subjects effects, and the plot), showing the moderating impact of community engagement on the relationship between venues interactivity and use of venues for purposive value, defined as the value derived from accomplishing some pre-determined instrumental purpose through virtual community participation. In particular, measures included in this case are the use of the venue to get information, to generate ideas, to negotiate or bargain, to learn how to do things, to provide others with information, to get someone to do something for them, to solve problems, to make decisions, to contribute to a pool of information.

If consumers have high engagement, they heavily use the venues for purposive value both in high and low interactivity venues. In this case, the use of venues for purposive values does not depend on the level of interactivity. Instead, when the level of engagement is low, the use of venues for purposive values does depend a lot on the level of interactivity. In particular, when venues allow for interactivity in real time the use of the venues for purposive value is very low.

Previous interactions and discussions are validated by this result. If companies are able to increase the level of consumers' engagement in the community, they can get many good feedbacks from their customers. They can also get many reviews and suggestions about how to improve their product or services and they can help potential consumers to purchase companies' products. Furthermore, companies might be able to provide their advertising to a larger number of people through not interactivity venues if the engagement is low.

For participants of interactivity venues in real time with high engagement, purposive value is a key driver of participation. From a managerial perspective, such purposive motives can be characterized as complementary to each others. For instance, in measuring informational value, one item that we used was to get information, whereas another was to provide information to others. It can be argued that an information-seeker will find the online community helpful, practical, and supportive only if he or she can find another participant with the complementary motive of providing that information. As a result, an important task of online community managers may be defined in terms of matching of participants' complementary motives effectively and maintaining a balance, so that the purposive goals of most participants are achieved. This topic will be central in paper number two of the dissertation.

It is also essential to point out the importance of "we-intentions" for purposive value, since people reported to use the venue to make decisions. In fact we intentions may lead to joint behaviors. We-intentions are more appropriate than "I intentions" in online communities and should be measured instead by marketers for predictive or inferential purposes.

Online groups, once formed, are very influential in shaping and changing the consumer's opinions, preferences, and following actions. Rather than focusing on the product or service, per se, these findings suggest that marketers should focus on providing the right conditions for consumers to come together and meet often enough for such groups to form, and then naturally exert their influence on participating consumers.

A related topic is to convince the leading members to adopt a special product in order to create a new "fashion". Marketers should focus on identifying leading consumer community members, because if they are able to influence them, the market impact will be much higher. Leading consumers may collaborate not only in idea generation and product design, but also in marketing communication effort itself. This is because interactivity in the Web gives consumers much greater control of the message.

Another marketing implication is that since consumers may trust more other consumers than company managers or community organizers, it becomes very important to get their collaboration. This topic will be studied in paper three of the dissertation. As an example, a new trends online are bookmark services such as http://bluedot.us/friends/dots or http://del.icio.us/ to see what friends find interesting on the Web. Blue Dot is a free service that helps consumers find, save, and share web content with friends and family. For a list http://www.listible.com/list/social-bookmarking-sites. Bookmarks have become a tool for users sharing similar interests to locate new websites that they might not have otherwise heard of, or to store their bookmarks in such a way that they are not tied to one specific computer.

Descriptive Statistics

Dependent Variable: Sum of the purposive value measures

Whether DSI is interactive in real time	median split engagment2	Mean	Std. Deviation	N
No, not interactive in real time	1,00	25,7937	5,24643	126
	2,00	27,8080	5,53828	125
	Total	26,7968	5,47673	251
Yes, it is interactive in real time	1,00	23,4110	7,16184	146
	2,00	27,8843	6,66857	121
	Total	25,4382	7,28004	267
Total	1,00	24,5147	6,44647	272
	2,00	27,8455	6,10792	246
	Total	26,0965	6,49880	518

Tests of Between-Subjects Effects

Dependent Variable: Sum of the purposive value measures

Source	Type III Sum of Squares	df	Mean Square	F	Sig.
Corrected Model	1817,424(a)	3	605,808	15,555	,000
Intercept	354372,298	1	354372,298	9099,293	,000
Interact	171,317	1	171,317	4,399	,036
rengagment2	1355,546	1	1355,546	34,807	,000
Interact * rengagment2	194,737	1	194,737	5,000	,026
Error	20017,750	514	38,945		
Total	374608,000	518			
Corrected Total	21835,174	517			

a R Squared = ,083 (Adjusted R Squared = ,078)

Estimated Marginal Means of Sum of the purposive value measures

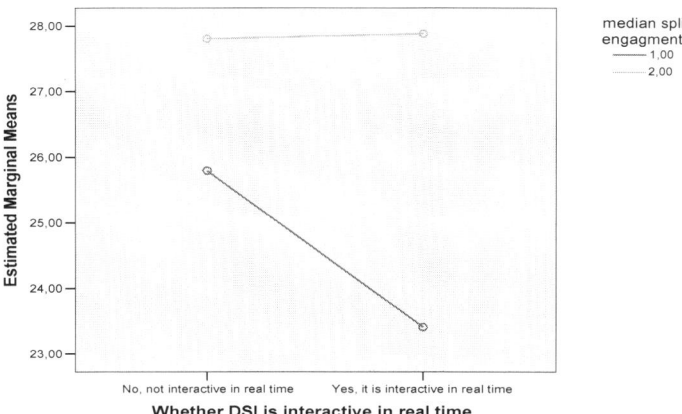

10.4 The moderating impact of community engagement on the relationship between venues interactivity and entertainment value

The last value we included is entertainment value, derived from fun and relaxation through playing or otherwise interacting with others in the virtual community (McKenna & Bargh, 1999). Studies have shown that many participants engage in online social interactions for entertainment through exploring different fictional identities (McKenna & Bargh, 1999), encountering and solving virtual challenges (Balasubramanian & Mahajan, 2001), etc. We consider the social influence variables in our model next.

Measures included in this case are the use of the venue to be entertained, to play, to relax, to pass the time away when bored, and to feel less lonely.

Effects provided by our results (see descriptive statistics, tests of between-subjects effects, and the plot) imply that virtual community organizers will need to thoughtfully decide on which tools and functionalities to provide in their venues if they want to be successful. In fact, in high-interactivity venues, consumers find applications of purpose to be valuable (tools, application, and content that enable them to achieve their entertainment goals successfully). Examples of such applications include: emoticons, avatars, winks, moods, games, videos, messengers, tool bar, greetings, downloads, news, FAQs lists, organization of past responses from community members in transparent and easily accessible hierarchies, query-tools to match information-seekers to information providers, and so on. Other features to increase interactivity include: blogging, message boards, live chat, dating, personal web pages, groups, events calendar and much more.

Additionally, if the site is free, many networks are a great way for people to stay in touch and share information such as convention dates and locations, group meetings, or an awesome way to just have fun chatting or exchanging pictures with other people from all over the world. Many website enables members to bookmark, introduce and even ignore other online members via a user-friendly member panel. Companies should have something new for their visitors on a daily basis to tie them to the network or their brand.

A chat interface for example brings the users together in a real time chat room allowing instant communication between users. Additionally, the events calendar is one of the best features of many sites allowing any user to post an event to the public calendar viewable by any member on the page.

It is crucial for companies to notice the lack of social resources for some categories of people if they want to develop a new business, because they can bring more people with same interests together by taking advantage of the full potential of the internet.

This has important implications for the types of commercial Web sites that are designed to attract new consumers. For example, the fun experience facilitates consumers learning about how to use the Web and become comfortable with it over time. The engagement of new web users is a new frontier.

In reality, it often happens that consumers complain that a site is slow and does not meet expectations. Complaints might include minutes-long loading times, broken stats pages, disappearing HTML, publishing problems, browser incompatibilities, and so on. Companies should identify the problems, work hard and quickly resolve the issues, since people search for websites where they can be entertained, play, and relax.

Descriptive Statistics

Dependent Variable: ENTERTAINMENT1: average of first two entertainment items

median split engagment2	Whether DSI is interactive in real time	Mean	Std. Deviation	N
1,00	No, not interactive in real time	2,8200	1,09875	125
	Yes, it is interactive in real time	4,0377	,77256	146
	Total	3,4760	1,11570	271
2,00	No, not interactive in real time	3,4800	1,06899	125
	Yes, it is interactive in real time	4,3760	,68093	121
	Total	3,9207	1,00347	246
Total	No, not interactive in real time	3,1500	1,13120	250
	Yes, it is interactive in real time	4,1910	,75033	267
	Total	3,6876	1,08576	517

Tests of Between-Subjects Effects

Dependent Variable: ENTERTAINMENT1: average of first two entertainment items

Source	Type III Sum of Squares	df	Mean Square	F	Sig.
Corrected Model	174,717(a)	3	58,239	68,906	,000
Intercept	6958,110	1	6958,110	8232,583	,000
rengagment2	32,035	1	32,035	37,903	,000
interact	143,594	1	143,594	169,895	,000
rengagment2 * interact	3,325	1	3,325	3,934	,048
Error	433,583	513	,845		
Total	7638,750	517			
Corrected Total	608,301	516			

a R Squared = ,287 (Adjusted R Squared = ,283)

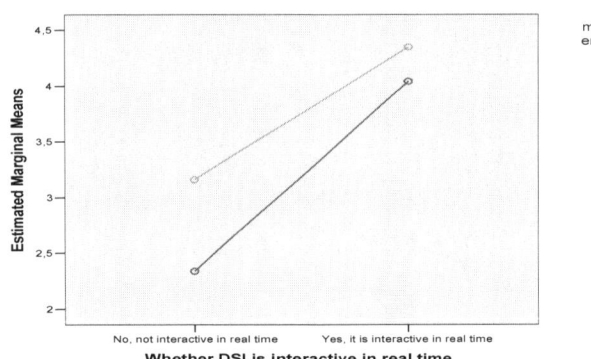

Estimated Marginal Means of Entertainment2

10.5 The moderating impact of community engagement on the relationship between venues interactivity and group norms, cognitive social identity, affective social identity, and evaluative social identity

Group norms and social identity are two key social influence variables that impact virtual community participation. We find the level of engagement to be a moderator, influencing not only the reasons why members participate, but also the strengths of their impact on group norms and social identity.

Results (see descriptive statistics, tests of between-subjects effects, and the plot) indicate that the influence of engagement on group norms would be definitely greater for individuals with high engagement no matter the level of venues interactivity. It would be lower for consumer with low engagement using low interactivity venues. As we can see, individuals with low engagement are affected by the level of venues interactivity, because group norms are higher when the venues are interactive in real time.

Individuals with high engagement are not affected by the level of venues interactivity. When the level of engagement is low the strength to which a respondent holds a goal does depend a lot on the level of interactivity. In particular, when venues allow for interactivity in real time this strength is higher.

An interesting marketing guideline is that companies, if they want their consumer to hold the goal they want (such as to buy their product, be loyal to the company and so on), they have to start using high interactivity venues as well and contacting their costumers through high interactivity venues. This can be done creating brand communities in their website, and using different functions as chat rooms, message boards, and newsletters to contact their customers. This topic will be discussed and studied in the third paper of the dissertation.

Descriptive Statistics

Dependent Variable: sum of group norms

Whether DSI is interactive in real time	median split engagment2	Mean	Std. Deviation	N
No, not interactive in real time	1,00	5,8485	2,19779	120
	2,00	7,9840	1,81267	121
	Total	6,9207	2,27657	241
Yes, it is interactive in real time	1,00	6,4070	1,94742	146
	2,00	7,8766	1,56916	122
	Total	7,0760	1,92694	268
Total	1,00	6,1550	2,07887	266
	2,00	7,9301	1,69214	243
	Total	7,0025	2,09908	509

Tests of Between-Subjects Effects

Dependent Variable: sum of group norms

Source	Type III Sum of Squares	df	Mean Square	F	Sig.
Corrected Model	421,387(a)	3	140,462	39,040	,000
Intercept	24981,643	1	24981,643	6943,422	,000
interact	6,431	1	6,431	1,787	,182
rengagment2	410,748	1	410,748	114,164	,000
interact * rengagment2	14,012	1	14,012	3,894	,049
Error	1816,933	505	3,598		
Total	27196,823	509			
Corrected Total	2238,319	508			

a R Squared = ,188 (Adjusted R Squared = ,183)

63

Estimated Marginal Means of GRPNORM1: strength to which resp holds goal

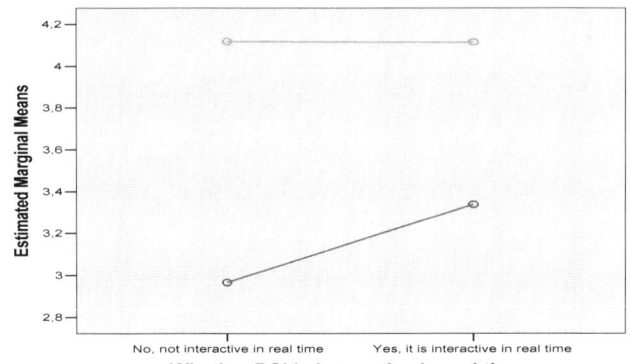

Whether DSI is interactive in real time

Furthermore, it has been shown that stronger group norms lead to a stronger social identity regarding the virtual community (Dholakia et al, 2004).

Social identity, in contrast to personal identity, is an integral part of group membership and confers a collective sense of who one is. Social identity consists of three highly related, yet distinct, dimensions: awareness of group membership, affective commitment to the group, and evaluative significance of group membership.

Awareness of group membership is a cognitive sense of oneself as an instance of a social category. Such thoughts concern judgments about similarities to in-group members and dissimilarities to out-group members. Surprisingly, cognitive social identity for a highly engaged member decrease if there is interaction in real time. On the contrary, cognitive social identity without engagement increase if there is interaction in real time. These results reinforce the previous idea about online groups, which once formed, are very influential in shaping and changing the member's opinions, preferences, and following actions.

Tests of Between-Subjects Effects

Dependent Variable: cognitive social identity

Source	Type III Sum of Squares	df	Mean Square	F	Sig.
Corrected Model	86,374(a)	3	28,791	10,240	,000
Intercept	5375,605	1	5375,605	1911,926	,000
rengagment2	77,595	1	77,595	27,598	,000
interact	,978	1	,978	,348	,556
rengagment2 * interact	9,823	1	9,823	3,494	,062
Error	1439,548	512	2,812		
Total	6892,000	516			
Corrected Total	1525,922	515			

a R Squared = ,057 (Adjusted R Squared = ,051)

Descriptive Statistics

Dependent Variable: cognitive social identity

median split engagment2	Whether DSI is interactive in real time	Mean	Std. Deviation	N
1,00	No, not interactive in real time	2,66	1,571	125
	Yes, it is interactive in real time	3,03	1,672	144
	Total	2,86	1,633	269
2,00	No, not interactive in real time	3,72	1,801	124
	Yes, it is interactive in real time	3,53	1,656	123
	Total	3,62	1,730	247
Total	No, not interactive in real time	3,19	1,767	249
	Yes, it is interactive in real time	3,26	1,680	267
	Total	3,22	1,721	516

Estimated Marginal Means of COGSI2

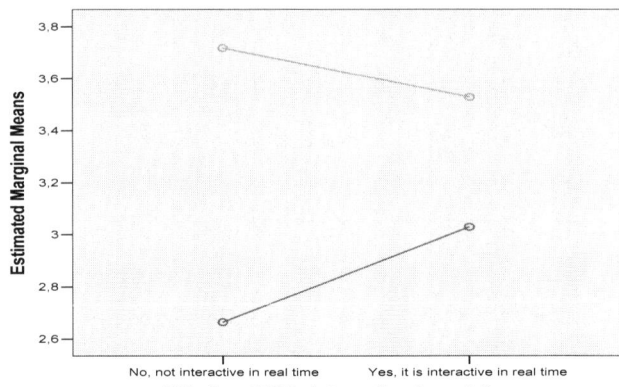

Affective commitment to a group is manifested in two senses of emotionality. One is feeling attachment to the group. Another is experiencing a feeling of belongingness to the group. Even though interactivity in real time does not influence affective social identity when there is a high level of engagement, instead it does when the level of engagement is low. In particular, it increases when there is interaction in real time. These results again reinforce the previous idea about online groups, which are very influential for consumers. Furthermore, it reinforces the idea about the use of other tools to increase the level of interactivity and entertainment. If consumers enjoy participating, they will be more willing to cooperate, assist other members, share knowledge and information, and ask suggestions to other members, such as purchase decision questions (see paper 2 of the dissertation for deeply discussion).

Descriptive Statistics

Dependent Variable: Affective social identity

INTERACT Whether DSI is interactive in real time	RENGAG_A median split engagment2	Mean	Std. Deviation	N
.00 No, not interactive in real time	1.00	3.86	1.764	124
	2.00	5.55	1.381	124
	Total	4.71	1.792	248
1.00 Yes, it is interactive in real time	1.00	4.56	1.689	143
	2.00	5.63	1.337	122
	Total	5.05	1.625	265
Total	1.00	4.24	1.756	267
	2.00	5.59	1.358	246
	Total	4.88	1.715	513

Tests of Between-Subjects Effects

Dependent Variable: Affective social identity

Source	Type III Sum of Squares	df	Mean Square	F	Sig.
Corrected Model	267.189(a)	3	89.063	36.588	.000
Intercept	12268.482	1	12268.482	5039.975	.000
INTERACT	19.391	1	19.391	7.966	.005
RENGAG_A	242.733	1	242.733	99.716	.000
INTERACT * RENGAG_A	12.029	1	12.029	4.941	.027
Error	1239.025	509	2.434		
Total	13748.000	513			
Corrected Total	1506.214	512			

a R Squared = .177 (Adjusted R Squared = .173)

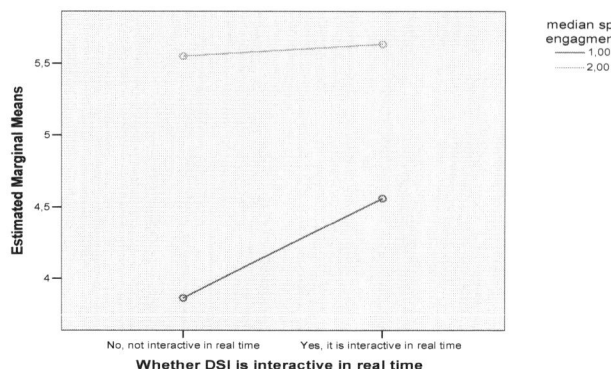

Estimated Marginal Means of AFFSI2

Evaluative significance of group membership is expressed in two related forms: a sense that one is an important member of the group and that one is a valuable member of the group. Again this result proves that interactivity is very importance, both with high engagement and without. In addition, it adds a very important feature. If a person considers him/herself important this may imply this person is a leader in the group. For marketers is very important to identify who the leaders in a group are. If they are able to contact and influence them, they will be able to contact and influence other members and so on. This result is significant, since it proves the internet has changed overall patterns of business communications. This is particular important, because it should be avoid the development of homogenized content that would appeal to a mass audience, since it has negative implications for niche audience. Leaders should be targeted with their needs in order to get a global, widespread response.

Descriptive Statistics

Dependent Variable: evaluative social identity

INTERACT Whether DSI is interactive in real time	RENGAG_A median split engagment2	Mean	Std. Deviation	N
.00 No, not interactive in real time	1.00	4.07	1.923	126
	2.00	5.30	1.680	125
	Total	4.68	1.904	251
1.00 Yes, it is interactive in real time	1.00	4.97	1.643	145
	2.00	5.62	1.404	122
	Total	5.27	1.571	267
Total	1.00	4.55	1.831	271
	2.00	5.46	1.556	247
	Total	4.98	1.763	518

Tests of Between-Subjects Effects

Dependent Variable: evaluative social identity

Source	Type III Sum of Squares	df	Mean Square	F	Sig.
Corrected Model	166.955(a)	3	55.652	19.866	.000
Intercept	12834.052	1	12834.052	4581.398	.000
INTERACT	48.049	1	48.049	17.152	.000
RENGAG_A	114.147	1	114.147	40.747	.000
INTERACT * RENGAG_A	10.366	1	10.366	3.700	.055
Error	1439.888	514	2.801		
Total	14467.000	518			
Corrected Total	1606.844	517			

a R Squared = .104 (Adjusted R Squared = .099)

Estimated Marginal Means of EVALSI1

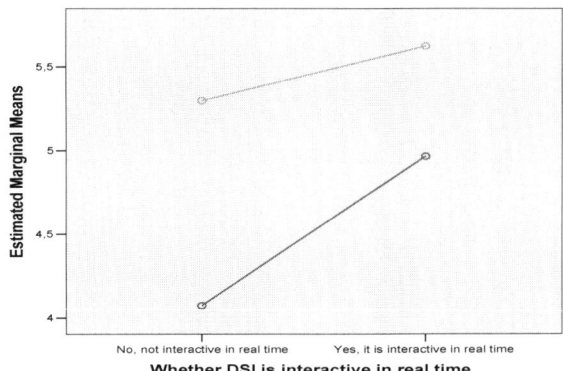

Whether DSI is interactive in real time

10.6 The moderating impact of gender (1=female, 2=male) on the relationship between venues interactivity and engagement

Highly engaged members are mostly females, in particular for real time interactions. Instead, if there is interaction in real time and people are males there is usually low engagement. Females are more engaged if there is interaction in real time, instead males are more engaged if there is not interaction in real time. Low levels of interactions and gender do not affect much the level of engagement. It is just slightly lower for males than females. Nevertheless, the huge difference in the level of engagement is between male and female, if there is interaction in real time. In this case, the level of engagement is definitely lower for males.

This is a crucial difference for manager to learn how to deal with female and male, in particular if they would like to use high interactivity venues as a tool to contact their customers. An interesting future research could be to study if males' online brand community members are less loyal compared to female, members as well of the same community.

There are some implications of our findings. Men are more engaged with their internet use in not-interactivity groups than women are. Men are more likely than women to participate in low interactivity groups in a vast selection of special interest groups such as fan clubs, product enthusiast people, community groups, brand communities, technological issues, games, and so on. They are online more frequently, because they probably have high-speed connection at home. Pew internet and American life project (2005) results show that men and women are equally likely to access the internet from home (89% of men and 87% of women) but men are more likely than women to have high speed connection at home (52% of men and 48% of women). Men use group and web to get information- such as get news, check the weather, get sport information, do new job related-search, use online reputation systems- play lottery or gamble, share files, buy products, search for an hobby, solve problems, make decisions and so on. Men search for information on a more extensive diversity of subjects and issues online than women do. Pew internet and American life project (2005) confirms these results and show men use search engines to get political information and news as well.

In Pew internet and American life project (December, 2005), they affirm men use the internet more than women as a destination for recreation. Our results sustain this finding. However, even though men are more willing to be part of a high interactivity venue and Instant Messaging, Web-Base Chat Rooms, Multiplayer Virtual, and Multi-User Domains (MUD), and these venues are mostly used for entertainment and recreation, they are less engaged in the community. They play games, share files, listen to audio clips and watch video clips, as women do, but they also practice their hobbies, participate in sport fantasy leagues, downloading files, remixing files and so on. The key difference is that women are more engaged when they do such activities.

Furthermore, shopping online differences between males and females begin as early as the teen years[13] (2006).

13

http://home.businesswire.com/portal/site/google/index.jsp?ndmViewId=news_view&newsId=20060816005135&newsLang=en

Descriptive Statistics

Dependent Variable: engagment

INTERACT Whether DSI is interactive in real time	GENDER Category	Mean	Std. Deviation	N
.00 No, not interactive in real time	1.00 Female	1.5210	.50167	119
	2.00 Male	1.4844	.50172	128
	Total	1.5020	.50101	247
1.00 Yes, it is interactive in real time	1.00 Female	1.5810	.49577	105
	2.00 Male	1.3631	.48242	157
	Total	1.4504	.49848	262
Total	1.00 Female	1.5491	.49870	224
	2.00 Male	1.4175	.49402	285
	Total	1.4754	.49989	509

Tests of Between-Subjects Effects

Dependent Variable: RENGAG_A median split engagment2

Source	Type III Sum of Squares	df	Mean Square	F	Sig.
Corrected Model	3.409(a)	3	1.136	4.645	.003
Intercept	1102.344	1	1102.344	4506.326	.000
INTERACT	.117	1	.117	.480	.489
GENDER	2.018	1	2.018	8.248	.004
INTERACT * GENDER	1.023	1	1.023	4.183	.041
Error	123.534	505	.245		
Total	1235.000	509			
Corrected Total	126.943	508			

a R Squared = .027 (Adjusted R Squared = .021)

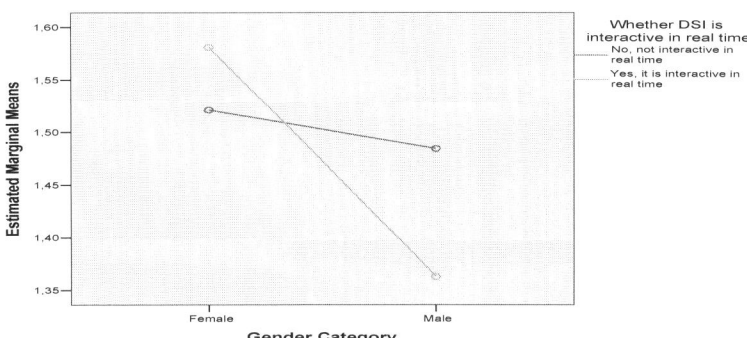

Estimated Marginal Means of median split engagment2

10.7 The moderating impact of community engagement on the relationship between venues interactivity and participation behavior (time in hours per session)

Descriptive Statistics

Dependent Variable: Time in hours per session during most recent two-week period

RENGAG_A median split engagment2	INTERACT Whether DSI is interactive in real time	Mean	Std. Deviation	N
1.00	.00 No, not interactive in real time	.966	1.2738	27
	1.00 Yes, it is interactive in real time	2.052	1.3936	38
	Total	1.601	1.4398	65
2.00	.00 No, not interactive in real time	.617	.5703	38
	1.00 Yes, it is interactive in real time	2.498	1.9038	31
	Total	1.462	1.6322	69
Total	.00 No, not interactive in real time	.762	.9366	65
	1.00 Yes, it is interactive in real time	2.252	1.6449	69
	Total	1.529	1.5377	134

73

Tests of Between-Subjects Effects

Dependent Variable: Time in hours per session during most recent two-week period

Source	Type III Sum of Squares	df	Mean Square	F	Sig.
Corrected Model	79.668(a)	3	26.556	14.702	.000
Intercept	308.456	1	308.456	170.771	.000
RENGAG_A	.076	1	.076	.042	.837
INTERACT	72.204	1	72.204	39.974	.000
RENGAG_A * INTERACT	5.180	1	5.180	2.868	.093
Error	234.813	130	1.806		
Total	627.887	134			
Corrected Total	314.481	133			

a R Squared = .253 (Adjusted R Squared = .236)

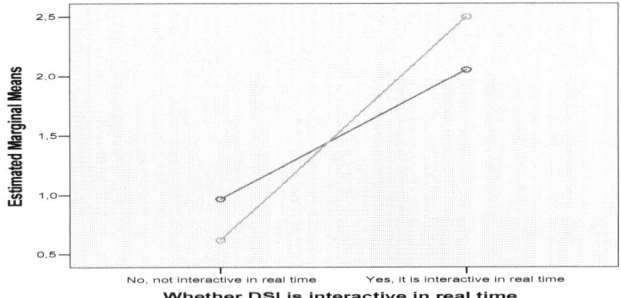

Estimated Marginal Means of Behavior second wave Measure 2: Time in hours per session during most recent two-week period

Results (see descriptive statistics, tests of between-subjects effects, and the plot) indicate that consumer participation behavior online, defined as time in hours per session, is clearly influenced by engagement and venue interactivity.

As expected, the influence of engagement on consumer participation would be greater for individuals with high engagement using high interactivity venues. Nevertheless, unexpected, it would be lower for consumer with high engagement using low interactivity venues.

Individuals with high engagement are heavily affected by the level of venues interactivity, because their venues participation is clearly higher when the venues are interactive in real time. With low engagement, the use of venues will be higher for high interactivity group and slightly lower for low interactivity venues.

These results have immediate implications for companies.

Online communities can help people form dynamic, self-motivated, and productive relationships. Unfortunately, this potential is not always satisfied: many online communities fail, and organizers are not able to understand why. Butler (2001) found 50% of social, hobby, and work mailing lists have no traffic over a 122 day period and even in communities that do survive: in a majority of active mailing lists, fewer than 50% of subscribers posted even a single message in a 4-month period. Even in successful communities, questions can go unasked or unanswered.

Varieties of online communities suffer from a deficit of content contribution, and sharing behavior in particular in firm-managed brand communities. Although there are many ways to participate in online communities including simply reading posts (Preece, 2000) the next two papers of the dissertation will focus specifically on understanding mechanisms of consumer online sharing behaviors and overcoming problems caused by lack of content contribution in firm-managed brand communities compared to consumer-managed. We want do develop innovative techniques and practical guidelines designers can use to increase positive contributions to online communities. The trick is to inspire participation in the first place. For example, companies have to provide interactive in real time functions in their website, if they want people to participate and they have jointly try to engage people in their website activities. Companies should provide Instant Messaging, Web-Based Chat-Rooms, Networked Video Games, and other high interactivity functions.

11. General discussion

The goal of this research was to contribute to the growing curiosity and comprehension concerning online group interactions in developing countries. First, we were able to better understand how involving in online social interactions relates to the member's online and offline social behavior. Second, we pointed out similarities and differences in participant's online and offline social behavior if interactions occur in high or low interactivity venues. Third, we identify similarities and differences in user's online and offline social behavior, if there is high engagement with the group or if the engagement is not so high. Through the study of specific differences between online group participants, our contribution was to the promising literature on the effects of internet use for group interactions (e.g., Bagozzi, Dholakia, & Pearo, 2005; Dholakia & Bagozzi, 2004; Flanagin & Metzger, 2001; Kraut et al., 2002; Shah et al., 2001; The UCLA Internet Report, 2003).

Forth, many interesting key interactions emerged and were discussed.

As discussed above, many positive effects emerge from group engagement and group interactivity. Our findings have theoretical and practical value. Contrarily to expectations, group engagement and high interactivity are a positive factor in everyday life. Our empirical survey based-study, conducted across seven different venues, found overall support for our proposed sets of hypotheses.

The first contribution was to study how online social interaction influence online and offline members' behavior.

While participation in online social groups has always been considered a time-consuming activity, our results have proved that is not always the case. People highly engaged in online group and participating in high- interactivity venues seems to have time to enjoy their lives in offline activities. Results show many significant differences in members' behavior online and offline.

Another contribution is that significantly gender differences allow us to obtain a user profiling to better understand participants' online characteristics.

As another important outcome of this research, many interesting differences between high- and low- interactivity groups and high- and low- engagement groups were uncovered. The following different effects were found in both set of results: mutual behaviors, such as mutual accommodation, support, commitment, agreement and liking, positive and negative anticipated emotions, past and current participation behavior, use of communication media, use of Email and Web, we-intentions, social identity, purposive value, self-discovery value, maintaining interpersonal interconnectivity, social enhancement value, entertainment value, subjective norms, positive attitude, perceived behavioral control.

Additionally, many interesting key interactions emerged, were discussed, and showed that the monitoring and management of online communities is best viewed as an ongoing task by their organizers. The most significance of them will be deeply discussed in the other two papers of the dissertation.

In conclusion, other marketing researchers showed optimism expressed by studying online communities (e.g., Balasubramanian and Mahajan 2001), and suggested that these online communities are only likely to grow in importance, magnitude, influence, power, and the range of activities for which they are used, as consumers become more comfortable, at ease, and adapted with these environments. Online communities deserve persistent and increasing attention from both practitioners and marketing researchers.

12. Future research

Future researches examining these interactivity and engagement group differences in a structural equation model may favorably help our understanding of participants' online and offline behaviors.

Assuming the cooperation distinction proposed in Bagozzi et al. (2006), and in Bagozzi and Lee (2002) between fully cooperative, partially cooperative and minimally cooperative group action, other two potential research opportunities emerge about cooperative and non-cooperative social interactions.

First, since we assume high interactivity and high engagement in-group participation, another interesting future research opportunity is to study sharing behavior or cooperative behavior in consumer communities. This topic may give a theoretical and practical contribution to the social psychology and marketing literatures, as well as significant managerial implications.

Second, future research should study free riding or non- cooperative mechanism in consumer communities to provide an actionable framework to marketers, organizers of communities, copyright holders and consumers through which to encourage or discourage free- riding behavior in all types of consumer networks. Free rider is defined as an individual who consume resources of the social group interaction without contributing (McKenna and Bargh, 1999). Both these two issues will be studied in this dissertation, both from theoretical and managerial point of view.

Another research opportunity required future theoretical and practical attention. More developments are needed into understanding offline behaviors modifications in other activities not included in this study. It is noteworthy to explain why high engagements in online social participation lead to more offline activities. Is social group participation decreasing the minimum time to perform some tasks? Or is the web in general decreasing the minimum amount of time to get information, make decisions and perform other tasks? Assuming a positive answer to the two previous questions, they may lead us to include our findings in a more comprehensive framework and model.

For example, can we conclude that both online social group and the web decrease time spending on learning during high-school and college? Can we also conclude that group venues members are more proficient in their education because of online social interactions? Or do they have time for doing other activities because interaction in collaborative venues decreases time to complete other tasks? In conclusion, do we need to assume there are some other antecedents, moderators, and variables not predicted yet that we should include in a model? Following these directions, more developments and studies are needed about this topic, including other potential significant variables in both online and offline behavior.

Moreover, many interactions emerge in this study. In the previous discussion about interactions it has been pointed out that in particular other two topics deserve a deep discussion and understanding.

The first topic is consumer sharing behavior. It will be studied in the second paper of the dissertation where I seek to better understand why consumers contribute content, and share their resources in customer communities. It is noteworthy that online sharing behaviour has not been systematically analyzed in the literature. The digital-content and related industries have to further understand the consumers who share files, information, material and so on.

The second topic is online brand communities. It will be analyzed in the third paper of the dissertation, where I study firm-managed and customer-managed brand communities of many large firms such as National Instruments and Microsoft. Marketers have become more and more interested in organizing, nurturing, and monitoring such brand communities, where their customers can interact with one another. Little research has examined differences between firm-managed and customer-managed brand communities. Some unanswered questions that we focus on are: do customers favor a particular type of community and are they entrenched within it? Does company involvement reduce the enthusiasm of customers? Which communities have a greater number of social interactions and are more effective in disseminating knowledge? Do these communities favor different sorts of interactions?

References

Ajzen, I. (1991). The theory of planned behavior. Organization Behavior and Human Decision Processes, 50, 179-211.

Allen, N. J., & Meyer, J. P. (1996). Affective, continuance, and normative commitment to the organization: An examination of construct validity. Journal of Vocational Behavior, 49, 252-276.

Algesheimer Rene, Utpal M. Dholakia, and Andreas Herrmann. 2005. "The social influence of brand community: Evidence from European Car Clubs." Journal of Marketing 69 (3) 19-34.

Richard P. Bagozzi, Utpal M. Dholakia, Lisa R. Klein Pearo (2006). Antecedents and Consequences of Online Social Interactions. Forthcoming.

Bagozzi, R. P., & Dholakia, U. M. (2002). Intentional social action in virtual communities. Journal of Interactive Marketing, 16(2), 2– 21.

Bagozzi, R. P., Baumgartner, H., & Pieters, R. (1998). Goal-directed emotions. Cognition and Emotion, 12, 1-26.

Bagozzi, R. P., & Lee, K. H. (2002). Multiple routes for social influence: The role of compliance, internalization, and social identity. Social Psychology Quarterly, 65, 226-247.

Balasubramanian, S., & Mahajan, V. (2001). The economic leverage of the virtual community. International Journal of Electronic Commerce, 5(3), 103–138.

Baumeister, R. F. (1998). The self. In D. T. Gilbert, S. R. Fiske, & G. Lindzey (Eds.), The Handbook of Social Psychology (pp. 680-740). New York: McGraw-Hill.

Bhattacharya and Sankar Sen (2003), "Consumer–Company Identification: A Framework for Understanding Consumers' Relationships with Companies," Journal of Marketing, 67 (April), 76–88.

Bergami, M., & Bagozzi, R. P. (2000). Self-categorization, Affective Commitment, and Group Self-Esteem as Distinct Aspects of Social Identity in an Organization. British Journal of Social Psychology, 39 (4), 555-577.

Bratman, M. E. (1993). Shared intention. Ethics, 104, 97-113.

Bratman, M. E. (1997). I intend that We J. In G. Homström-Hintikka and R. Tuomela. Dordrecht (Eds.), Contemporary Action Theory, Volume II (pp. 49-63). The Netherlands: Kluwer.

Butler, B. Membership Size, Communication Activity, and Sustainability: A Resource-Based Model of Online Social Structures. *Information Systems Research 12*, 4 (2001), 346-362.

Burgoon, J. K., Bonito, J. A., Bengtsson, B., Ramirez, A., Dunbar, N. E., & Miczo, N. (2000). Testing the interactivity model: Communication processes, partner assessments, and the quality of collaborative work. Journal of Management of Information Systems, 16 (3), 33-56.

Burgoon, J. K., Bonito, J. A., Ramirez, A., Dunbar, N. E., Kam, K., & Fischer, J. (2002). Testing the interactivity principle: Effects of mediation, propinquity, and verbal and non-verbal modalities in interpersonal interaction. Journal of Communication (September), 657-677.

Burnett, G. (2000). Informational exchange in virtual communities: A typology. Information Research, 5, 4.

Catterall, M., & Maclaran, P. (2001). Researching consumers in virtual worlds: A cyberspace odyssey. Journal of Consumer Behaviour, 1(3), 228– 237.

Dholakia, U. M., & Bagozzi, R. P. (2004). Motivational antecedents, constituents and consequents of virtual community identity. In S. Godar, & S. Pixie-Ferris (Eds.), Virtual and collaborative teams: Process, technologies, and practice (pp. 252– 267). London7 IDEA Group

Dholakia, U. M., & Bagozzi, R. P., Pearo L.K. (2004). A social influence model of consumer participation in network- and small-group-based virtual communities International Journal of Research in Marketing 21, 241–263.

Eagly, A. H., & Chaiken, S. (1993). The psychology of attitudes. Fort Worth, TX: Harcourt Brace Jovanovich.

Fallows, D. (2005). How Women and Men Use the Internet, Pew Internet and American Life Project. Available online at:
http://www.pewinternet.org/pdfs/PIP_Women_and_Men_online.pdf

Flanagin, A. J., & Metzger, M. J. (2001). Internet use in the contemporary media environment. Human Communication Research, 27(1), 153– 181.

Gleicher, F., Boninger, D.S., Strathman, A., Armor, D., Hetts, J., & Ahn, M. (1995). With an eye toward the future: The impact of counterfactual thinking on affect, attitudes, and behavior. In Roese, N. J. & Olson, M. M. (Eds.), What Might Have Been: The Social Psychology of Counterfactual Thinking. (pp. 283-304), Mahwah, NJ: Lawrence Erlbaum Associates

Hars, A., & Ou, S. (2002). Working for free? Motivations for participating in open-source projects. International Journal of Electronic Commerce, 6 (3), 23-37.

Kelman, H. C. (1974). Further thoughts on the processes of compliance, identification, and internalization. In J.T. Tedeschi (Eds.), Perspectives on social power (pp. 126-171). Chicago: L. Aldine.

Kraut, R., Kiesler, S., Boneva, B., Cummings, J., Helgeson, V., & Crawford, A. (2002). Internet paradox revisited. Journal of Social Issues, 58 (1), 49-74.

Kozinets, R.V. (1999). E-tribalized marketing? The strategic implications of virtual communities of consumption. European Management Journal, 17 (3), 252–264.

Langerak, Fred, Peter C. Verhoef, Peeter W. Verlegh, and Kristine de Valck (2003), "The Effect of Members' Satisfaction with a Virtual Community on Member Participation," ERIM Report Series Research in Management, 2003-004-MKT, Erasmus Research Institute of Management, Erasmus University Rotterdam.

Lombard, M. (2001). Interactive Advertising and Presence: A Framework. Journal of Interactive Advertising, 1 (2).

Luhtanen, R., & Crocker, J. (1992). A collective self-esteem scale: Self-evaluation of one's social identity. Personality and Social Psychology Bulletin, 18, 302-318.

Mantel, S. P., & Kardes, F. R. (1999). The Role of Direction of Comparison Attribute Based-Processing and Attitude Based-Processing in Consumer Preference. Journal of Consumer Research, 25(4), 335-352.

McKenna, K. Y. A., & Bargh, J. A. (1999). Causes and consequences of social interaction on the internet: A conceptual framework. Media Psychology, 1, 249– 269.

McKenna, K. Y. A., Green, A. S., & Gleason, M. E. J. (2002). Relationship formation on the internet: What's the big attraction? Journal of Social Issues, 58 (1), 9-31.

Morrison, D. F. (1990). Multivariate Statistical Methods, New York: McGraw Hill.

Oulette, J.A., & Wood, W. (1998). Habit and intention in everyday life: The multiple processes by which past behavior predicts future behavior. Psychological Bulletin, 124, 54–74.

Postmes, T., Spears, R., & Lea, M. (2000). The formation of group norms in computer-mediated communication. Human Communication Research, 26(3), 341– 371.

Preece, J. *Online Communities: Designing Usability, Supporting Sociability.* John Wiley and Sons, Ltd., England, 2000.

Rafaeli, S., & Sudweeks, F. (1996). Networked Interactivity. Journal of Computer-Mediated Communication, 2 (4).

Searle, J. R. (1990). Collective intentions and actions. In P. R. Cohen, J. Morgan, & M. E. Pollack (Eds.), Intentions in Communication (pp. 401-415). Cambridge, MA: MIT Press.

Shah, D. V., McLeod, J. M., & Yoon, S-H. (2001). Communication, context, and community: An exploration of print, broadcast, and internet influences. Communication Research, 28 (4), 464-506.

Spears, R., & Lea, M. (1994). Panacea or Panopticon? The hidden power in computer-mediated communication. Communication Research, 21, 427-459.

Spears, R., Postmes, T., Lea, M., & Wolbert, A. (2002). When are net effects gross products? The power of influence and the influence of power in computer-mediated communication. Journal of Social Issues, 58 (1), 91-107.

Tabachnick, B.G., Fidell L.S., 1983. "Using multivariate Statistics." Harper and Row Publishers, New York.

The UCLA Internet Report: Surveying the Digital Future Year Three (2003) UCLA Center for Communication Project, January.

Tuomela, R. (1995). The importance of us: A philosophy study of basic social notions. Stanford, CA7 Stanford University Press.

Tuomela, R. (2000). Cooperation: A philosophical study. Dordrecht, NL: Kluwer Academic Publishers.

Walther, J.B. (1996). Computer-mediated communication: Impersonal, interpersonal and hyperpersonal interaction. Communication Research, 23, 1, 3–43.

Wellman, B. (1999). The network community: An introduction. In B. Wellman (Ed.), Networks in the global village: Life in contemporary communities (pp. 1 –48). Boulder, CO7 Westview Press.

Wellman, B., & Gulia, M. (1999). Net-surfers don't ride alone: Virtual communities as communities. In B. Wellman (Ed.), Networks in the global village: Life in contemporary communities (pp. 331–366). Boulder, CO7 Westview Press.

Wellman, B., Salaff, J., Dimitrova, D., Garton, L., Gulia, M., & Haythornthwaite, C. (1996). Computer networks as social networks: Collaborative work, telework, and virtual community. Annual Review of Sociology, 22, 213–238.

Williams, R. L., & Cothrel, J. (2000). Four smart ways to run online communities. Sloan Management Review, 81–91

Table 1.

Constructs and Measures

Mutual Agreement (Two measures)
"How strong would you say the explicit or implicit agreement is among each of the following to interact with on the internet as a group sometime during the next two weeks? And how strong is the agreement of the whole group? (5-point "very weak-very strong" scales)
   ➤   Strength of self's agreement
   ➤   Average of the strength of other group members' agreement
   ➤   Whole group's agreement

Mutual Commitment (Two measures)
"How strongly committed would you say the following are to interacting together as a group on the internet sometime during the next two weeks or so? And how committed is the whole group?" (5-point "very weak-very strong" scales)
   ➤   Strength of self's commitment
   ➤   Average of the strength of other group members' commitment
   ➤   Whole group's commitment

Mutual Accommodation (Two measures)
"How willing are each of the following to accommodate or adjust to the needs of the others in the group so as to choose a time and place to interact together on the internet sometime during the next two weeks or so? And how willing is the whole group to accommodate or adjust? (5-point "not at all willing – very strongly willing" scales)
   ➤   Strength of self's willingness to accommodate
   ➤   Average of the strengths of other group members' willingness to accommodate

➤ Whole group's willingness to accommodate

Mutual Support (Two measures)

"How inclined are each of the following to support or help other members in doing whatever it takes to facilitate interacting together on the internet as a group sometime during the next two weeks? And how inclined is the whole group willing to help others?". (5-point "not at all inclined-very strongly inclined" scales)

      ➤ Strength of self's inclination to support

      ➤ Average of the strengths of other group members' inclination to support

      ➤ Whole group's inclination to support

Mutual liking (Two measures)

"How strongly do you like the members of your group and the group as a whole" (5-point "do not like at all-like very, very much" scales)

      ➤ Strength of self's liking

      ➤ Average of the strengths of group members' liking

      ➤ Whole group's liking

Participation Behavior (Two measure)

      ➤ "How many times in the *past 2 weeks* did you interact together on the internet with the group of friends you identified above?"

      ➤ "How much time do you spend on average when you interact together on the internet with the group of friends identified above?"

Past Behavior (One measure)

      ➤ "How many times did you interact together on the internet with the group of friends you identified above in a *typical 2-week* period over the past 6 months?"

Group norms (Two measures)

"Interacting together sometime within the next two weeks with the group of friend you often chat with can be considered a goal. For each of the people listed below, please estimate the strength to which each holds this goal" (5-point "very weak-very strong" scales)

      ➤ Strength of self's goal

➤ Average of the strength of group members' goal	

Positive Anticipated Emotions	*Negative Anticipated Emotions*
(Nine measures)	*(Twelve measures)*
"If I am able to interact together on the Internet with the group of friends I identified above during the next 2 weeks, I will feel:" (7-point "not at all-very much" scales)	"If am unable to interact together on the Internet with the group of friends I identified above during the next 2 weeks, I will feel:" (7-point "not at all-very much" scales)

➤ Relief	➤ Angry
➤ Contentment	➤ Frustrated
➤ Excited	➤ Guilty
➤ Delighted	➤ Ashamed
➤ Happy	➤ Sad
➤ Glad	➤ Disappointed
➤ Satisfied	➤ Depressed
➤ Proud	➤ Worried
➤ Self-assured	➤ Uncomfortable
	➤ Anxious
	➤ Agitated
	➤ Nervous

Perceived Behavioral Control (Four measures)

➤ "How much control *do you have* over interacting together on the Internet with the group of friends you identified above during the next two weeks?" (7-point "no control-total control" scales)

➤ "*For me* to interact together on the internet with the group of friends I mentioned above during the next 2 weeks is:" (7-point "difficult-easy" scales)

➤ "If I chose to, it would be unproblematic for me to interact together on the internet with the group of friends I mentioned above" (7-point "very unlikely-very likely" scales)

➤ "For my group, interacting together on the internet during the next two weeks is" (7-point "difficult- easy" scales)

Attitudes (Four measures)

"On the following scales, please express your attitude toward interacting together on the internet with the group of friends you identified above sometime during the next two weeks". (7 point "foolish– wise," "harmful–beneficial," "bad–good," "punishing– rewarding." Scale)

Subjective norms (Two measures)

"Please express how strongly most people who are important to you feel you should or should not interact together on the internet with the group of friends you normally interact with".

> Most people who are important in my life think I (circle appropriate number): should 1: 2: 3: 4: 5: 6: 7: should not interact together on the Internet with friends sometime during the next two weeks.

> Most people who are important to me would (circle appropriate number): approve 1: 2: 3: 4: 5: 6: 7: disapprove of me interacting together on the Internet with friends sometime during the next two weeks.

Desires (Three measures)

> "I desire to interact on the internet with the group sometime during the next two weeks" (7 point "disagree-agree" scale)

> "My desire for interacting together on the internet with the group can be described as:" (7-point "not desire at all – very, very strong desire" scale)

> "I want to interact together on the internet with my group during the next two weeks." (7-point "does not describe me at all – describes me very well" scale)

We-intentions (Two measures)

> Mutual intentions: "How strong would you say is your intention and the intention of each of the following people to interact with together on the internet sometime during the next two weeks or so? And how strong is the whole group intention?"

    o   Strength of self's intentions

    o   Average of the strength of group members' intentions

>   ➢   "I intend that our group (i.e., the group that I identified before) interact on the internet together sometime during the next two weeks" (5-point "strongly disagree-strongly agree" scale)
>
>   ➢   "Please express the degree to which you might intend to interact together on the internet with the group of friends mentioned above during the next two weeks" (7-point "extremely unlikely-extremely likely)
>
>   ➢   We (i.e., the group that I identified above) intend to interact on the internet together sometime during the next two weeks." (5-point "strongly disagree-strongly agree" scale)

Cognitive social identity (Two measures)

    ➢   Please indicate to what degree your self-image overlaps with the identity of the group of friends as you perceive it (7-point "not at all – very much" scale)

    ➢   How would you express the degree of overlap between your personal identity and the identity of the group you mentioned above when you are actually part of the group and engaging in group activities? (8-point "far apart – complete overlap" scale)

Affective social identity (Two measures)

    ➢   How attached are you to the group you mentioned above? (7-point "not at all: I have no positive feelings toward the group – attached very much: I have very substantial positive feelings toward the group" scale)

    ➢   How strong would you say your feelings of belongingness are toward the group you mentioned? (7-point "not at all strong – very strong" scale)

Evaluative social identity (Two measures)

    ➢   "I am a valuable member of the group" (7-point "does not describe me at all-describe me very well" scale)

    ➢   "I am an important member of the group" (7-point "does not describe me at all-describe me very well" scale)

"How often do you use your online group (identified above) for satisfying the following needs? And "How often do you use <u>the Internet in general</u> for satisfying the following needs?

Purposive value (Nine measures)

- ➢ to get information
- ➢ to generate ideas
- ➢ to negotiate or bargain
- ➢ to learn how to do things
- ➢ to provide others with information
- ➢ to get someone to do something for me
- ➢ to solve problems
- ➢ to make decisions
- ➢ to contribute to a pool of information

Self-discovery value (Two measures)

- ➢ to learn about myself and others
- ➢ to gain insight into myself

Maintaining interpersonal interconnectivity (Three measures)

- ➢ to have something to do with others
- ➢ to stay in touch
- ➢ to get to know others

Social enhancement value (Two measures)

- ➢ to impress
- ➢ to feel important

Entertainment value (Five measures)

- ➢ to be entertained
- ➢ to play
- ➢ to relax
- ➢ to pass the time away when bored
- ➢ to feel less lonely

Offline behavioral outcomes of social interactions

Other activities and interactions

"Participating in group interactions on the internet often influences other activities and interactions of individuals". "How the amount of interactions with others have changed now when compared to before you engaged in internet-based group interactions".

(5-point scale, "Very much less than before-Very much more than before")

- ➢ Visiting with family members
- ➢ Visiting with friends
- ➢ Going out with family members
- ➢ Going out with friends
- ➢ Activities with neighbors
- ➢ Activities with hobby groups (book clubs, sports teams, etc.)
- ➢ Telephone conversations with family
- ➢ Telephone conversations with friends
- ➢ Writing letters to family and friends

Use of media

"Participating in group interactions on the Internet also often influences how individuals use other media such as television, radio, etc. how your use has changed now when compared to before you got on the internet" (5-point scale "very much less than before-very much more than before)

- ➢ Watching television
- ➢ Listening to the radio
- ➢ Reading newspapers
- ➢ Reading magazines
- ➢ Watching movies in movie theaters
- ➢ Renting videos and DVDs
- ➢ Reading fiction and non-fiction books

"How many days per week do you use the following communication media? And "On each day you do use these media, how many hours on average per day do you use it?

- ➢ Television
- ➢ Radio
- ➢ Newspaper
- ➢ Magazines
- ➢ Email
- ➢ Web (non-e-mail)
- ➢ Telephone

Table 3.

Hypothesis number	Variable name	Low interactivity means	High interactivity means	Significance level
1a	Strenght of self's intention	3.92	4.13	F (1, 520) =4,951**
	Intention to interaction whole group	4.14	3.75	F (1, 463) =15,315***
1a	Average we-intentions	8.004	7.71	F (1, 519) =3,739*
1b	Behavior second wave (Measure 1): How many different sessions in the most recent two-week period?	30.65	15.71	F (1, 138) =8,519**
1b	Behavior second wave (Measure 2): Time in hours per session during most recent two-week period	.747	2.242	F (1, 138) =43,489**
1b	Behavior second wave Measure 3: How many different sessions on avg in a two-week period during last 6 months?	30.07	15.85	F (1, 138) =7,316**
1b	Hours	1.5829	3.5683	F (1, 479) =30,801***

1b	TotalBehavior - Number of times * hours each time	24.8747	41.2409	F (1, 138) =4,045***
2a	Group norms: strength to which friends hold goal (average)	3.6517	3.4716	F (1, 493) = 4,251 **
2b	Agreement self	3.6773	3.9745	F (1, 523) = 7,985**
	Agreement whole group	3.92	3.66	F (1, 470) = 6,474**
	Sum of agreement	7.2289	7.5622	F (1, 525) =3,032*
2b	Committed whole group	4.00	3.53	F (1, 464) =20,023***
	Commitment - average of group members	3.9717	3.6214	F (1, 505) = 15,323***
2b	Support whole group	3.74	3.44	F (1, 452) =7,402**
	Support- average of group members	3.7943	3.4970	F (1, 505) =9,598 **
2b	Like members of group (me)	4.25	4.39	F (1, 501) =3,591 *
	Like whole group	4.10	4.26	F (1, 512) =4,754 **
2c	Affective Social identity	4.68	5.05	F (1, 513) =5,956 **
	Sum of affective social identity	9.5787	10.156	F (1, 138) =4,919**
2c	Evaluative social identity (first measure)	4.69	5.27	F (1, 518) =14,342 ***

	Evaluative social identity (second measure)	4.16	5.06	F (1, 514) =31,218 ***
	sum of evaluative social identity	8.7412	10.253	F (1, 521) =24,882***
3a	Positive Anticipated Emotions	3.9173	4.2299	F (1, 519) =5,372 **
3b	Negative Anticipated Emotions	1.7849	1.9779	F (1, 512) =3,240 *
4a	Days of TV use	5.17	4.33	F (1, 533) =16,386 ***
	Tv use (hours)	15.9815	12.0370	F (1, 506) =7,702 ***
4a	Days of radio use	4.88	4.36	F (1, 534) =6,363 **
4a	Days of newspaper use	3.97	2.95	F (1, 534) =21,939 ***
4a	Newspaper use (hours)	4.5198	3.5374	F (1, 515) =4,543 **
4a	Days of magazine use	2.81	1.93	F (1, 533) =28,963 ***
4a	Magazine use (hours)	3.2044	2.1314	F (1, 508) =31,218 ***
4a	Hrs/ day of magazine use	1.06	.81	F (1, 492) =13,082***
4b	Days of email use	6.60	6.08	F (1, 534) =18,788 ***
4b	Email use (hours)	16.5473	13.8268	F (1, 509) =2,865 *
4b	Hrs/ day of web use	2.90	3.86	F (1, 497) =12,921 ***
4b	Webuse	18.7826	24.8446	F (1, 501) =10,706 ***
4c	Visiting with family members	3.05	2.84	F (1, 522) =15,460 ***

4c	Going out with family members	2.96	2.83	$F_{(1, 519)} = 7,165$ ***
4c	Visiting with friends	3.11	2.96	$F_{(1, 520)} = 4,694$ **
4c	Going out with friends	3.06	2.94	$F_{(1, 520)} = 3,330$ ***
4c	Average of going out with family and friends	3.0079	2.8866	$F_{(1, 521)} = 7,009$ **
4c	Activities with neighbors	2.93	2.84	$F_{(1, 519)} = 3,180$ *
4c	Activities with hobby groups (book clubs, sports teams, etc,)	3.23	2.91	$F_{(1, 520)} = 18,122$ ***
4c	Telephone conversations with family	2.84	2.60	$F_{(1, 521)} = 13,415$ ***
4c	Average of conversations with family and friends	2.8098	2.6524	$F_{(1, 522)} = 7,009$ **
4c	Social activity: average of first four items	3.0444	2.8950	$F_{(1, 522)} = 12,492$**
	Social activity: Average of all nine social interactions change measures	2.9521	2.8716	$F_{(1, 521)} = 4,841$**
4c	Watching movies in movie theatres	2.81	3.03	$F_{(1, 521)} = 8,735$**

5	INFORMATIONAL1: average of first two inform items	3.523	3.149	$F_{(1, 525)} = 22,093***$
	INFORMATIONAL2: average of second two inform items	3.6157	2.9945	$F_{(1, 524)} = 55,804***$
	Average of the informational value measures	3.5723	3.0720	$F_{(1, 526)} = 46,008***$
5	INSTRUMENTAL1: average of first three instrumental items	2.3817	2.6218	$F_{(1, 524)} = 13,798***$
5	ENTERTAINMENT1: average of first two entertainment items	3.1240	4.1827	$F_{(1, 523)} = 159,257***$
	ENTERTAINMENT2: averag of last two entertainment items	2.8234	3.7963	$F_{(1, 520)} = 125,868***$
5	Sum of the self-discovery value measures	5.1423	5.4945	$F_{(1, 522)} = 3,245*$
5	Sum of the MII value measures	5.7866	7.0000	$F_{(1, 522)} = 38,853***$
5	Sum of the social enhancement measures	3.3889	4.0258	$F_{(1, 521)} = 7,316**$
5	Sum of the	11.7953	15.8893	$F_{(1, 523)} = 168,375***$

	entertainment value measures			
5	Sum of the purposive value measures	26.7422	25.4280	F (1, 526) =5,464**
6b	Perceived behavioral control	6.00	5.74	F (1, 524) =4,201 **
6a	Attitude: average of measures	5.2411	4.8063	F (1, 512) =21,968 ***
7	Social norm1: reverse of q14a	5.5913	4.9333	F (1, 520) =23,591 ***
7	Social norm2: reverse of q14b	5.9407	5.4502	F (1, 522) = 13,22***
	Gender Category	1.5195	1.6067	F (1, 521) =4,058**
	Age	39.93	26.52	F (1, 523) =174,001***

Table 4.

Hypothesis number	Variable name	Low engagement means	High engagement means	Significance level
1a	Agreement self	3.44	4.29	F (1, 513)=74,408***
	Agreement whole group	3.44	4.18	F (1, 460) = 55,708***
	Agreement average of group members	3.38	4.09	F (1, 498) = 70,047***
1a	Sum of agreement	6.6846	8.2774	F (1, 515)=80,286***
1a	Intention to interact (me)	3.67	4.47	F (1, 508) =78,259***
	Intention to interaction (whole group)	3.61	4.33	F (1, 453) =58,976***

1a	sum of we-intentions	6.8571	8.9357	F (1, 520)= 288,99***
1a	WEINTENT1	3.43	4.52	F (1, 517) =288,908***
	WEINTENT2	3.46	4.47	F (1, 518) =212,863***
1a	Commitment - average of group members	3.44	4.36	F (1, 511) = 94,634***
	Commitment self	3.43	4.36	F (1, 511) = 94,634***
1a	Accommodate - Self	3.1	3.86	F (1, 512) =59,941 ***
	Accommodate - average of group members	3.06	3.64	F (1, 487) =40,992***
1a	Sum of accommodation	6.0230	7.39	F (1, 505)=53,234***
1a	Support whole group	3.23	3.96	F (1, 452) =48,138***
	Support self	3.45	4.13	F (1, 509) =47,069***
	Support average of group members	3.33	3.95	F (1, 496) =44,451***
1a	Like members of group me	4.13	4.55	F (1, 492) =30,801***
	Like whole group	3.94	4.45	F (1, 440) =54,139 ***
1a	Group Norm1: strength to which resp holds goal	3.17	4.12	F (1, 500) =105,290***
	Group norm2: strength to which friends hold goal (average)	3.1845	3.9619	F (1, 490) = 92,694***

1a	sum of group norms	6.1544	7.9301	F (1, 508)=110,853***
1a	We- intentions	3.426	4.5223	F (1, 517)= 288,908***
	We-intentions2	3.4559	4.4677	F (1, 518)=212,863***
1b	COGSI1	3.44	4.30	F (1, 518) =24,765***
	COGSI2	2.85	3.62	F (1, 515) =27,203***
	AFFSI1	4.49	5.76	F (1, 518) =112,525***
	AFFSI2	4.23	5.59	F (1, 512) =95,399***
	EVALSI1	4.54	5.46	F (1, 518) =37,351***
	EVALSI2	4.19	5.11	F (1, 512) =32,021***
1b	Sum of Cog si	6.2757	7.9113	F (1, 518)= 31,249***
1b	Sum of aff si	8.6117	11.2811	F (1, 520)=130,231***
1b	Sum of eval si	8.6374	10.5000	F (1, 519)=38,953***
2a	Behavior second wave Measure 1: How many different sessions in the most recent two-week period?	13.20	32.64	F (1, 133) =14,196***
2a	Behavior second wave Measure 3: How many different sessions on average in a two-week period during last 6 months?	12.91	32.57	F (1, 133) =13,826***
2b	Informational1: average of first two informational items	3.1593	3.5203	F (1, 133) =20,170***
	Informational2:	3.0938	3.5122	F (1, 516) =23,350***

	average of second two inform items			
2b	Instrumental1: average of first three instrumental items	2.3866	2.6369	F (1, 516) =14,825***
	Instrumental2: average of last two instrumental items	2.4707	2.9796	F (1, 516) =35,238***
2b	Entertainment1: average of first two entertainment items	3.4706	3.9207	F (1, 516) = 23,08***
	Entertainment2: average of last two entertainment items	3.1292	3.5449	F (1, 515) = 18,927***
2a	Total Behavior - Number of times * hours each time	22.9802	45.905	F (1, 457) = 7,767**
2b	Average of the informational value measures	3.1300	3.5163	F (1, 517)= 25,924***
	Average of the instrumental value measures	2.4335	2.8103	F (1, 517)=31,767***
2b	Sum of the self-discovery value measures	4.7426	6.0286	F (1, 516)= 46,81***
2b	Sum of the MII value measures	5.7757	7.1260	F (1, 516)=48,409***
2b	Sum of the social enhancement	3.500	3.9837	F (1, 516)= 8,131**

	measures			
2b	Sum of the entertainment value measures	13.1066	14.8780	F (1, 516)= 25,012***
2b	Sum of the purposive value measures	24.4945	27.845	F (1, 517)= 36,767***
3a	Positive Anticipated Emotions (average of first four measures)	3.4238	4.8044	F (1, 515) =129,230***
	PAE2: Positive Anticipated Emotions (average of last five measures)	3.6917	4.9906	F (1, 517) =134,529***
3a	NAE1: Negative Anticipated Emotions (average of first six measures)	1.9305	2.9948	F (1, 520) =100,270***
	NAE2: Negative Anticipated Emotions (average of last six measures)	1.5483	2.2786	F (1, 507) = 49,896***
4b	Perceived behavioral control1	5.41	6.35	F (1, 520) =61,229***
	Percevied behavioral control2	5.27	6.15	F (1, 516) =39,685***

4a	Attitude1: Average of first two measures	4.63	5.44	$F (1, 520) =83,547***$
	Attitude: Average of last two measures	5.06	5.94	$F (1, 516) =113,447***$
5	Subjective norms1: reverse of q14a	4.82	5.72	$F (1, 521) =45,97***$
	Subjective norms2: reverse of q14b	5.4109	5.9960	$F (1, 523) =19,037***$
6a	Days of radio use	4.40	4.78	$F (1, 523) =3,257*$
6a	Radio use (hours)	11.14	14.31	$F (1, 489) =3,954**$
6b	days of email use	6.20	6.52	$F (1, 523) =6,98**$
6b	Email use (hours)	13.2619	17.4815	$F (1, 500) =6,737**$
6b	Days of web use	6.00	6.42	$F (1, 523) =10,701***$
6b	WEB use (hours)	18.6553	25.68	$F (1,491) =14,035***$
6a	hrs/ day of radio use	2.00	2.45	$F (1, 483) =3,78**$
6b	hrs/ day of email use	2.03	2.59	$F (1, 499) =6,020**$
6b	hrs/ day of web use	3.00	3.85	$F (1, 487) =9,697**$
6c	Visiting with family members	2.9	2.99	$F (1, 512) =2,92**$
	Going out with family members	2.84	2.94	$F (1, 509) =4,27**$
6a	Reading magazines	2.67	2.54	$F (1, 510) = 3,213*$
6	Watching movies in movie theaters	2.98	2.85	$F (1, 511) =3,065*$
	Gender Category	1.62	1.49	$F (1, 508) = 9,037**$

Table 5.

Hypothesis Number	Hypothesis	Result
1a	Greater levels of interactivity lead to stronger We-Intentions to interact with on the Internet as a group.	Supported
1b	Higher levels of interactivity lead to stronger currently and past online participation behavior both for average number of interactions and average time spent each interaction with the group of friends.	Supported
2a	Higher levels of interactivity lead to stronger group norms.	Reversed
2b	Higher levels of interactivity lead to stronger mutual behaviors. i. Mutual agreement ii. Mutual commitment of members to interact with on the internet as a group and stronger commitment of the whole group. iii. Mutual accommodation iv. Mutual support v. Mutual liking	Supported
2c	Higher levels of interactivity lead to stronger i. Cognitive social identity ii. Affective social identity iii. Evaluative social identity	Partially supported
3a	Higher levels of interactivity lead to stronger positive anticipated emotions	Supported
3b	Higher levels of interactivity lead to	Supported

	stronger negative anticipated emotions	
4a	Higher levels of interactivity imply a lower use of other communication media such as television, radio, newspapers, magazines, books, telephone	Supported
4b	Higher levels of interactivity imply a higher use of email and web	Partially Supported
4c	Higher levels of engagement lead to low activities with family and friends.	Supported
5a	Higher levels of interactivity lead to stronger use of online group of friend and/or the Internet for satisfying needs such as: Purposive value	Supported
5b	Self discovery value	Supported
5c	Maintaining interpersonal interconnectivity	Supported
5d	Social enhancement value	Supported
5e	Entertainment value	Supported
6a	Higher levels of interactivity lead to stronger positive attitude toward interacting together on the internet with the group.	Partially supported
6b	Higher levels of interactivity lead to stronger perceived behavioral control over interacting together on the internet with the group.	Supported
7	Higher levels of interactivity lead to	Supported

	stronger subjective norms.	

Table 6.

Hypothesis Number	Hypothesis	Result
1a	Higher levels of engagement lead to: i. Mutual agreement ii. Mutual commitment iii. Mutual accommodation iv. Mutual support v. Mutual liking	Supported
1b	Higher levels of engagement lead to stronger i. Cognitive social identity ii. Affective social identity iii. Evaluative social identity	Supported
2a	Higher levels of engagement lead to stronger online participation both for number of interactions and average time spent each interaction.	Partially Supported
2b	Higher levels of engagement lead to stronger use of online group and the Internet in general for satisfying needs: i. Purposive value ii. Self discovery value iii. Maintaining interpersonal interconnectivity iv. Social enhancement value v. Entertainment value.	Supported
3a	Higher levels of engagement lead to	Supported

	stronger positive anticipated emotions	
3b	Higher levels of interactivity lead to stronger negative anticipated emotions	Supported
4a	Higher levels of engagement lead to stronger positive attitude toward interacting together on the internet with the group.	Supported
4b	Higher levels of engagement lead to stronger perceived behavioral control over interacting together on the internet with the group.	Supported
5	Higher levels of engagement lead to stronger subjective norms.	Supported
6a	Higher levels of engagement imply a lower use of other media such as television, radio, newspapers, magazines, books, and telephone.	Partially Reversed
6b	Higher levels of engagement imply a higher use of email and web.	Supported
6c	Higher levels of engagement lead to low activities with family and friends.	Partially Reversed

Figure 1.

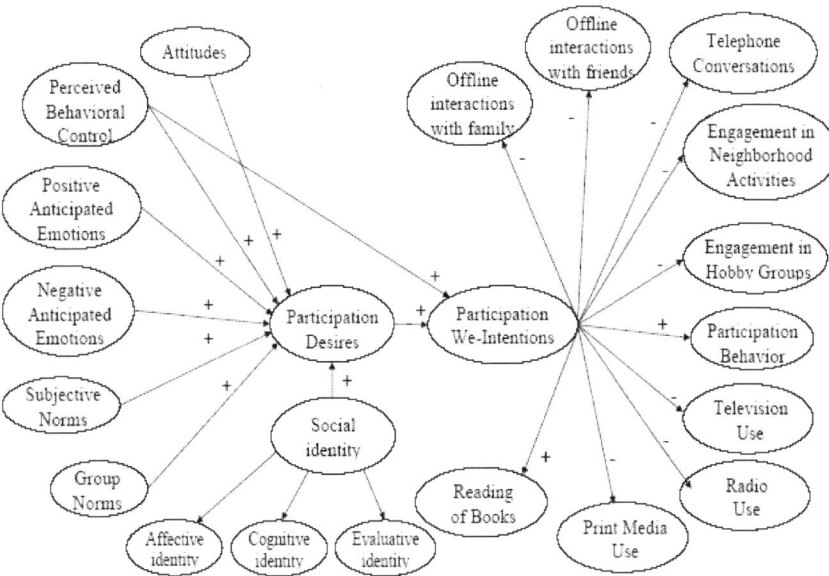

Chapter 3. A Study of Sharing in Online Consumer Communities

Abstract:

A key ingredient for customer community success is active and enthusiastic contribution and participation by customers. In this research, we seek to better understand why consumers contribute content, and share their resources in customer communities. We make the distinction between sharing behaviors that are intrinsically motivated, and those that are spurious. We then propose a causal model detailing the antecedents of these different sharing behaviors. In our model, motivated sharing is influenced positively by identification with other members, customers' sense of personal responsibility, their overall engagement in the community, their sense of reciprocity, their belief in the sponsoring organization's principles, and beliefs that they will gain personally from sharing, and it is influenced negatively by perceptions of costs associated with making contributions to the community. Spurious sharing is influenced by economic benefits, increase in social stature and reputation enhancement. Managerial implications include free-riding-mitigating mechanisms that can be employed in consumer communities to increase sharing behavior.

Keywords: Consumer Networks, Sharing Behavior, Consumer Communities, Motivation

1. Introduction: Statement of the Problem Area to Be Researched

Over the last decade or so, consumer communities have been steadily growing in popularity (e.g., Kozinets, 2002; Muniz & O'Guinn, 2001). These communities take many forms. Some consumer communities, such as those found on the eBay web site, have primarily commercial purposes of buying and selling gainfully. Others, such as Gnutella and BitTorrent, are peer-to-peer (P2P) networks of consumers who share digital information like music or video files, software programs, videogames, images, documents etc., with one another. Still other consumer communities are found in the chat rooms, bulletin boards, and user groups that congregate to discuss experiences, and share knowledge regarding a particular product or service. For example, in the MUSE chat-room devoted to the Apache server software[14], experienced developers help novices with specific software installation and usage issues. Similarly, Slyck.com is a popular file sharing community, offering news, reviews, and opinions, and has very active user forums. It tracks the latest versions of file sharing clients and file sharing network traffic. Others, such as MacIntosh computer enthusiasts and Star Trek "trekkie" fans, are brand communities, organized by admirers of a particular brand, that meet to engage in social interactions and accomplish joint goals (e.g., Bagozzi & Dholakia, 2006).

Marketers are very interested in organizing and managing consumer communities, since they offer attractive alternatives to traditional marketing programs like advertising or sales promotions (Algesheimer, Dholakia, & Herrmann, 2005; McAlexander, Schouten, & Koenig, 2002). This is because consumer communities allow firms to identify and interact with their loyal and engaged customers (Algesheimer et al., 2005), socialize new customers to the brand ethos (McAlexander et al., 2002), and provide low cost service support to their newer customers through the assistance of experienced community volunteers instead of paid employees (see the MUSE chat-room example above).

---

[14] http://ws.apache.org/muse/contact_info

Perhaps the most interesting aspect of consumer communities is that they rely on cooperation among members and in particular, on ongoing effortful contributions by a significant number of them, for their continued functioning (Nonnecke & Preece, 2000). It is often said that people never stop looking for sharing things with others, belonging to various groups or establishing new relationships (De Cremer, 2002; De Cremer & Van Vugt, 1999; Baumeister, & Leary, 1995; Komorita & Parks, 1994). This obviously reflects the need of socialization which is a never ending process through which people develop their values, motivations and habits (Blackwell et al., 2001).

Customer-generated contributions are essential for the continued functioning of customer communities. For example, in eBay auctions, unless a significant number of buyers and sellers take the time to evaluate their trading partners' performance and provide feedback, the reputation mechanism will no longer work (Dholakia, 2005). Similarly, epinions.com and other recommendation sites rely on their users to provide thoughtful and honest product reviews in large numbers. P2P networks rely on their users to upload (i.e., share) their files so that others can download them. The MUSE chat-room relies on its experienced users to take the time and the effort to answer a majority of technical questions and solicitations for help that are posed by novice users. In the present dissertation, we call the effortful contributions that are volunteered by users of consumer communities as sharing behavior.

It is noteworthy that even though sharing by members is essential, a vast majority of consumer communities do not compensate users for their contributions in any tangible way. Moreover, at the individual level, consumers do not have to share resources with others in order to benefit from the resources that are available in the community (Karau & Williams 1993; 2001). For example, a consumer can read product reviews posted by others on epinions.com without posting a review. Under such circumstances, why do consumer community members share their resources with other members? In particular, what are the types and drivers of sharing in consumer communities? We attempt to answer these questions in the present research. At least two aspects of sharing in consumer communities are relevant to our subsequent analysis. The first is that in most instances, sharing involves generating or transmitting digital information (e.g., recommendations, reviews, songs, movies, software, etc.), and therefore the sharer typically does not give up the good he or she possesses, but simply shares a perfect copy in the case of songs, movies and software, or in cases like reviews and recommendations, generates original content. In fact, this is an important argument used by observers to encourage sharing in many consumer communities: "The community's innovative power results from accumulating member-generated expertise and multiplying it by giving it away." (Hemetsberger, 2002, p.354).

Secondly, previous research reveals considerable variation in the amount of sharing in different consumer communities. For instance, one study of P2P networks found that over a 24 hour period, almost 70% of Gnutella users shared no files at all, whereas the top 1% shared 50% of the files (Adar & Huberman, 2000). However, another study showed that 58% of Gnutella users shared at least some of their files with others (Asvanund et al. 2003). Other studies have shown that in open source development communities, only 4% of users account for more than half the responses given to help other members (Lakhani & Hippel, 2003), and 4% of developers contribute 88% of new code and 66% of code fixes (Mockus, Fielding, & Andersen 2002). We argue that by borrowing insights from the knowledge-sharing literature, especially regarding individual knowledge-sharing behavior, and applying them in an online context, additional explanations can be found regarding why file sharing in online networks is often not realized.

Until now, online sharing behavior has not been systematically analyzed in the literature. The digital-content and related industries have to further understand the consumers who share files. What facilitates online sharing behavior? The present study, therefore, aims to present a model that will help academics and practitioners to understand consumer-sharing behavior in the online community file-sharing phenomenon.

Our larger goal is to provide an actionable framework to marketers, organizers of consumer networks, copyright holders of information goods, and consumers through which to encourage or discourage sharing behavior and free-riding behavior in all types of consumer networks. Our second goal in this research is to comprehend why consumers share (provide contributions) and not share (free ride) in online customer communities.

Our third goal is to comprehend if we want consumers to share, how we can get them to share.

Information sharing behavior is one of the more intriguing and fascinating behaviors online. Our fourth goal in this research is to understand what the types of sharing behavior are. In particular, we make the distinction between sharing behaviors that are intrinsically motivated, and those that are spurious.

Fifth, we intend to study if there are differences in drivers of sharing across different types of customer communities. In the present research, we study sharing behaviors in different types of communities including peer-to-peer networks, eBay customer communities, blogs, review web-sites, and online forums. We wish to examine if the drivers of sharing behaviors vary across the different customer communities.

This paper is part of a doctoral dissertation. We present the proposed causal model that we developed as a result of preliminary qualitative analysis. In the second phase of the research, we conducted a large-scale survey of a variety of consumer community users, to test our proposed model of sharing using Structural Equation Modeling.

2. Relevant Theory Addressing the Topic: Theory of Information Sharing and Social Exchange Theory or Interdependence Theory

Kelley & Thibaut's (1978) interdependence theory distinguishes sharing between two individuals acting alone and sharing between two individuals influenced by their social and organizational environment. In the first case, rational self-interest and simple reciprocity theoretically predict behavior: "I help you if you help me; I withhold help if you act destructively". In the second case, the reciprocation of negative behavior does not necessarily take place. People may overcome their initial impulse to get revenge for a negative behavior because of the social and organizational circumstances. The environment affects their apprehension for future relations with others, their power, how others will see them, the impact of their behavior on other desirable goals and so on. In our context, a community member may decide that acting constructively is the appropriate thing to do, because of these reasons.

Increased information sharing could improve efficiency, learning, innovation, flexibility, and understanding of community goals for the sharer (e.g., Walton 1989, Malone & Rockart 1991, Sproull & Kiesler 1991, Nickerson, 1992). Communications and sharing among people are strongly influenced by their friendships and personal contacts with others, and by their commitment to the community (Kraut et al. 1990, O'Reilly & Chatman 1986). For example, employees in some organizations share knowledge and help others, including organizationally remote people they will never meet in person (Finholt & Sproull 1990, Constant et al, 1996). The Theory of Information Sharing (TIS) originated through the study of the attitudes and norms that affect information sharing. According to this theory, information as know-how belongs to a special category of shared information that contributes to the formation of self identity and the sharing of this knowledge is derived from the need for self-expression (Constant, Kiesler, & Sproull, 1994). Thus, as a form of self-expression, sharing can provide personal benefits such as reinforcing self-esteem and pride, improving sense of self-efficacy, personal identity within the group, and gaining of respect and reputation (Constant, Kiesler, & Sproull, 1994). Chan, Bhandar & Chan (2004) demonstrated that the TIS is applicable in a social-oriented context of virtual community.

The TIS is based on the Social Exchange Theory. Social Exchange Theory (Kelley & Thibaut's, 1978) assumes that people review and weigh their relationships in terms of costs and rewards (West & Turner, 2001). Economic exchange theories focus on economic capital such as goods and money, instead social exchange theory focuses on sharing of social capital such as power and trust (Blau, 1964). Originally, Social Exchange Theory did not concern the sharing of knowledge and information (Jarvenpaa, & Staples, 2000). Through the TIS, Constant et al. (1994) contextualized Social Exchange Theory to the organizational environment of information sharing. Consequently, Jarvenpaa and colleagues (Jarvenpaa & Staples 2000, Jarvenpaa & Staples, 2001, Staples & Jarvenpaa, 2000) developed the TIS to comprehend the determinants that affected the use of collaborative electronic media for information sharing within the organizational boundary. Participation in an online consumer community often requires members to share and seek knowledge and information on a particular joint interest. Therefore, participation in an online consumer community can be considered as a form of information sharing and knowledge exchange (Ridings, Gefen, & Arinze, 2002; Wasko & Faraj, 2000).

3. Online consumer community

There is no accepted definition of online community. The term means different things to different people (Preece & Maloney-Krichmar, 2003; Preece, 2000, 2001). Rheingold describes virtual communities as cultural aggregations that materialize when enough consumers bump into each other often enough online (Rheingold, 2000). Many virtual community definitions are found online: is a community of people sharing common interests, ideas, and feelings over the Internet or other collaborative network[15]; or a community made of people who have no contact in the real world, but only over a technological system, by engaging on discussions or by communicating or by having the same interests they share in the virtual world[16]; or a group whose members are connected by means of information technologies, typically the Internet. Similar terms include online community and mediated community[17].

In the past, a multidisciplinary group of academics tried to identify the following common characteristics of online communities (Whittaker, Issacs, & O'Day, 1997, p. 137): members have a shared goal, interest, need, or activity that provides the primary reason for belonging to the community; they are engaged in repeated, active participation; there are often intense interactions, strong emotional ties and shared activities between consumers; they have access to shared resources and there are policies for determining access to those resources. Reciprocity of information, support and services between consumers is important. There is a shared context of social conventions, language, and protocols.

Furthermore, sociologists consider the strength and nature of relationships between individuals to be the useful basis for defining community (Hamman, 1999; Haythornthwaite & Wellman, 1998; Wellman & Gulia, 1999). In this dissertation,

---

[15] http://www.creotec.com/index.php?page=e-business_terms
[16] http://mobileman.projects.supsi.ch/glossary.html
[17] http://en.wikipedia.org/wiki/Virtual_community

consistent with prevailing definitions (e.g., Dholakia, Bagozzi, & Pearo, 2004; Rheingold, 2002; Wellman & Gulia, 1999), online communities are viewed to be composed of customer aggregations of varying sizes that meet, participate, contribute and interact online for achieving personal as well as shared goals of their members, and for sharing interests, ideas, opinions and feelings.

4. Different types of Online Consumer Community

In the empirical study to validate our proposed theoretical framework and for the sake of generalization, we will include members from a total of five different types of online consumer communities where online sharing behavior occurs: P2P networks, eBay community, web logs, review websites, and message boards. We chose them because although each virtual community is unique and has its own characteristics, these communities present some shared characteristics we will describe in the next section. Additionally, we chose these communities because all of them have some particular functions that facilitate sharing behaviors.

4.1 P2P Networks

P2P networks refer to distributed information-sharing systems used by consumers to share digital information goods such as music or video files, software programs, video games, etc. as well as idle storage and processing capacity of their computers (e.g., Andrade, Brasileiro, & Cirne, 2004). Examples of P2P networks are Gnutella, BitTorrent, and eDonkey. The "peers" are computer systems connected to each other via the Internet. In P2P networks, files can be shared directly between systems on the network without a central server because each computer on the network becomes a file server as well as a client. There is no central server managing the network and there is no central router. For example, Kazaa uses P2P technology: individual users connect to each other directly, without need for a central point of management. A computer needs P2P software, such as Kazaa, Limewire, BearShare, Morpheus, and internet connection to join the P2P network.

The P2P software connects to the P2P network, such as Gnutella, Freenet and Napster, which allows the computer to access other systems on the network to search for files on other people's computers. Users can search for a file on each shared folder on each connected computer. People design the folder to share on their computer[18].

P2P networks are chosen because there is converging evidence of widespread use. For example, recent estimates from Big Champagne (June 2006), a P2P tracking firm, indicate that in Germany alone, approximately 9.7 million individuals simultaneously use P2P networks at any given time. Adding BitTorrent (which is not included), augments this estimate by an additional 3 million[19]. In USA 40 to 60 million Americans admit to having swapped music files over the Internet.[20] World-wide, estimates of P2P network users range in the hundreds of millions, and this number is constantly growing[21]. Although most of the popular attention has been given to the "underground" illegal sharing of copyrighted information goods through these networks (e.g., Einhorn & Rosenblatt, 2005; Helm, 2005), experts have noted the beneficial and high market potential applications of P2P networks such as distributed computing, internet telephony (VoIP), online video conferencing, and other collaboration-fostering applications for the workplace (e.g., Baset & Schulzrinne, 2004).

Over the last five years or so, a considerable amount of research has studied P2P networks, considering technological issues in setting up and running such networks (e.g., Androutsellis-Theotokis & Spinellis, 2004; Ripenau, Foster, & Iamnitchi, 2002; Subramanian & Goodman, 2005). Moreover, P2P consumer networks are chosen because they are (for the most part) decentralized; consequently, the identities of individual consumers within the networks are anonymous. Furthermore, to function smoothly and effectively, P2P networks rely on contributions, in particular, sharing, from its individual members. For example, unless a user uploads a song or video file to the network, others cannot download it. Yet, users of most P2P networks have no clear incentives for doing so (Ramaswamy & Liu, 2002: Krishnan et al., 2004; Beenen et al., 2004).

---

[18]. http://www.sharpened.net/glossary/definition.php?p2p
[19]. http://www.slyck.com/news.php?story=1229
[20] William Fisher, The New York Times, June 25, 2004
[21] http://internet-filter-review.toptenreviews.com/peer-to-peer-file-sharing.html

Such conditions are conducive to free-rider behavior, which economists have described as follows: "Each consumer has an incentive to enjoy the benefits of the public good provided by others while providing it insufficiently herself" (Mas-Colell, Whinston, & Green, 1995, p. 362; see Ledyard, 1995, for a review). Social psychologists too have noted the analogous "social loafing effect" wherein participation in a collective activity (such as a distributed information sharing network) leads to reduced effort by individuals than when they are engaging in an individualistic task (Karau & Williams, 1993).

We include P2P networks also because free-riding behavior by participants is detrimental to the functioning of P2P networks for several reasons. Firstly, when few consumers contribute resources and many take them, the network's performance degrades significantly, making it cumbersome to use for everyone (Ramaswamy & Liu, 2002). Secondly, inadequate contributions lead to a reduced assortment of available resources, making the network less appealing to its members. Thirdly, the greater the free-riding behavior in a network, the more vulnerable those who share will be, which in turn may dissuade them from further sharing their resources (Adar & Huberman, 2000). This issue is especially significant when the information good being shared is copyrighted or otherwise protected, and sharers face the risk of being prosecuted.

4.2 EBay Community

The consumer community on the eBay web site has primarily commercial purposes of buying and selling gainfully. The eBay Community is composed by eBay members, buyers and sellers, as well as eBay staff. It encourages open and honest communication among all its members. In their website they say: "respect and communication are the cornerstones of eBay's dynamic Community"[22].

First, eBay community is chosen since it is the largest digital auction, facilitating the buying and selling of items in more than 4000 different categories, markets in over 20 countries, and 181 million registered users around the world at the end of 2005[23]. Second,

---

[22] http://pages.eBay.in/help/newtoeBay/community_overview.html

[23]. http://investor.eBay.com/annual.cfm

over 75% of all transactions through digital auctions are conducted on eBay (Lucking-Reiley, 2000). Third, data from eBay have been used in recent digital auction research (e.g., Bajari & Hortac, 2000; Wilcox, 2000). Fourth, we want to consider an e-business website community since 52% of the 104 million American adults who have Internet access have bought a product online (Pew, 2001). Fifth, e-business companies seek to build a new kind of relationship with their customers through online communities (Hagel & Armstrong, 1997). People who buy from eBay want value for money, their personal information to be secure and private, and to receive the product in a timely manner (Preece & Maloney-Krichmar, 2003). 'Credit card fear' is the most important deterrent to online shopping. Non-shoppers are afraid that their credit card information will be stolen and that product will not be delivered[24] (IBM, 2005). eBay's reputation system and eBay community help to mitigate some of these fears. We study the eBay reputation system in this research as a sharing information tool provided by the Community. The infrastructure for eBay is designed to make it easy for users to use the website without sacrificing their trust about reliability, security and privacy (Venkatraman, 2000).

4.3 Blogs or Web Logs

The blogosphere refers to the distributed network of user opinions published on the WWW. Blogging software allows users to publish opinions on any topic without constraint (Avesani, Cova, Hayes & Massa, 2005). Web logs, blogs or online diaries are utilized by consumers to publicly broadcast what in the past would have been private writings regarding one's emotions and experiences (Brynin & Kraut, 2006). We include blogs in our study because Weblogging has become an important part of the information economy found on the Internet (Nardi, Schiano & Gumbrecht, 2004; Schiano, Nardi, Gumbrecht, & Swartz, 2004). "Blogging has come a long way since the medium burst on the scene in 1999. Weblogs aren't merely vehicles for personal expression; many of them frequently break news, shape public opinion, and serve as lively channels for discussion" (Tweney, 2006). Review sites are topic-centric, instead blog sites are user-centric,

---

[24]. http://www.bankrate.com/brm/news/cc/20021011a.asp

publishing the user's perspective on multiple topics, defined and categorised in a local way by the user (Mathes & Folksonomies, 2004).

As an example of sharing information in blogs, on April 27, 2006, AOL kicked off bloggingstocks.com, a new blogging network that features bloggers posting about individual stocks, ranging from Google to Time Warner. AOL encourages users to be stockholders, if not necessarily in the companies they are writing about. Consumers have to sign a code of ethics, disclose their holdings and not trade on insider information. This is a new world. It is up to people following these blogs to decide whether they feel any stock manipulation is happening in the comments and to decide how good the shared information is. This example illustrates that blogs have become very influential components of the Internet, and their importance is growing exponentially. In fact, Blogs also can be used as tools for creating online consumer communities of people with same interests or interested in each other's. Any consumer can describe opinions, feelings, activities and reactions, and thereby share them with others who participate on the blog, but since blogs are normally publicly available sites, some customers called "lurkers" can read them without contributing any thoughts or materials of their own. "Lurkers" often outnumber the active "bloggers". For this reason, it is important to include them in our research and study sharing behavior in Blogs. Furthermore, because during the past two years, some blogs have become "news sources," publishing stories like newspapers, radio stations and TV stations.

4.4 Review websites

Centralized review sites such Amazon.com allow users to post opinions regarding books, CDs, and other product categories. Their significant advantage is that reviews regarding a single topic are collected together in one place, allowing readers to access a diverse range of opinions conveniently (Avesani, Cova, Hayes & Massa, 2005). Ordinary consumers easily publish opinions and reviews based on their experiences. Reviews have great value for other consumers since they can use them to choose between different options or simply to inform themselves.

For example, Epinions helps people make informed buying decisions. It is a consumer reviews platform on the Web and a reliable source for valuable consumer insight, unbiased advice, in-depth product evaluations and personalized recommendations. Epinions is a service of Shopping.com, Inc., a leading provider of comparison shopping services.

We include review websites because, with millions of consumer reviews, they provide a platform for consumers to share their experiences. In addition to detailed product reviews, members can read and share buying guides (What should I consider when buying something?), product definitions, and 'how-to' guides (How do I install …?). Review websites often include reputation mechanisms. For example Epinions uses biography pages, review lists, and the ability to comment on reviews to allow consumers to discount certain members' advice and stop seeing advice from unreliable reviewers. Additionally, Epinions has launched "tickets" to flag users who have violated the user agreement.

4.5 Message Boards

A message board, also referred as discussion boards, discussion forums, discussion groups, bulletin boards or web forums, is an online community where members may read and post topics of a shared interest. This group can be either closed, private, or open if public. It allows free sharing of ideas, thoughts, comments, information, and opinions. Online forums provide potential for new forms of collaborative work, study, and community that reduce barriers of time and distance (Kanuka, & Anderson, 1998). For example, a typical technical support forum allows customers to post technical questions and receive answers from their peers (Gu & Jarvenpaa, 2003). Additionally, communication forums can reduce complexity, help consumers make judgments about what is important, and build shared beliefs (Schultz, 2000). We include forums in our research because in many cases, they are not mere information boards, but arenas of discussions, places to meet other community members, and get help with personal editing questions. It is noteworthy that many forums facilitate sharing by allowing members: (1) to take time to reflect, compose and edit items posted to the list; (2) to find an existing group with sharing interests; (3) to offer separate topics for each conversation and is excellent for in-depth discussion; (4) good search facilities that enable participants to search on topics, or people, or messages sent on or between particular dates.

5. Common Characteristics of Consumer Communities

Although each community is unique and has its own characteristics, the consumer communities that we study share several common characteristics. First, consumer communities considered in this research are all network-based consumer communities. A network-based virtual community is a "specialized, geographically dispersed virtual community based on a structured, relatively sparse, and dynamic network of relationships among participants sharing a common focus" (Bagozzi, Dholakia & Pearo, 2004). Previous studies found virtual community type to be a moderator, influencing the reasons why members participate, and the strengths of their impacts on group norms and social identity (e.g. Bagozzi, Dholakia & Pearo, 2004).

For example, a member may log into a P2P, and participate because he is interested in downloading files, but have no expectation or inclination to meet, chat or communicate with any particular individual therein. Similarly, an engaged Epinion.com member may read and benefit from reviews offered by other customers, without any personal knowledge of, or relationships with, the reviewers. In network-based communities members are more likely to participate mostly to achieve functional goals (e.g., to download files, to get benefits and so on) and may have weak, short-lived, and easily disconnected relationships with others. Consequently sharing is expected to be a crucial variable to study in this type of communities since willingness to share is expected to be lower than in small-group based communities. When members cannot communicate with each other, contributions do not tend to increase over time and converge to less than 30 percent of the socially optimal contribution (e.g., Saijo & Nakamura, 1995).

In our research, we decided to consider network-based virtual communities because increasing group size tend to decrease efficiency (Pruitt, 1998; Brewer &

Kramer, 1986; Sato, 1988; Yamagishi, 1992). Sharing and generally cooperation decrease in large groups, mainly because people feel less effective, are less identifiable, and may feel less responsibility to pursue the group's interests (Kerr, 1989; Liebrand, 1984). When social constraints that promote cooperation are absent, cooperation may depend on psychological and emotional needs, such as personal self interest or the need to belong (De Cremer, Leonardelli, 2003).

For example, Isaac and Walker (1988) studied the relationship between variations in group size and "free-riding" behavior in voluntary contributions. They examined experimentally the marginal return to an individual from contributions, and the actual number of members in the group. Results show that increasing group size implies a reduction in efficiency when accompanied by a decrease in marginal return from the good provided.

The second common characteristic of these types of communities is that sharing is effortful. Members have to deliberately act to share. Consumer communities rely on ongoing effortful contributions by a significant number of them, for their continued functioning (Nonnecke & Preece, 2000). For example, in eBay auctions, unless a significant number of buyers and sellers take the time to evaluate their trading partners' performance and provide feedback, the reputation mechanism will no longer work (Dholakia, 2005). Similarly, epinions.com relies on its customers to provide thoughtful and honest product reviews in large numbers. P2P networks rely on their consumers to upload (i.e., share) their files so that others can download them, and the MUSE chat-room relies on its experienced users to take the time and the effort to answer a majority of technical questions and solicitations for help that are posed by novice consumers. Travelocity.com and expedia.com rely on their users' opinions and reviews. Many reviews are provided by users for the benefit of fellow travelers. The motto is "get the truth before you go". With this system, people can get unbiased hotel reviews, photos and travel advices for hotels and vacations.

Third, sharing is a voluntary action in these communities, not forced or compelled. Communities members offer to perform a service (e.g. upload a file, provide a review or a feedback, or provide their knowledge, experience or opinion) out of his/her own free will. This offer is without payment, and refers to a community member's decision to participate and to continue to participate in the virtual activity. Macintosh (2002) found that members with strong interpersonal relationships displayed high levels of dedication behavior, including extra role voluntary behavior that was functional to the service provider, such as enhancement, identification, co-operation and advocacy. Other authors empirically examine the role of active communication as a mechanism for improving economic efficiency in a voluntary-contribution, public-goods environment. Voluntary communication is shown to significantly improve group optimality (Isaac and Walker, 1988). Volunteers may be motivated to help a group out of a wish to have friends, or because they feel commitment to the local neighbourhood, church, work organization, or cause for which they volunteer (Callero, Howard, & Piliavin, 1987; Deaux & Stark, 1996; Grube & Piliavin, 1996; Omoto & Snyder, 1995; Snyder & Omoto, 1992).

In the online world, these opportunities for real world contact and local impact may be rare or absent but online consumer community still exist and are extremely vital because people participate in by sharing and consuming. Sharing content plays a crucial role in sustaining an online group (Butler et al., 2002). In addition contribution rates increase if communication between consumers is allowed before each use of the network (for economics literature, see for example Isaac and Walker, 1988a or Elinor Ostrom et al., 1992) and the level of contribution declines with repetition use of the network (for economics literature of this phenomenon, Mark R. Isaac et al. 1985; Isaac and James M. Walker, 1988b; Andreoni, 1988, 1996; Weimann, 1994; Keser, 1996). Andreoni (1989) and Glazer (1996) point out that members may also contribute goods, services or information due to intrinsic motivation ("warm glow" effect) in contribution itself. Voluntary contributions to public goods have been studied extensively in laboratory settings (for example, for surveys see Dawes & Thaler, 1988; Ledyard, 1995). The behavioral research question is how much a virtual community member will voluntary contribute to the network in such an environment. Recently economists have taken experiments out into the field in an attempt to study human behavior in a more natural setting (List & Lucking-Reiley 2002, Frey & Meier 2004, Richard Martin John Randalz, 2005).

The fourth common characteristic is that sharing is essential to the community's long-term survival, otherwise the situation might imply a market failure. Market failure is a situation in which marketers do not efficiently organize or allocate resources to community members. In this case, market failure is a claim that the market is failing to create maximum efficiency, but it also means that the network might cease to exist. This is the case when a shared information good is non-excludability and for this reason it is not possible to provide a file and information or, generally speaking, sharing something online to one person without it thereby being available for others to enjoy in the network. Second when a shared information good is non-rivalry: the consumption of a shared file/information by one person will not prevent others from enjoying it.

Some authors provided preliminary evidence that volunteer contributors consider contributions to online technical support forums as private goods rather than public goods. This finding helps explain survivals of many P2P networks despite presence of free riders (Gu & Jarvenpaa, 2003).

6. Research Hypotheses: Typology of Sharing in Customer Communities

This paper presents a conceptual model of sharing behavior through a set of hypotheses. Our qualitative research, along with a review of the social science (economics, social psychology, sociology, anthropology, and marketing) literature on sharing led us to propose a causal model of sharing behavior (see Appendix: Figure 1). In our framework, sharing behavior in consumer communities is constituted of two types of sharing: (1) motivated sharing, and (2) spurious sharing.

We make this distinction between sharing behaviors that are intrinsically motivated, and those that are spurious because, from our preliminary analysis, we realized many customers share not because they are intrinsically motivated. Their sharing behavior is false, inauthentic and they intend to deceive. Spurious sharing is not genuine, consumers share for example to get some benefits in return.

[Insert Figure 1 about here]

6.1. Motivated sharing

Consistent with goal-directed views of consumer behavior (Bagozzi & Dholakia, 1999), motivated sharing is the deliberate sharing of resources useful to other community members by the consumer. Motivated sharing is the most important type of sharing in our proposed model because it reflects true customers' motivation to share resources. We hypothesize that motivated sharing will be a predictor of sharing behavior. In particular we hypothesize it will influence positively consumer sharing behavior. Additionally, understanding the antecedents of motivated sharing is important since it is likely to provide significant managerial implications regarding how to make online consumer communities useful, functional and influential for their customers. We describe below each antecedent of motivated sharing.

6.2 Identification with community members

A key aspect for sharing is the extent to which people feel they belong to and identify with the online group (e.g., De Cremer & Van Vugt, 1999; Kramer & Brewer, 1984). Consumers with strong group identification with community members have been found to invest more in sharing and cooperate for the group than weak-identifying group consumers. Identification with community members may serve several functions (Deaux, Reid, Mizrahi, & Cotting, 1999), such as to increase belongingness. We predict that consumers with a strong need to belong should share the most, because this satisfies their need to belong. Moreover, Baumeister and Leary (1995) argue that need to belong applies equally to strangers and to specific and known members. A strong need to belong motivates people to invest time and energy for the continuation of social relationships, for this reason it can be hypothesized that under such circumstances people will be more likely to share. This is consistent with recent studies showing that sharing can increase feelings of inclusion and satisfy the need to belong (De Cremer, 2002). Consequently, we test that people with a high need to belong will attempt to increase their feelings of inclusion by focusing more on the joint interests and sharing with others.

Thus, we test that motivated sharing is impacted positively by identification with community members (Bagozzi & Dholakia, 2002; Bhattacharya & Sen, 2003). Identification may stem from different sources. Some members may be driven to share because they know others personally within the community. Further, identification is derived from shared goals, shared values, and shared lifestyles with other community members. The goals shared by the community may be functional, such as the give-and-take of useful information regarding a particular subject, or hedonic, simply the creation and consumption of a pleasant experience (Dholakia, Bagozzi & Pearo, 2004). A strong sense of community and the ability to identify with the online consumer community have been found to increase the likelihood of members' contribution and participation in a community (Blanchard & Markus, 2002; Butler, Sproull, Kiesler, & Kraut, 2002; Hars & Ou, 2002; Koh & Kim, 2001).

Members benefit from participating in online social relationships, and people who identify with a group feel personally gratified when the group benefits (Baym, 1999; Cummings, Sproull & Kiesler, 2001; Galegher, Sproull & Kiesler, 1998). Online groups offer a place to build and maintain social relationships with people that one already knows offline as well as those that one has met online. Online social relationships generate trust and increase credibility of the information that the group shares. Members who value sharing benefits are likely to provide content and manage social sharing behavior by encouraging others. They are also likely to be more engaged in the online consumer community, because following others' social sharing and online conversations can encourage their own participation (Butler, Sproull, & Kiesler, 2002).

Perceptions of costs are likely to influence motivated sharing negatively. They decrease identification with community members. To the extent that sharing is seen as involving risks and/or effort, consumers are likely to share less. Previous researches identified three types of costs: (1) procedural costs, primarily involving the loss of time and effort; (2) financial costs, involving the loss of financially quantifiable resources; and (3) relational costs, involving psychological or emotional discomfort due to the loss of identity and the breaking of bonds (Burnham, Frels, Mahajan, 2003). Thus, the perception of costs variable is a belief regarding the access to resources, i.e. time, money and efforts needed to perform behavior (Taylor & Todd, 1995; Triandis, 1979). In this study, it refers to the availability of resources (time and effort) needed to share files or information goods and the risk related with sharing. The perceived risk is the degree of risk associated with sharing. Risk derives from both the uncertainty and potential side effects which cannot be completely foreseen (Dunphy & Herbig, 1995). The risk of sharing mainly concerns privacy issues and copyright.

Based on the above considerations, in our theoretical framework, we hypothesize that:

Hypothesis 1: *Identification with community members* will be a significant predictor of motivated sharing.

Hypothesis 2: *Shared lifestyle, Shared goals, Shared values* will influence motivated sharing through identification with community members.

Hypothesis 3: *Personal knowledge of members* will influence motivated sharing through identification with community members.

Hypothesis 4: *Perception of costs of sharing* will influence negatively identification with community members and consequently motivated sharing.

6.3 Emotional attachment

Prior research has shown that emotional attachment to the community is an important factor, influencing online consumer behavior (Algesheimer et al., 2005). Unfortunately, it is becoming harder and harder to find applications that make consumers feel emotionally attached. These communities should dig into emotional connections with members to increase their sharing behavior intentions. The goal of organizers should be to create emotional attachment, in order to create community loyalty, because that means they can stick heavy users. In particular, we hypothesize that:

Hypothesis 5: *Emotional attachment* will influence positively motivated sharing.

6.4 Overall engagement in the community

Overall engagement in the community differs from identification with community members. In fact, engagement refers to the general degree of customer involvement, including the more active processes in which consumers play a greater role in actually formulating plans or influencing community developments, instead of the merely consciously or unconsciously attribution to oneself of the characteristics of another person, or community of consumers. The user's overall engagement in the community is posited to influence motivated sharing positively. This is based on prior research which has shown that the greater the consumer's community engagement, the higher his or her participation intentions, and intentions to continue membership within the community (Algesheimer et al., 2005). Furthermore, stronger engagement is likely with greater degrees of conspicuous participation within the community (e.g., Langerak et al. 2003). Interesting, owners are usually expected to show greater audience engagement than any involved group member and will do significantly more community building work than will other members of the community (Butler, Sproull, & Kiesler, 2002). Hence, we hypothesize the following:

Hypothesis 6: A stronger overall engagement in the community leads to higher levels of motivated sharing.

6.5 Consumer's sense of reciprocity

The consumer's sense of reciprocity drives motivated sharing with other community members. Reciprocity can be considered a sense of obligation, i.e., the need to return favours that others have accorded one in the past, perceptions of fairness, altruism, and expectations of getting assistance in the future if one shares now. Reciprocity means also trading resources: the consumer chooses to share a particular rare resource, say, a rare file, hoping that he or she will meet someone who shares their arcane interest, and will be able to exchange hard-to-find resources with them in the future.

In economics, traditional theories of altruism are consistent with a negative correlation between a member's contribution and the contributions of others (Becker 1974; Andreoni, 1989, 1990). Instead, theories of reciprocity (Sugden, 1984) imply a positive correlation. In a study, members' contributions were significantly positively related both to the contributions of others and to beliefs about those contributions, providing support for reciprocity theories over theories of altruism (Croson, 1999).

The social exchange literature (e.g., Davenport & Prusak, 1998; Tiwana, & Bush, 2000; Butler et al, 2002; Lui, Lang & Kwok, 2002; Obreiter & Nimis, 2003) suggests members perceives the efficacy in sharing knowledge as a public good and they share for social altruism, especially when contributions are seen as important and relevant. In our theoretical framework, we hypothesize that:

Hypothesis 7: Sense of reciprocity, measuring as *perception of obligation, perception of fairness, and expectation of future assistance,* will positively influence motivated sharing through consumer's sense of reciprocity.

6.6 Consumer's belief in the community principles

In our model, motivated sharing is driven by the consumer's belief in the organizational principles on which the community is based. This follows from a prior research that has shown such beliefs in the founding principles for the Open Source Movement to drive participation in open source user communities (Bagozzi & Dholakia, 2006). Community Principles refer to community ideology of what should or should not be done that describes the rules, parameters or guidelines for community participation. For example, P2P networks discourage any of the following activities: infringes anyone else's intellectual property rights; repeatedly uses language inconsistent with the community standards; contains highly explicit or graphic descriptions of sexual acts; contains vulgarities; depicts violence; contains or facilitates the transfer of software viruses or spywares; incites illegal activity; solicits for exchange, sale or purchase of sexually explicit images, and/or material harmful to minors.

Similarly, eBay provides Polices in the website[25]. eBay has created policies to guard against inappropriate feedback, buyer rules assist buyers in doing the right thing in a transaction, seller rules help selling with integrity and reliability to build trust among buyers, and encourages them to do business with the seller again. eBay also provides a list of prohibited and restricted items as well as protection of intellectual property.

---

[25]. http://pages.eBay.com/help/policies/hub.html

Likewise, Blogs provides some rules and conditions of participation such as: do not post any defamatory, abusive, profane, threatening, offensive, or illegal information or material, and do not utilize the blog in any illegal manner; do not post any information or other material protected by copyright; do not post any confidential information or any information that would infringe upon the proprietary, privacy or personal rights of others; blog shall not be utilized in any manner that violates laws; all postings shall be of an informational nature and for informational purposes only; commercial use or any other unauthorized use is prohibited; do not use the blog to solicit or conduct business; do not provide information, materials, products, or services in exchange for compensation of any kind.

Epinions and the other review websites also provide their policies[13]. As an example, they specify the following as inappropriate: creating more than one account, re-establishing an account on Epinions.com after the account has been terminated, defaming a third party, using emails tools (such as "Email this page") to send spam, sharing password with a third party and so on. Similarly, each message board provide guidelines, rules and policies, for example they prohibit: spamming; materials that violate the law such as copyright infringements; flooding: any action apparently intended to consume board space or to hamper other member postings, including the posting of essentially identical messages into different threads or repeatedly over time; posts encrypted to prevent other members from reading them; trolling: posting of any content with the intention of disrupting the forum or inflaming members, this includes flaming, flamebaiting, registration of multiple accounts or impersonation of another member and so on. We hypothesize that:

Hypothesis 8: Consumer's beliefs in the community principles will positive predict motivated sharing.

6.7 Spurious sharing

A second distinct type of sharing is one in which the consumer shares resources that are not useful to others to achieve one's own objectives. For example, the customers of a P2P community may upload a file without any useful information to satisfy uploading requirements imposed by the community. In our framework, spurious sharing is influenced positively by the beliefs that one is going to gain personally from sharing in the sense of fulfilling requirements or of raising one's stature within the community to avail of greater resources from it. While such sharing may be detrimental to the larger community's well-being, it is likely to benefit the user significantly. In our theoretical framework, we hypothesize that reputation enhancement, increase in social stature and economic benefits will be significant predictors of spurious sharing and spurious sharing will be a significant predictor of sharing behavior.

6.8 Reputation and Social stature

The existence of a reputation system is an incentive for community members to be trustworthy because of the damaging effects of acquiring a bad reputation (Kollock, 1999). Online reputation mechanisms or reputation systems (Resnick, Zeckhauser, Friedman, & Kuwabara, 2000) utilize the Internet's bi-directional communication capabilities to artificially obtain large-scale word-of-mouth networks in online consumer communities. Reputation systems allow members of an online consumer community to submit their opinions regarding other members.

The social exchange literature (e.g., Davenport & Prusak, 1998; Tiwana, & Bush, 2000; Butler et al, 2002; Lui, Lang & Kwok, 2002; Vassileva, 2002; Obreiter & Nimis, 2003) suggests that a crucial variable for sharing is personal reputation: member feels he can improve his visibility and influence to others in the network, e.g. leading to more work or status in the future.

In addition to providing information and social benefits, online consumer communities provide opportunities for members to be visible beyond the boundaries of their local work or geographical community (Lerner & Tirole, 2000). In online communities, sharing topics of personal interest, being seen as skilled, knowledgeable or respected may have benefits. Informational benefits come from the typically invisible work of audience engagement, instead the benefits of personal visibility increase to those who share content, and those who do social encouragement and external promotion (Butler, Sproull, & Kiesler, 2002).

Based on the above discussion, we hypothesize the following:

Hypothesis 9: Reputation will significantly influence sharing behavior through spurious sharing.

Hypothesis 10: Social stature will significantly influence sharing behavior through spurious sharing.

6.9 Benefits, Paybacks, Remunerations, Priorities, Gains

In contrast to sharing behavior for collaborative purposes, it is essential to acknowledge that consumers may enter online networks with hidden motives, such as is reflected in online "lurkers", participants who pursue only personal benefits, attempt to damage or disrupt cooperation, or people who adopt false identities for deceptive purposes (called "whitewashing attacks") or people who simply do not contribute anything to the community.

The beliefs that one is going to gain personally from sharing are likely to influence motivated sharing positively. Such gains can take many forms. One is that the sharer's reputation is enhanced due to sharing. Such privileges may involve a priority in downloading resources or in accessing information, or an increase in downloading speed, or availability of more resources than lower-ranked members. The sharer can also get economic benefits. For example, epinions.com pays customers for contributing high-quality reviews whereas the U2 fan website offers consumers who posted reviews the opportunity to go backstage before and after the concert to meet the band.

In offline communities, volunteers have different motivations for volunteering (e.g., Omoto & Snyder, 1995). The benefits people expect influence the types of community building work that they do, their effort, and how long they continue to volunteer (e.g., Deaux & Stark, 1996; Penner & Finkelstein, 1998). Prior studies of online groups suggest that people often participate as a way to gain access to otherwise obscure or inaccessible information that is relevant to their work, hobbies, health, and other topics in which they are personally interested in (Ogan, 1993; von Hippel, 2001; Galegher, Sproull, & Kiesler, 1998).

The social exchange literature (e.g., Davenport & Prusak, 1998; Tiwana, & Bush, 2000; Butler et al, 2002; Lui, Lang & Kwok, 2002; Obreiter & Nimis, 2003) suggests that members have a pre-existing expectation that he will receive actionable and useful extra benefit in return; this phenomenon is called personal access, or anticipated reciprocity; additionally it suggests that members negotiate to get some kind of more tangible asset or tangible rewards in return. Other distinctions have been made between: individual (access, reputation, reward) versus interpersonal factors (altruism) (Deci, 1975; Deci & Ryan, 1985); hard (e.g., access, money) versus soft (e.g., satisfaction, altruism) rewards (Hall, 2001); quantitative versus qualitative gain, intrinsic versus extrinsic factors, and others. Receiving recognition, either in the form of status or financial reward, also encourage participation in virtual community (Andrews, 2002; Evans, Wedande, Ralston, & Hul, 2001; Hars, & Ou, 2002).

Based on the above discussion, we hypothesize the following:

Hypothesis 11: Benefits will significantly influence sharing behavior through spurious sharing.

7. Methodology to Be Employed: First phase, Qualitative Research Methodology

The initial portion of our research was exploratory, and employed qualitative methods (Calder, 1977). We interviewed a total of 24 active customers of various consumer communities. Each interview lasted between 45 minutes and an hour. We asked questions regarding which consumer communities the individuals participated in, details of their sharing activities, and their motives for doing so. In addition, we conducted a focus group of 8 active consumer community participants to elaborate on the findings of the interviews.

In addition, we conducted Netnographic observation and analysis (Kozinets, 2002) of a number of prominent web sites (http://p2pnet.net, http://www.slyck.com, http://www.zeropaid.com, http://www.abxzone.com, http://www.infoanarchy.org, http://best2p.com, http://www.filesharingtalk.com, http://reviews.cnet.com, http://38.119.65.153/~p2punited). We chose Netnography since this method was designed specifically to study "the language, motivations, consumption linkages, and symbols of consumption-oriented online communities" (Kozinets, 2002, p. 70). As a marketing research technique, Netnography uses information already available in online forums to "identify and understand the needs and decision influences of relevant online consumer groups" (Kozinets, 2002, p.62). On the basis of this analysis, we developed our model of sharing (see Figure 1).

7.1 Results of the Explorative Analysis

Motivated sharing. Some members may be driven to share because they know others personally within the community. For example, one of our interviewees [K, male, age = 24] told us that he shared files through P2P networks with "... my friends that come over to watch or ask me to share whatever I dl w/ them." Further, identification is derived from shared goals, shared values, and shared lifestyles with other community members. In describing his view of the community in a P2P network, T, m, 26, said "they typically share the culture of file swapping; mostly business with little interaction between the individuals concerned." Another interviewee, K, f, 18, said her view of the P2P group to which she belonged to be "...i guess just a community of typical college students who download off of each other so they don't have to pay to watch movies or music, etc". Another user, M, m, 32, said "you can feel that in this world u are not alone, if you are online u are never alone, u can stay in front of your laptop night and day and u will always find someone to talk to…you can meet a lot of people from different parts of the world, share not only files but culture also, and u can learn different ways of living."

Second, the user's overall engagement in the community is posited to influence motivate sharing positively. A Morpheus user, L, m, 27 told us "it is unbelievable that online there are people sharing 100, 200, 500, 1000 gigs of different stuff, they are constantly in front of their laptop ready to help other people".

Third, the consumer's sense of reciprocity drives motivated sharing with other community members. Reciprocity, in turn, stems from a sense of obligation, i.e., the need to return favors that others have accorded one in the past, perceptions of fairness, and expectations of getting assistance in the future if one shares now. For example, in describing his perception of fairness within BitTorrent, Y, Male, 26, said "... [I picture

134

public torrent communities as]... hmmm... kind of like a health insurance company. Paying your monthly premiums is like maintaining an upload quota. Everyone contributes to the pot and if someone needs something, it is taken out of the pot. If no one contributes there is no pot." Similarly, T, Male, 26 said "someone let me complete downloads from them, there shouldn't be any reason why i don't allow others to complete downloads from me," indicating a sense of obligation toward community members. Another consumer, M, m, 32 who uses idc, emule, and morpheus, said "I share everything because it is a system where you have to give and take as much as u can, everything must be in equilibrium..u can have new friends and get free advice." Another element of reciprocity is trading resources where the user chooses to share a particular rare resource, say, a rare file, in the hopes that he or she will meet someone who shares their arcane interest, and will be able to exchange hard-to-find resources with them in the future. Y, m, 26, who uses BitTorrent said "I usually at least maintain a 1:1 ratio basically, upload as much as i download. so for any particular file i download, i leave it up until the ratio is 1:1...(Q: Why a 1:1 ratio?)...well, a bittorrent network wouldn't survive without sharing. The benefit of torrents lies in the number of simultaneous people sharing... it's file-swarming more than file-sharing." Another Emule user, M, m, 29, said "I share everything I download and then after awhile when I am sick of what I am sharing I hide everything and I start again from the beginning...so my library is always new and people can periodically find a lot of different materials."

Forth, in our model, motivated sharing is driven by the consumer's belief in the organizational principles on which the community is based. An eBay user and other consumer communities told us " I share and I take because everything is there for free or cheaper than everywhere else..i do it because my salary is not in line with needs we have for everyday life..i mean everything in general.. everyone tries to spend less and to get the best...communities offer exactly this... and I do not feel any regret because even if you do not use communities outside there is a lot of black market, for food we use discount..etc etc, am I clear? ..When I needed some stuff for my heating I spent 48 dollars and I found them online for 14...I need to tell everybody that they have to use communities because society is cheating us."

Fifth, perceptions of costs are likely to influence motivated sharing negatively. To the extent that sharing is seen as involving risks and/or effort, users are likely to share less. For example, one BitTorrent user, T, m, 26, told us that he was inclined to share less because "...aside from the witch hunt propaganda perpetuated by RIAA and the MPAA, ... there's always the threat of malicious programs finding their way on your system." Another P2P user, M, m, 32 "I do not use Limewire and Kazaa anymore because they are full of viruses even if they are faster and easier to use than other programs. It is also dangerous if they caught you but it could be even more dangerous if someone else is going to be dangerous for your computer, because when you are sharing is an open door for other users" .

Spurious Sharing. The second distinct type of sharing is one in which the consumer shares resources that are not useful to others. For example, users of a P2P community may upload a file without any useful information to satisfy uploading requirements imposed by the community. In our framework, spurious sharing is influenced positively by the beliefs that one is going to gain personally from sharing in the sense of fulfilling requirements or of raising one's stature within the community to avail of greater resources from it. While such sharing may be detrimental to the larger community's well-being, it is likely to benefit the user significantly. An Emule user, M, m, 29 said "My friends are real and not virtual, they are here and not online, I know them personally...sharing file does not mean to know each other or talk each other etc.. in my opinion it is only courtesy...we only divide the loot...but no one knows how I am contributing to the pot..." The beliefs that one is going to gain personally from sharing are likely to influence motivated sharing positively. Such gains can take many forms. One is that the sharer's reputation is enhanced due to sharing. For example D, Male, 24, a member of the mirc P2P community told us: "in most rooms, sharing on mirc can give you a higher ranking, allowing you to have a few privileges (sic) the "non-sharing leechers" don't have". Such privileges may involve a priority in downloading resources or in accessing information, or an increase in downloading speed, or availability of more resources than lower-ranked members. The sharer can also get economic benefits, as when some communities pay their contributors in cash or kind for their contributions. For example, epinions.com pays users for contributing high-quality reviews whereas the U2 fan website offers consumers who posted reviews the opportunity to go backstage before and after the concert to meet the band.

7.2 Second phase: Quantitative Research Methodology

We collected a large survey of Italian online consumer community members, included P2P users, blog readers, eBay feedback givers, and recommendation and bulletin boards website customers. Questions were customized to context of user group. The survey was conducted in two waves.

The first wave was approximately half an hour long; included series of questions about antecedents of sharing behaviors. In the second wave, participants maintained a diary recording details of their online interactions for two weeks. Diaries were collected after two weeks and they provided the dependent measures of sharing behaviors.

Analysis to be performed on the data collected

When the data collection was complete, we tested our proposed model of sharing behavior using Structural Equation Modeling. First, we checked for constructs' reliability and we performed a confirmatory factor analysis. Then, we tested the proposed structural equation model in LISREL.

Results

Participants and Procedure

Participants in our empirical study were existing members (and regular participants), belonging to one of the 5 online consumer communities described before.

Data were collected by conducting an internet-based survey, which was publicized by posting a message in many message boards, blogs, chats related to the particular type of community and encourage people to participate. The use of an internet-based survey does not permit us to assess response rates, since we cannot determine how many potential respondents were reached through our posts. Thus, the nature and extent of response bias are unknown. Nevertheless, as the number of specific instances of groups from each venue and the total sample are large, we think that the convenience sample is relevant for testing hypotheses, although we cannot make any conclusions as to generalizability. Anyways, the sample size can be increased, and surveying methods may move away from the on-line survey, which may account for a disproportionately tech-savvy sample. In fact, additionally, data were collected at the University of Venice. Students were encouraged to participate in class and by posting a message in the university's message board.

The study was introduced to participants as an "opinion survey" regarding sharing behavior on the internet in different types of online consumer communities.

Before participation, participants were first asked to answer where they most frequently share online with other consumers. This gave them the opportunity to complete the survey regarding the type of sharing behavior in the online community with which they were most familiar.

Participants described their online community in some details such as the name of the community, times per week they use on average the community and how much time they spend on average when they log in on the internet in the community. Questions were customized to context of community group.

The sample size was 366 and 58,7% were male. Measures of sharing behavior were collected by emailing respondents approximately two weeks later.

Sample Characteristics

Table 1 provides details of the sample for each of the online communities. After the survey was completed, we found that only few individuals had responded for the review websites. These responses were therefore combined with the message boards' sub-sample and are reported in that category in Table 1. Respondents ranged in age from 16 to 59 years, with a mean age of 22,75 years (median = 21, s.d. = 4,589). Our sample is composed by 100% of Italy residents.

Community	Sample size	%	Female % Respondents	Male % Respondents	Average age
Blog	68	18,6	37,3	62,7	24,97 (SD 7,451)
eBay	71	19,4	35,3	64,7	23,10 (SD 3,922)
forum/rev	92	25,1	54	46	21,73 (SD 2,475)
P2P	135	36,9	38	62	22,42 (SD 4,228)
Total	366	100,0	41,3	58,7	

To give the reader a better sense of the data, examples of some of the online communities represented in the sample are useful. Among P2P networks represented in our survey included Limewire, eMule, DC++, iMesh, Gnutella, Kazaa, eDonkey, iTunes, Winmx, Razoback, Acqualime, BitTorrent, Bearshare. Among website bulletin boards, forum free, alfemminile, P2P forum, tiscali, corrieradellasera, musicforum, politicaforum, forumcommunity, freeforumzone, kataweb, techforum, zdnet, universitas, tuttocalcio. Among webblogs, BeppeGrillo, Personalblogs, BlogItalia, Spriz.id, Boing, Tiscali, Nero, Soccerblog, politicablog, messenger MSNspace, blogofjack, Raulken, Liberoblog, Repubblica, Xerobio, tuttogratis, azpint.net, blogger. Among review websites, epinions, amazon, tripadvisor, expedia, Travelocity, music and movies review websites.

Details of the measures are provided in Table 2. We provide in the table the questionnaire for P2P networks members.

Example of Constructs and Measures for P2P

Community principles	Please answer to the following questions about P2P Community Principles. Community Principles refer to community ideology of what should or should not be done that describes the rules, parameters or guidelines for community participation. For example, P2P networks discourage any of the following activities: infringes anyone else's intellectual property rights; repeatedly uses language inconsistent with the community standards; contains highly explicit or graphic descriptions of sexual acts; contains vulgarities; depicts violence; contains or facilitates the transfer of software viruses or spywares; incites illegal activity; solicits for exchange, sale or purchase of sexually explicit images, and/or material harmful to minors. On a scale of 1-7 (1=Strongly Disagree to 7=Strongly Agree), rate these statements	I agree with P2P principles I consider P2P principles important I follow P2P principles P2P Network rules are too strict P2P Network rules are fair
Positive emotional attachment	A: "When I interact with my P2P Network, I feel" :	Happy, Contented, Glad, Delighted, Relieved, Excited, Satisfied, Proud, Self-assured
Negative emotional attachment	B: If I am not able to interact with my P2P Network, I feel:	Angry, Frustrated, Guilty, Ashamed, Sad, Disappointed, Depressed, Worried, Uncomfortable, Anxious, Agitated, Nervous
Shared goals	Please indicate to what degree your goals overlap with goals of others P2P members, as you perceive it.	My goal of sharing files such as music, movies, and games overlaps with those of other P2P members in my network My goal of getting something I want overlaps with those of other P2P members in my network

		My goal of meeting new people overlaps with those of other P2P members in my network
Shared values	Please indicate to what degree your values overlap with values of others P2P members, as you perceive it.	Fairness, Reliability, Concern for others, Love of Accuracy, Respect for others, Equality, Friendship, Fun, Love of Speed, Love of Pleasure, Love of Money, Freedom
Shared lifestyles	Please indicate to what degree your lifestyle overlap with lifestyle of P2P members, as you perceive it.	Economic level, Political ideas, Religion, Dietary habits, Physical activity, Education, Fashion, Smoking, Alcohol habits, Social activity, Motivation/ambitions, Music tastes, Videogame tastes, Movie tastes
Personal knowledge of members	Please express your extent of agreement or disagreement with the following statements. Chose number corresponding to your reaction. On a scale of 1-7 (1=Strongly Disagree to 7=Strongly Agree), rate these statements:	I use functions, such as chat room, or instant messaging, to contact other P2P members I upload a file only if someone asks me for it in a chat or instant messaging I have personal relations with other members, such as regular contacts or online friends I have no relations with other members; I use the P2P purely to download files I communicate a lot with other P2P members
Costs perceptions	Please express your extent of agreement or disagreement with the following statements (chose number corresponding to your reaction to these statements):	**Risk perceptions:** It is very risky to share (i.e. to be caught by authorities, to be contacted by unreliable individuals, others)

		I feel sharing files has little or no risk
		Effort perceptions:
		I feel sharing within P2P networks takes a lot of time (for example, to upload a file, to change program's default options, others)
		I feel sharing within P2P networks takes a lot of effort
		I feel sharing files is not at all costly
Reciprocity	Please express your extent of agreement or disagreement with the following statements (chose number corresponding to your reaction to these statements):	When I am using a P2P network, I feel I do not have to upload files
		When I am using a P2P network, I feel it is fair to share on the community
		When I am using a P2P network, I feel I want to upload new files
		Freeloaders (who consumes resources without providing others) are not honest
		P2P networks cannot survive without sharing
		I download files much more than what I upload
		I upload junk files to find good quality resources
Reciprocity	Please express your extent of agreement or disagreement with the following statements (chose number corresponding to your reaction to these statements):	If I need something, I am sure other P2P members will assist me to resolve my problems
		I feel I have to help P2P

		member if they ask me for it
		I expect to receive future assistance from P2P members
		I feel obligated to share from P2P members
Overall Community Engagement	Please express your answer to the following questions (chose the number corresponding to your reaction to these questions)	How attached are you to the P2P network you mention above?
		Do you have positive feelings toward the P2P network?
		How strong would you say your feelings of belongingness are toward the P2P you mentioned?
		Do you feel you are a valuable member of the P2P network?
		Do you feel you are an important member of the P2P network?
Benefits	How often do you share within the P2P network for each of the following purposes?	To get information
		To get new files
		To get practical advice
		To get rare files/information
		To get easily what you search for
		To be entertained
		To get to know others
		To learn how to do things
		To provide others with information

		To get someone to do something for me
		To solve problems
		To play
		To stay in touch
		To relax
		To make decisions
		To contribute to a pool of information
		To pass the time away when bored
		To feel less lonely
		To feel important
Reputation	How often do you upload files within the P2P network for each of the following purposes?	To improve your reputation
		To learn about others
		To feel you belong to the P2P network
		To improve the general opinion of the other members towards you
Social stature	How often do you upload files within the P2P network for each of the following purposes?	To increase your social stature
		To be consider a valuable member and not a freeloader
		To improve your position within the P2P network
		To improve your power, influence, or leadership in the P2P network

		To impress people

Structural equation modeling (SEM) was used to test the model presented in Figure 1. The LISREL 8.52 program (Jöreskog & Sörböm, 1999) was employed for the SEM analyses.

A SEM model represents a series of hypotheses. Parameters include regressions, variances, and means. A model is estimated from the data to obtain unknown parameters and fit statistics are used to evaluate model adequacy.

The goodness-of-fit of the models was assessed with chi-square tests, the root mean square error of approximation (RMSEA), the non-normed fit index (NNFI), and the comparative fit index (CFI). Discussions of these indices can be found in Bentler (1990), Browne & Cudeck (1993), and Marsh, Balla, and Hau (1996). Two indicators were used to operationalize each latent construct in the SEM. For latent constructs where more than two measures were available, these were combined to produce two indicators according to the so-called partial disaggregation model (Bagozzi & Edwards, 1998). This yielded models with less parameters to estimate, and reasonable ratios of cases to parameters, while smoothing out measurement error to a certain extent. All analyses were performed on covariance matrices (Cudeck, 1989).

Results

Table 3 summarizes the number of measures, the means, standard deviations, and Cronbach alpha reliabilities of the constructs. The reliabilities were adequate in all cases except for the spurious sharing construct where it was .637. It is useful to note here that this low value would most likely make it more difficult to find any significant relationships with this variable in the SEM.

Means, Standard Deviations, and Reliabilities of Construct Measures

Scale	# of Items	Mean	Std. Dev.	Reliability
Belief in Community principles	5	26.09	5.255	.762
PEA	8	36.32	10.016	.908
NEA	12	34.82	18.817	.955
Personal	4	17.36	5.653	.762

knowledge of members				
Shared goals	3	16.43	3.695	.765
Shared values	12	51.59	13.124	.852
Shared lifestyle	14	53.96	18.478	.916
Reputation	4	13.73	6.539	.821
Increase social stature	4	12.86	6.438	.807
Benefits	16	67.97	20.109	.896
Overall community engagement	5	22.55	7.009	.854
Motivated sharing	3	15.33	3.491	.695
Perception of cost of sharing	4	17.95	5.488	.738
Reciprocity	7	32.38	6.75	.714
Motivated sharing	3	15.33	3.49	.695
Identification with community members	4	16.44	5.92	.743
Spurious sharing	7	24.23	6.471	.637

Standardized path coefficients for structural model

Hypothesis	Path	Path Coefficient	T-value
1	Identification with community members → motivated sharing	1.26	2.90
2	Shared goal, values and lifestyle → identification with community members	0.12	2.39
3	Emotional attachment (positive and negative) → motivated sharing	0.20	3.36
4	Personal knowledge of members → identification with community members	0.15	3.53
5	Overall engagement in the community→ motivated sharing	0.27	2.96

6	Sense of reciprocity (perception of obligation, perception of fairness, expectation of future assistance) → motivated sharing	0.06	0.63
7	Consumer's beliefs in community principles → sharing behavior	0.55	1.57
8	Perception of costs→ (negative) identification	-0.06	-2.51
9	Reputation → spurious sharing	2.24	2.15
10	Social stature→ spurious sharing	-2.29	-2.42
11	Benefits→ spurious sharing	0.76	3.18
12	Motivated sharing→ sharing behavior	0.97	3.15
13	Spurious sharing→ sharing behavior	0.24	1.48

Goodness of Fit Statistics

Statistics	Full Sample (n = 366)
χ^2	860.88 (P = 0.0)
RMSEA	0.058
NNFI	0.89
CFI	0.92
NFI	0.86
IFI	0.92
RFI	0.82
GFI	0.87
AGFI	0.82

Many indicators are calculated by LISREL, which can be used to evaluate the global model-fit. Five common measures for judging goodness-of-fit are the Chi-square ($\chi2$), the goodness-of-fit index (GFI), the adjusted goodness-of-fit index (AGFI), the root mean square error of approximation (RMSEA), and the root mean square residual (RMR).

The most fundamental measure of overall fit is the likelihood-ratio Chi-square statistic, the only statistically based measure of goodness-of-fit available in a structural equation model.

LISREL provides two different Chi square: the minimum fit function Chi square (C1) and the normal theory weighted least squares Chi-square (C2).

Results showed that the overall fit of the structural model of Figure 1 was good: Minimum Fit Function Chi-Square χ^2 (394) = 860.88 p $\approx$ .00, Normal Theory Weighted Least Squares Chi-Square χ^2 (394) = 878.12 p $\approx$ .00 Root Mean Square Error of Approximation RMSEA = .058, Non-Normed Fit Index NNFI = .89 , Comparative Fit Index CFI = .92.

The goodness-of-fit index (GFI) is a non-statistical measure ranging in value from 0 (poor fit) to 1.0 (perfect fit), which measures the degree to which the actual input matrix is predicted by the estimated model. Higher values indicate a better fit, but no absolute threshold levels for acceptability have been established. In our case, we can observe that the goodness-of-fit index (GFI) has a value of 0.87. It shows a good fit.

The adjusted goodness-of-fit index (AGFI) differs from the GFI only in the fact that it adjusts for the number of degrees of freedom in the specified model. In our case, we have that in the good model the adjusted goodness-of-fit index (AGFI) has a value of 0.82. The value means an acceptable fit.

The fourth indicator, the root mean square error of approximation (RMSEA) takes into account the error of approximation in the population. The RMSEA value is the discrepancy per degree of freedom, and is measured in terms of the population, not just the sample used for estimation. The value is representative of the goodness-of-fit that could be expected if the model were estimated in the entire population, not just the samples drawn for estimation.

It is commonly considered that values less than 0.05 indicate a good fit; values from 0.05 to 0.08 represent a fair fit; values ranging from 0.08 to 0.10 indicate a poor fit; and those greater than 0.10 indicate a very poor fit.

In our case we have that the root mean square error of approximation (RMSEA) has a value of 0.058. The value is very close to 0.05, this indicates a good fit.

Then we have other indices: the NFI, the RFI, the IFI, the NNFI, and the CFI.

The NFI is the normed fit index, which varies from 0 to 1, with 1 indicates perfect fit. We have that in our model the value of the NFI is 0.86, this indicates good fit.

RFI is the relative fit index, which is not guaranteed to vary from 0 to 1.

RFI close to 1 indicates a good fit. In our model we have that the value of RFI is 0.82, this indicates an acceptable fit.

IFI is the incremental fit index, which is not guaranteed to vary from 0 to 1. IFI close to 1 indicates a good fit and values above 0.90 an acceptable fit. In our model we have that the value of IFI is 0.92, this indicates a good fit.

The non-normed fit index (NNFI) is not guaranteed to vary from 0 to 1. NNFI close to 1 indicates a good fit. In our model we have that the value of NNFI is 0.89, this indicates an acceptable fit.

CFI is the comparative fit index, which varies from 0 to 1. CFI close to 1 indicates a very good fit, and values above 0.90 an acceptable fit. In our model, we have that the value of CFI is 0.92, this indicates a good fit.

8. Discussion and managerial relevance of the results

The strength of our research lies in the comprehensiveness of our proposed model of online sharing behavior, which has been developed through extensive qualitative research and drawing upon existing studies of sharing behaviors and confirmed by our quantitative analysis. We expect it to make a significant theoretical contribution to the social psychology and marketing literatures. This research has also significant managerial implications given the increasing interest in establishing, sponsoring, and managing consumer communities in many firms.

We aimed to provide a conceptual framework for thinking about how to use information sharing theory to assist in the design of a community, a network, a website, an online auction, an online advertising and so on. Additionally, understanding the antecedents of sharing behavior is important since it is likely to provide significant managerial guidance regarding how to make virtual communities useful, functional, valuable, and influential for their participants. Our empirical study was not limited to one virtual community but it was broader and considered and elaborated the distinctions between different types of virtual communities and their implications for marketers.

The topic is significant since, for example, recent surveys have indicated that as many as 35 million American adults and 30 million American teenagers use P2P networks (Harrison, 2003). World-wide, estimates of P2P network users range in the hundreds of millions, and this number is constantly growing. Over the last five years or so, a considerable amount of research has studied virtual communities we included in our study, considering technological issues in setting up and running such communities (e.g., Androutsellis-Theotokis & Spinellis, 2004; Ripenau, Foster, & Iamnitchi, 2002; Subramanian & Goodman, 2005). However, a problem arises because for example an important characteristic of P2P consumer networks is that they are (for the most part) decentralized; consequently, the identities of individual consumers within the networks are anonymous. To function smoothly and effectively, online consumer communities rely on contributions, in particular, sharing, from its individual members.

As the other side of the coin, instead of sharing such conditions are conducive to free-rider behavior. The importance of understating sharing behavior drivers is shown by many studies of consumer communities that have provided evidence of free-riding behavior. For example, Adar and Huberman (2000) found that almost 70% of Gnutella users shared no files at all, whereas the top 1% shared 50% of the files. Similarly, Asvanund et al. (2003) reported that 42% of Gnutella v0.6 users are free-riders.

Free-riding behavior by participants is detrimental to the functioning of online communities for several reasons. Firstly, when few consumers contribute resources and many take them, the community's performance degrades significantly, making it cumbersome to use for everyone (Ramaswamy & Liu, 2002). Secondly, inadequate contributions lead to a reduced assortment of available resources, making the community less appealing to its members. Thirdly, the greater the free-riding behavior in a community, the more vulnerable those who share will be, which in turn may dissuade them from further sharing their resources (Adar & Huberman, 2000). This issue is especially significant when the information good being shared is copyrighted or otherwise protected, and sharers face the risk of being prosecuted.

Furthermore, it is noteworthy that the free-rider problem is significant for all types of consumer communities beside P2P such as those that provide recommendations concerning products and services (e.g., Beenen et al., 2004), evaluations and reputations of members (e.g., eBay's reputation system, see Dholakia, 2005), and information regarding product/ service development and use (e.g., Lakhani & von Hippel, 2003; see Wasko, 2003 for a review).

Given the growing popularity of consumer communities, and the importance of tackling the free-rider problem for their continued success, we studied drivers of online sharing behavior in the present research. In particular, based on a review of the literature, extensive observation of evolving trends in the design and modification of existing online communities, and a quantitative study, we develop a model of sharing behavior in online consumer communities.

Through this research, our larger goal was to provide an actionable framework to marketers, organizers of online consumer communities, copyright holders of information goods, and consumers through which to encourage or discourage free-riding behavior and consequently sharing behavior (depending on the constituent) in all types of consumer communities.

Summarizing, we discovered that *identification with community members* is a significant positive predictor of motivated sharing. *Personal knowledge of members', Shared lifestyle, Shared goals, Shared values* positively influence motivated sharing through identification with community members. *Emotional attachment* positively influence motivated sharing. A stronger overall engagement in the community leads to higher levels of motivated sharing. Sense of reciprocity, measuring as *perception of obligation, perception of fairness, and expectation of future assistance,* positively but not significantly influence motivated sharing through consumer's sense of reciprocity, the T-value is low (0.63) . *Consumer's beliefs in the community principles* predict sharing behavior, the result is almost significant, the T-value is low (1.57). *Perception of costs of sharing* is a significant negative predictor of motivated sharing because decrease identification with community members. *Reputation and social stature* significantly influences sharing behavior through spurious sharing. Social stature is a significant predictor, but in the opposite expected direction. It negatively influences sharing behavior through spurious sharing. A possible explanation could be that consumers do not want to be visible online. They prefer to maintain anonymity.

As we pointed out, some t-values are low in our model, but as suggested by Jöreskog, and Sörbom (1999, p.275): "eliminating a parameter on the basis of its t-value may be dangerous, especially in a small sample. Even non-significant parameters may be of practical importance. If the substantive theory suggests that a particular parameter should be included in the model, it is probably better to retain it even thought it is not significant, because the sample size may be too small to detect its real significance."

Anyways, an evaluation based on the t-value must take in consideration that LISREL assume people are using sample sizes above 120, the point at which most tables of the t-distribution assign a value of infinity to the t-distribution. At this point, the t-distribution can be approximated by the z (standard normal) distribution. For the z distribution, an obtained value less that -1.96 or larger than +1.96 suggests a statistically significant result at the alpha = .05 level, two-tailed. The critical value is -/+ 1.64 for a one-tailed test.

As you can see in table of the standardized path coefficients for structural model, identification with community members is the greatest predictor of motivated sharing and personal knowledge of members is the greatest predictor of identification with community members.

Both reputation and social stature have a great impact on spurious sharing, but they act in the opposite direction, reputation increases spurious sharing, instead social stature decreases it.

9. Managerial implications: free-riding-mitigating mechanisms

Our findings provide many managerial implications on how to motivate people to share in online consumer communities. We organize them in Figure 2. It provides a graphical summary depicting free-riding-mitigating mechanisms that can be employed in consumer communities to increase sharing behavior. As can be seen, at the broadest

152

level, we make the distinction between two types of free-riding-mitigating mechanisms: (1) those that force users to share their resources, and (2) those that encourage sharing behaviors. The key distinction is that in the former case, the mechanism *mandates* (through a particular means) that the consumer share his or her resources in order to participate in the network, whereas in the later, the mechanism appeals to the consumer's self-interest, sense or fairness, or heightens his/her awareness of individual contributions and their importance, to *voluntarily* share his or her resources with the network. We describe these mechanisms in more detail next.

Mechanisms that force reciprocity behaviors

We distinguish between three types of forced reciprocity mechanisms: (1) reward mechanisms, (2) penalty mechanisms, and (3) trade and ratio systems. Note that whereas all three mechanisms require sharing on the consumer's part, their differences lie in the way they force the consumer to share. In a nutshell, reward mechanisms explicitly reward sharing behaviors of consumers, penalty mechanisms explicitly penalize non-sharing by users, and trade and ratio systems explicitly link the giving of resources to the network with the getting of resources from it. Each of these systems is now considered in-depth.

Reward mechanisms that force reciprocity. Reward is one of the extrinsic motivations to induce contribution. It is very common to use a reward as an incentive to motivate Internet community participants to contribute to the group.

One way to reward sharing is to give priority to those who share their resources with others in the consumer communities. Priority can take different forms. One is priority in receiving needed resources ("priority first"). Take the example of P2P network KaZaa. In KaZaa, each consumer's priority is calculated based on how much information (i.e., aggregate size of files) s/he has uploaded to the network. This metric is then used to determine the order in which consumers can download a particular file.

This procedure is perhaps better explained using the following example. Imagine a consumer is node N in a distributed file sharing system like KaZaa. He gets two requests for a particular file, from nodes (consumers) A and B. He will process these requests according to how these nodes have benefited him in the past. One that has sent him lots of correct files in response to requests will be helped before the one that has not. Furthermore, if N doesn't have the requested file, he will pass on the request to other nodes. When passing on the request to node C say, N will tell C that the request from A has a higher priority than the one from B. Thus, the information regarding the user's priority will propagate down the network, and the request from A will be honored first. The reward from this mechanism is that consumers who share more gain earlier access to new resources in the consumer network. Consumers who don't share at all will not have their requests honored by the network (see Adar & Huberman, 2000, for details). Note that instead of aggregate file size, other measures such as number of files shared, number of new files shared, number or size of popular files shared, etc. may also be used in assigning priority to users in such a mechanism (Ramaswamy & Liu, 2002).

Another way in which reward is delivered to sharers is through speed with which resources can be downloaded ("Priority faster"). Take the example of BitTorrent, another popular P2P network. It uses a share rating system to force reciprocity. The download speed, i.e., the rate at which a consumer can download a needed resource from the network, is determined by how much (in terms of size) the consumer has uploaded. Thus, the more the consumer shares (i.e., the greater the aggregate size of uploaded files), the faster his/her download speed will be. The upshot of such a mechanism is that if a consumer is responsive to others, s/he will get useful and higher-quality resources back faster; to the extent that s/he is unresponsive, s/he will get ignored by others in the network.

Other reward systems can take forms that are more indirect. For example, consumers who share their resources may get invited by organizers of private (and higher-value) communities such as Grouper, Groove, and QNext where resources of higher quality and greater variety are available to its members (Metz, 2005).

As another example, Hummel et al (2005) examine how to encourage learners in LN4LD to contribute their knowledge, and whether incentive mechanisms can increase the level of consumers' active participation. Results show that the level of participation was increased by the introduction of the reward system. They describe an incentive mechanism based on constructivist principles and Social Exchange Theory, and experimentation using the mechanism designed to increase the level of consumers' active participation. The incentive mechanism allows consumers to gain personal access to additional information through the accumulation of points earned by making contributions.

Reward can be tangible or intangible. Examples of tangible rewards can be monetary rewards, discount rates for subscription or purchase, bonus points for prize remedy, add-value service, gifts, and coupons. Monetary rewards are incentives used in online consumer communities, for example, spedia.com (Janis, 2005) pays users who connect to the Internet and view the advertisement bar while surfing the web. Instead, intangible rewards include self-benefit or indirect benefits from the contribution and top contributors ranking. This ranking feature is important since contributions could get one better reputation from others (see reputation mechanisms). An example is Amazon.com, which has a top reviewer chat that persuades customers to write books reviews. The 10 top reviewers in terms of the number of reviews that they have posted are shown in the chat with small icons to point out their accomplishment and contribution to the site.

Penalty mechanisms that force reciprocity. Many consumer communities impose penalties on consumers who do not share their resources. Some networks do not allow users to join the network or participate in it unless they have resources to share with others. Others impose monthly fees on users that do not share. A variation of this mechanism is an imposition of one IP (Internet Protocol) per account with fees charged for additional accounts. Such an approach can help to prevent "whitewashing" attacks by free-riders, whereby a free-rider repeatedly re-joins the communities using new identities to avoid penalties imposed on free-riders such as fees (Feldman et al., 2004).

Another type is a system when a consumer can download a certain type of file only during the time when s/he is uploading another similar file. For example, if downloading a song, the consumer must be sharing another song at the same time; if reading a review or discussion, the consumer must have posted a review before, and so on. More directly, some consumer networks block access to specific IP addresses that are known to belong to free-riders. In LimeWire, users can see the extent of uploading activity of other users, and determine whether s/he is a free-rider. They can then use this knowledge to block particular users that they deem as free-riders.

Another example, the IRC program contains two features. Every member has access to an "ignore" command, which blocks incoming messages from selected other consumers. Furthermore, each IRC channel is controlled by "operators." Channel operators have access to special commands, unavailable to ordinary people, to "kick" participants out of a channel or even "ban" them from entering a channel at all. Thus, individuals can ignore others whose comments they consider undesirable, and operators can kick and ban troublemakers so as to maintain order in their channels. These features are pretty common in most online consumer communities.

Instead, recently, eBay' makes punishment more flexible. Specifics about eBay's punishments were not made public. "The old system of warning after warning followed by a long suspension had to change," Bill Cobb, eBay's president of North American operations, said at the company's user conference last month. "It was creating fear and uncertainty even among good, honest sellers." Here are some of the potential punishments mechanisms eBay utilizes: A 15-minute questionnaire on eBay's rules, restriction from listing new items from a day to a few weeks, and forfeiting listing fees for suspended auctions.

Trade and ratio mechanisms that force reciprocity. In forced reciprocity mechanisms of this type, the consumer community establishes rules that link sharing of resources with receiving of resources. These rules can be of different types. According to one rule, which works as a barter system, a user will only share information with another user when s/he receives something of value in return. A second rule requires ratios specifying the proportion of upload to download activity that users must adhere to. The upshot is that for networks which specify 1:1 ratios, every megabyte of information that a user downloads must be balanced by sharing, i.e., uploading a megabyte of information. In another variation of this mechanism, the community forces sharing at certain times (e.g., Krishnan et al., 2004). For example, in eDonkey, consumers are forced to share the files that they are downloading while it is being downloaded. Some networks (for example eMule) employ a credit system, where sharing resources provides credits to the consumer, which s/he can then redeem by downloading the files of his/her choice.

<u>Mechanisms that encourage sharing behaviors</u>

An alternative approach, not using force, is to more subtly influence users' behavior by encouraging them to share their resources with others within the community. We identified three distinct mechanisms to encourage sharing behaviors in consumer communities: (1) reputation systems, (2) tracking systems, and (3) enhancing sense of community among users. We consider each one of these in more detail.

Status and Reputation systems. This mechanism comes from what in our model is called reputation enhancement and increase in stature in spurious sharing. For example, although most online networks are decentralized, recent research has shown that reputation scores of P2P users can be calculated and stored locally at the individual user level, and then utilized in his or her interactions with other users in the network during every session (Andrade et al., 2004). According to this mechanism, the user's reputation is incremented every time s/he uploads files. Variations of this mechanism may additionally reward the sharing of rare or popular files. When the user wants files, his/her reputation is used by other community members to decide whether to comply and share their resources with him/her. Considerable research on reputation mechanisms in consumer networks has shown that reputations can influence behaviors of transaction partners significantly (Dholakia, 2005; Khopkar, Li, & Resnick, 2005).

It is complicated to measure the value of each consumer contribution precisely since quality measures are generally subjective. Centralized moderation is reasonable and feasible only for small and narrowly focused communities, where members have very similar evaluation criteria. For that reason, decentralized mechanisms for quality measurement are required. The quality of resources used in online communities can be evaluated through explicit user ratings. This mechanism has two advantages. Firstly, it distributes the task of evaluating quality resources among the large consumer pool, thereby making achievable a job that would otherwise have been overwhelming. Second, the final ratings of resources are more unbiased since they are computed based on ratings from many consumers. Nevertheless, a study of the Slashdot community rating mechanism (Lampe and Resnick, 2004) showed that some worthy comments might receive insufficient attention and end up with an unfair score, in particular the ones with lower initial rating and those contributed late in the discussion. Therefore, the timeliness of contributing is important and a motivational mechanism should encourage early contributions. Additionally, since the needs of the community change in time, a motivational mechanism should adapt to the dynamic needs of the community and encourage users to contribute early.

A challenge in online communities that rely on decentralized moderation is to ensure that there are enough consumer ratings. MovieLens tried to motivate users to rate movies by sending them email-invitations (G. Beenen, et al. 2004).

On eBay, an online feedback mechanism that encourages buyers and sellers to rate one another have succeeded in encouraging cooperative behavior in an otherwise very risky trading environment.

The potential applications of online reputation mechanisms go beyond of trust building online. Reputation mechanisms facilitate cooperation without costly enforcement institutions and provide more efficient outcome in a setting where societies currently rely on the threat of litigation in order to induce cooperation.

Another technique of rewarding participation operates with points and status (community membership). For example, users can share something, or they can accumulate points and result in higher membership. Consumer status (membership) depends on earned points. Points for example can be earned by: contributing new files, reviews, suggestions, knowledge, links, pictures and so on, depending on the type of consumer community considered. Status can be computed as weighted sum of the points earned with each activity. The current value of earned points can be shown to the consumer, together with a personal message stating what is expected from him/her.

Tracking systems. Another approach is to increase the salience of users' behavior in online consumer communities. Considerable research in consumer behavior has shown that increasing accessibility of particular information elements increases the influence of those elements in the consumer's decisions and actions. For example, asking consumers to express their satisfaction with a firm induces them to form a judgment, which then influences behavior. Based on this process, tracking systems provide detailed and updated (in real time) information of each user's uploading and downloading behaviors as well as associated measures such as contribution (upload to download) ratio, sharing rank, etc. We hypothesize that making this information salient should increase sharing behaviors of online communities consumers. Experiments are needed to further develop and study this mechanism of discouraging free-riding behaviors.

Enhancing sense of community. Another voluntary approach to mitigating free-riding behaviors is to raise participants' sense of obligation toward the community to which they belong. One way to accomplish this is to create and sustain social identity, i.e., cognitive, evaluative, and emotional attachment to the community comprising the P2P network (Dholakia, et al., 2004). Many of the existing P2P networks, BitTorrent being a particular example, have been successful in creating a sense of community among users.

Online it is very easy to find witness about sense of online communities. For example, Haughey "I did my best to make the place as welcoming as possible, and eventually a few hundred people showed up and we had something good. Since then, I think the strong sense of community, the sense of belonging and getting something out of the participation, is what drives people to contribute. There are no points or karma or awards, but I think members enjoy sharing interesting links and comments with each other and seeing their name mentioned on the site." Matt Haughey is the founder of the popular group blog MetaFilter, in which the community decides what to link to and comment on each day.

One woman says about her experience as a forum moderator for CNN Interactive back in 1995 on Compuserve. "My work on the Internet has always been a second job/hobby; by day I'm a self-employed pension administrator. For me, the motivation was the same as my motivation for volunteering to build the marching band website for my son's school and my daughter's dance school. I saw the power that the Internet had to bring people together and wanted to have a hand in creating something that was meaningful in the larger scope of the term 'community.'"

At first, she was not paid, and then later she was paid a small sum when the boards became more commercialized. For this online moderator, the interactive nature of the web has always been what held her interest. "Many volunteers in online communities do it for the love of the conversation and the connections, and are willing to give up their time to make those communities more pleasant and interesting places to inhabit. I believe in the power of the Internet as an experience beyond just sucking up information — it's always been the interactivity that gets me going, and whether I'm paid or not, that's the part that keeps me interested."

Devlon, who blogs at Loaded Pun affirms: "I blog to share information, to hopefully help someone find something that they were looking for, or even find something they didn't know they could use. My pay? Comments. Comments and feedback are the currency of blogging in my opinion. Comments and that precious link-love."

Others have altruistic motives, believing their work would change the online community for the better.

"I work to do good…because I care…because I believe in making a difference and leaving this world slightly changed for the better," wrote O'Neil. "It sounds schlocky, but that is how it is…"

Donna Schwartz Mills, who blogs at SocalMom.net, says: "There's nothing altruistic about it. I blog because it is fun. I get to blather on about what is interesting to me, without worrying about pleasing a boss or editor. If someone reads it and likes it, and lets me know about it, that's an added bonus."

A blogger named Ben, who helps run the Tech Savvy Educator, noted his motivation comes down to the reward of working together and learning as a community. "Bloggers can start altruistically, but it takes a dedicated community to continue that purpose. I started blogging because I believed that others could benefit from my thoughts on educational technology (again, is the egotistical viewpoint of others benefiting from my thoughts altruistic?). What I found was that so many others shared my ideas, that including a forum on the site was a more democratic, and easier, way of filtering through all of the thoughts and providing a place for a wide range of voices. That is really what it comes down to: Working for no pay just is not engaging (at least not for me) without some communal or mutually beneficial reward that will not just benefit myself, but others searching for the same answers or looking for a forum to voice their own thoughts. The reward in blogging pro-bono is to find those that you can relate with beyond your own limited set of experiences, beyond your limited range of knowledge, and to create a whole that is much stronger and longer lasting than its parts."[26]

People find their motivation from the online community, the feeling that they get when help a group of people have a better experience or learn something new. It is a mix of belief in community principles, overall engagement in the community, identification with community members and reciprocity.

Additionally, to enhance a sense of community in consumer communities a motivational approach based on hierarchical memberships in the community (for example, gold, silver, and bronze) can be used, awarded to users depending on the quantity of their contributions to the community (Cheng and Vassileva, 2005; Vassileva, 2004). The different memberships implied different privileges and prestige in the community. To create a self-maintaining community, it is necessary to motivate users to contribute high-quality resources and simultaneously inhibiting the contribution of poor quality resources. Therefore, a mechanism of measuring the quality of user contributions is needed.

10. Conclusions

Designing incentives to ensure that online communities are sustainable is one of the most challenging and important problems for these consumer communities. As a result of our structural equation model, we proposed many mechanisms that take into account the needs of the online consumer community (e.g. more new contributions) and the user's personal style of contributing (e.g. fewer but higher-quality contributions versus many mediocre ones). We are confident that the use of these mechanisms can improve the quality and quantity of contributions, because for example they encourage the members who have a good reputation for sharing high quality resources to share more and inhibit the contributions from the users who does not have a good reputation. To ensure sustainability, the incentive mechanism needs to: reward participation, discourage excessive useless participation, guarantee a way to evaluate the quality of contributions,

---

26 http://www.pbs.org/mediashift/2006/03/your_take_roundupsense_of_comni.html

encourage timely contributions (when most needed by the online consumer community) and high-quality contributions (from people who tend to have higher standards), make the consumer aware of the rewards for different actions at any given time.

References

Adar, E., & Huberman, B. A. 2000. Free riding on Gnutella. First Monday, 5 (10). Retrieved July 25, 2005 from http://www.firstmonday.dk/issues/issue5_10/adar/

Alba, J.W., and Hutchinson, J.W. Dimensions of consumer expertise. 1987. Journal of Consumer Research, 13, 4 (March 1987), 411–454.

Ajzen, I. 1985. From intentions to actions: A theory of planned behavior. In J. Kulh & J. Beckmann (Eds.), Action control: From cognition to behavior (pp. 11–39). New York: Springer Verlag.

Andrade N., Brasileiro F., Cirne W., Mowbray M. 2004. Discouraging free riding in a peer-to-peer cpu sharing grid 13th IEEE International Symposium on High Performance Distributed Computing (HPDC-13 '04) pp. 129-137

Andreoni, J. 1996. Cooperation in Public-Goods Experiments: Kindness or Confusion? American Economic Review, 85(4), pp.891-904.

Andreoni, J. 1988. Why Free Ride? Strategies and Learning in Public Goods Experiments. Journal of Public Economics, 37(2), pp. 291-304.

Andreoni, J. 1989. Giving with Impure Altruism: Applications to Charity and Ricardian Equivalence. The Journal of Political Economy, Vol. 97, No. 6. (Dec., 1989), pp. 1447-1458

Andreoni, J. 1990. Impure altruism and Donations to Public Goods: a Theory of Warm--Glow Giving. The Economic Journal, 100: 464--477.

Andrews, D.C. 2002. Audience-Specific Online Community Design, Communications of the ACM (45:4), pp. 64-68.

Androutsellis-Theotokis, S., & Spinella, D. 2004. A survey of peer-to-peer content distribution technologies. ACM Computing Surveys, 36(4), 335-371.

Asvanund, A., Krishnan, R., Smith, M.D., Telang, R. (2003). Intelligent club management in peer-to-peer networks. Working paper, Carnegie Mellon University.

Avesani Paolo, Marco Cova, Conor Hayes, Paolo Massa, Learning Contextualised Weblog Topics, blogworkshop 2005.

Bagozzi, R.P., J.R. Edwards. 1998. A general approach for representing constructs in organizational research. *Organizational Research Methods* **1** 45-87.

Bajari, P., & Hortacsu, A. 2001. Winner's curse, reservation prices, and endogenous entry: empirical insights from eBay auctions. Working Paper, Stanford University.

Baset, S.A., & Schulzrinne, H. 2004. An analysis of the Skype peer-to-peer internet telephony protocol. Working paper, Columbia University.

Baym, N. 1999. Tune in, log on: Soaps, fandom, and on-line commmunity. Thousand Oaks, CA: Sage Publications.

Baumeister, R. F., & Leary, M. R. (1995). The need to belong: Desire for interpersonal attachments as a fundamental human motivation. Psychological Bulletin, 117, 497–529.

Becker, Gary S. 1974. A theory of social interactions, Journal of Political Economy 82, no. 6: 1063-1093

Beenen, G., Ling, K., Wang, X., Chang, K., Frankowski, D., Resnick, P., & Kraut, R.E. 2004. Using social psychology to motivate contributions to online communities. Proceedings of the CSCW'04, Chicago Illinois.

Bentler, P.M. 1990. Comparative fit indexes in structural models. *Psychological Bulletin* **107** 238-246.

Blackwell, R.D., Miniard, P.W. & Engel, J.F. 2001. Consumer Behavior, Orlando: The Dryden Press, 9th international edition

Blanchard, A.L. and Markus, M.L. 2002 "Sense of Virtual Community – Maintaining the Experience of Belonging", in Proceedings of the 35th Hawaii International Conference on System Sciences.

Blau, P.M. 1964 Exchange and Power in Social Life, Wiley, New York.

Brewer, M. B., & Kramer, R. M. (1986). Choice behavior in social dilemmas: Effects of social identity, group size, and decision framing. Journal of Personality and Social Psychology, 50, 543– 549.

Brynin, M. & Kraut, R. E., (In press) Social studies of domestic information and communication technologies. In R. Kraut, M. Brynin, and S. Kiesler (Eds). Computers, Phones and the Internet: Domesticating Information Technology. Oxford University Press.

Browne, MichaelW. and Robert Cudeck (1993), "AlternativeWays of Assessing Model Fit," in *Testing Structural Equation Models*, ed. Kenneth A. Bollen and J. S. Long, Newbury Park, CA: Sage, 136–62.

Butler, B., Sproull, L., Kiesler, S., & Kraut, R. 2002. Community Effort in Online Groups: Who does the work and why? In S. Weisband & L. Atwater (eds.). Leadership at a Distance. Mahwah, NJ: Erlbaum.

Callero, P. L., Howard, J. A., & Piliavin, J. A. 1987. Helping behavior as a role behavior: disclosing social structure and history on the analysis of prosocial action. Social Psychology Quarterly, 50, 247-256.

Chan, C., Bhandar, M., Oh, L., and Chan, H. Recognition and Participation in a Virtual Community. 2004. In Proceedings of the 37 the Hawaii International Conference on System Sciences (January 2004), IEEE Press, pp. 194-203

Cheng R., Vassileva, J. (2005) User Motivation and Persuasion Strategy for Peer-to-peer Communities. HICSS'2005

Constant, D., L. Sproull, and S. Kiesler. 1996. The Kindness of Strangers: On the Usefulness of Electronic Weak Ties for Technical Advice, Organizational Science, 7(2): p. 119-135.

Constant, D., Kiesler, S. and Sproull, L. 1994. "What's Mine Is Ours, or Is It? A Study of Attitudes about Information Sharing", Information Systems Research (5:4), pp. 400-421.

Crosby L, Evans K, Cowels D. 1990. Relationship quality in services selling: an interpersonal influence perspective. J Mark;54:68–81.

Croson, R.T.A. 1999. Contributions to Public Goods: Altruism or Reciprocity? University of Pennsylvania Working Paper #96-08-01.

Cudeck, R. 1989. Analysis of correlation matrices using covariance structure models. *Psychological Bulletin*, 317-327.

Cummings, J. N., Sproull, L., & Kiesler, S. 2001. Beyond hearing: Where real world and online support meet. Group Dynamics

Davenport, T., & Prusak, L. 1998. Working knowledge. How organizations manage what they know. Cambridge, MA: Harvard Business School Press.

Davis, D., & Holt, C. C. 1993. Experimental economics. Princeton: Princeton University Press.

Dawes, R. M. & Thaler, R. H. 1988, Anomalies: Cooperation, Journal of Economic Perspectives 2(3), 187–197.

Deaux, K., Reid, A., Mizrahi, K., & Cotting, D. (1999). Connecting the person to the social: The functions of social identification. In T. R. Tyler, NEED TO BELONG AND COOPERATION 173 R. M. Kramer, & O. P. John (Eds.), The psychology of the social self (pp. 91–113). Mahwah, NJ: Erlbaum

Deaux, K., & Stark, B. E. 1996. Identity and motive: an integrated theory of volunteerism. Paper presented at the annual meeting of the Society for the Psychological Study of Social Issues, Ann Arbor, MI.

Deci, E.L. 1975. Intrinsic motivation. New York: Plenum Press.

Deci, E.L., & Ryan, R.M. 1985. Intrinsic motivation and Self-Determination in Human Behavior. New York: Plenum Press.

De Cremer, D. 2002. Respect and cooperation in social dilemmas: The importance of feeling included. Personality and Social Psychology Bulletin, 28, 1335–1341.

De Cremer, D. & Leonardelli. 2003. Cooperation in Social Dilemmas and the Need to Belong: The Moderating Effect of Group Size. Group Dynamics: Theory, Research, and Practice, 2003, Vol. 7, No. 2, 168–174.

De Cremer, D., & Van Vugt, M. 1999. Social identification effects in social dilemmas: A transformation of motives. *European Journal of Social Psychology, 29,* 871–893.

Dholakia, U.M. 2005. The usefulness of bidders' reputation ratings to sellers in online auctions. Journal of Interactive Marketing, 19(1), 31-40.

Dholakia, U. M., Bagozzi, R. P., & Pearo, L. K. 2004. A social influence model of consumer participation in network- and small-group-based virtual communities. International Journal of Research in Marketing, 21 (3), 241-263.

Dholakia, Utpal M., Suman Basuroy, Kerry Soltysinski. 2002. Auction or agent (or both)? A study of moderators of the herding bias in digital auctions. International Journal of Research in Marketing 19 115-130

Dunphy, S., & Herbig, P.A. 1995. Acceptance of innovations: the customer is the key! The Journal of High Technology Management Research, 6, 193–209.

Einhorn, M. A. and Rosenblatt, B. 2005. Peer-to-Peer Networking and Digital Rights Management: How Market Tools Can Solve Copyright Problems, Cato Institute Policy Analysis, No. 534: 1-20.

Elinor, O.; Walker, James M. and Gardner, Roy. 1992. Covenants With and Without a Sword: Self- Governance is Possible. The American Political Science Review, 86(2), pp. 404-17.

Ellis, C. A., Gibbs, S. J., & Rein, G. L. 1991. Groupware: Some issues and experiences. Communications of the ACM, 34(1), 38-58.

Evans, M.; Wedande, G.; Ralston, L.; and Hul, S. 2001 Consumer interaction in the virtual era: Some qualitative insights. Qualitative Market Research, 4, 3 2001, 150–159.

Feldman, M., Papadimitriou, C., Chuang, J., Stoica, I. (2004). Free-riding and whitewashing in peer-to-peer systems. *3rd Annual Workshop on Economics and Information Security*, University of California at Berkeley.

Finholt and L. Sproull. 1990. Electronic groups at work, Organization Science, 1, 1, 41-64.

Folksonomies Mathes A. 2004. Cooperative classification and communication through shared metadata. Computer Mediated Communication, LIS590CMC (Doctoral Seminar), Graduate School of Library and Information Science, University of Illinois Urbana-Champaign.

Frey, B. S. & Meier, S. 2004, Social comparisons and pro-social behavior: Testing "conditional cooperation" in a field experiment, American Economic Review 94(5), 1717–1722.

Galegher, J., Sproull, L., & Kiesler. S. 1998. Legitimacy, authority, and community in electronic support groups. Written Communication, 15: 493-530.

Glazer, A., Kai A. K.. 1996. A Signaling Explanation for Charity, The American Economic Review, Vol. 86, No. 4, pp. 1019-1028

Grube, J. A., & Piliavin, J. A. 1996. Role-identity, organizational commitment, and volunteer performance. Paper presented at the annual meeting of the Society for the Psychological Study of Social Issues, Ann Arbor, MI.

Gu Bin and Sirkka Jarvenpaa. 2003. Are Contributions to P2P Technical Forums Private or Public Goods? – An Empirical Investigation, in 1st Workshop on Economics of Peer-to-Peer Systems.

Hagel, J. I., & Armstrong, A. G. 1997. NetGain: Expanding markets through virtual communities. Boston: MA: Harvard Business School Press.

Hall, H. 2001. Social exchanges for knowledge exchange. Paper presented at Managing knowledge: conversations and critiques, 10-11 April 2001. University of Leicester Management Centre.

Hamman, R. B. 1999. Computer networks linking network communities: Effects of AOL use upon pre-existing communities. Available: http://www.socio.demon.co.uk/cybersociety/.

Hars, A. and Ou, S. 2002. Working for Free? – Motivations of Participating in Open Source Projects", International Journal of Electronic Commerce (6:3), pp. 25-39.

Harrison Ann. Another P2P survey shows widespread file trading Survey says 35% Americans use P2P software Peer-to-Peer Newsletter, Network World, 09/04/03

Haythornthwaite, C., & Wellman, B. 1998. Work, friendship, and media use for information exchange in a networked organization. Journal of the American Society for Information Science., 49(12), 1101-1114.

Helm, B. 2005. A hard ride for eDonkey. Business Week, October 24, p.90.

Hoffman, D.L., and Novak, T.P. 1996. Marketing in hypermedia computer mediated environments: Conceptual foundations. Journal of Marketing, 60, 3, 50–68.

Hummel, H.G.K., D. Burgos, C. Tattersall, F. Brouns, H. Kurvers & R. Koper. 2005. Encouraging contributions in learning networks using incentive mechanisms. Journal of Computer Assisted Learning, Volume 21, 355.

IBM, Fear of Identity Theft and Credit Card Fraud Worry Consumers During the 2005 Holiday Season, According to IBM Survey, November 16, 2005 http://www.findbiometrics.com/article/153

Isaac, Mark R.; McCue, Kenneth F. and Plott, Charles R. 1985. Public Goods Provision in an Experimental Environment. Journal of Public Economics, 26(1), pp. 51-74.

Isaac, M. R. and Walker, J. M. 1988a. Communication and Free-Riding Behavior: The Voluntary Contributions Mechanism. Economic Inquiry, 26(4), pp.585-608.

Isaac, M. R. and Walker, J. M. 1988b. Group Size Effects in Public Goods Provision: The Voluntary Contributions Mechanism. Quarterly Journal of Economics, 103(1), pp. 179-99.

Isaac, R.M., and J. Walker. 1991. Costly Communication: An Experiment in a Nested Public Goods Problem, In T. Palfrey, ed., Laboratory Research in Political Economy, 269-286, University of Michigan Press, Ann Arbor, MI.

Janis M., "Spedia Unveils Surf+ tech," *Adweek*, 42(9), pp.55.

Jarvenpaa, S.L. and Staples, D.D. 2000. The Use of Collaborative Electronic Media for Information Sharing: An Exploratory Study of Determinants, Journal of Strategic Information Systems (9:2-3), 2000, pp. 129- 154.

Jarvenpaa, S.L. and Staples, D.D. 2001 Exploring the Perception of Organizational Ownership of Information and Expertise, Journal of Management Information Systems (18:1), 2001, pp. 151-183.

Johnson, D.G. Computer Ethics. Prentice Hall, Englewood Cliffs, N.J., 1985, 1994.

Johnson, D. G. 1997. Ethics Online in Communications of the ACM, 40, 1 (p. 60, 64 and p. 65)

Jöreskog, K., D. Sörbom 1999. *Lisrel 8: User's reference guide, Second Edition.* Scientific Software International, Chicago.

Karau, S. & Williams, K. 1993. Social loafing: A meta-analytic review and theoretical integration. Journal of Personality and Social Psychology, 65(4), 681-706.

Kanuka, H., & Anderson, T. 1998. Online social interchange, discord, and knowledge construction. Journal of Distance Education, 13(1), 57-74.

Kelley, H. H. and J. W. Thibaut. 1978. Interpersonal Relations: A Theory of Interdependence. Wiley, New York, 1978.

Kerr, N. L. (1989). Illusions of efficacy: The effect of group size on perceived efficacy in social dilemmas. Journal of Experimental Social Psychology, 25, 287–313.

Keser, Claudia. 1996. Voluntary Contributions to a Public Good when Partial Contribution is a Dominant Strategy. Economic Letters, 50(3), pp. 359-66.

Khopkar, T., Li, X., Resnick, P. (2005). Self-selection, slipping, salvage, and stoning: The impacts of negative feedback at eBay. *ACM EC 05 Conference on Electronic Commerce,* Vancouver Canada.

Koh, J. and Kim, Y. 2001. Sense of Virtual Community: Determinants and the Moderating Role of the Virtual Community Origin, in Proceedings of the 22nd International Conference on Information Systems, pp. 407-409.

Kollock P. 1999. The production of trust in online markets, in: E.J. Lawler, M. Macy, S. Thyne, H.A. WalkerŽEds.., Advances in Group Processes vol. 16, JAI Press, Greenwich, CT, 1999.

Komorita, S. S., & Parks, C. D. (1994). *Social dilemmas.* Dubuque, IA: Brown & Benchmark.

Kramer, R. M., & Brewer, M. B. (1984). Effects of group identity on resource use in a simulated commons dilemma. *Journal of Personality and Social Psychology, 46,* 1044–1057.

Krishnan, R., Smith, M.D., Tang, Z., & Telang, R. 2004. The impact of free-riding on peer-to-peer networks. Proceedings of the 37th Hawaii International Conference on System Sciences.

Kwax, H.; Fox, R.J.; and Zinkhan, G.M. 2002. What products can be successfully promoted and sold via the Internet? Journal of Advertising, 42, 1, 23–38.

Lakhani, K.R., & von Hippel, E.V. 2003. How open source software works: "Free" user to user assistance. Research Policy, 32, 923-943.

Lampe C. and P. Resnick: Slash(dot) and Burn: Distributed Moderation in a Large Online Conversation Space, in Proceedings of CHI'2004, Vienna, Austria, Apr. 24–29, 2004.

Ledyard, J. O. 1995. Public goods: A survey of experimental research. In J. Kagel & A. E. Roth (Eds.), Handbook of experimental economics (pp. 111–194). Princeton, NJ: Princeton University Press.

Liebrand, W. B. G. (1984). The effect of social motives, communication and group size on behavior in a n-person multi-stage mixed-motive game. European Journal of Social Psychology, 14, 239–264.

List, J. A. & Lucking-Reiley, D. 2002. The effects of seed money and refunds on charitable giving: Experimental evidence from a university capital campaign, Journal of Political Economy 110(1), 215–233.

Lucking-Reiley, D. 2000. Auctions on the internet: what's being auctioned and how? The Journal of Industrial Economics, 227–252.

Lui, S.M., Lang, K.R, & Kwok, S.H. 2002. Participation Incentive mechanisms in Peer-to-Peer Subscription Systems. Proceedings of the 35th Hawaii International Conference on System Sciences, IEEE.

Macintosh, G. 2002. Perceived risk and outcome differences in multi-level service relationships, Journal of Services Marketing, 16 (2). 143-57.

Malone, T. W. and J. F. Rockart. 1991. Computers, Networks, and the Corporation, Scientific American, 263, 128-137.

Market Wire Incorporated. RIAA Actions Spawn New Product Designed to Help Parents and Others Avoid Lawsuits. December 2, 2003. Available at www.marketwire.com/mw/release_html_b1?release_id=60599.

Marsh, H.W., J.R. Balla, K. Hau. 1996. An evaluation of incremental fit indices: A clarification of mathematical and empirical properties. G.A. Marcoulides, R.E. Schumacker, eds. *Advanced structural equation modeling: Issues and techniques.* Erlbaum, Mahwah, New Jersey, 315-353.

Martin Richard, Randal John. 2005. Voluntary contributions to a public good: a natural field experiment, Unpublished manuscript

Mas-Colell, A., Whinston, M.D., & Green, J.R. 1995. Microeconomic Theory. New York: Oxford University Press.

Metz, C. (2005). P2P goes private. *PC Magazine*, January.

Nickerson, R. S., 1992. Looking Ahead: Human Factors Challenges in a Changing World, Lawrence Erlbaum Associates, Hillsdale, NJ.

Novak, T.P.; Hoffman, D.L.; Yung, Y. 2000. Measuring the customer experience in online environments: A structural modeling approach. Marketing Science, 19, 1 (2000), 22–42

Obreiter, P.& Nimis, J. 2003. A Taxonomy of Incentive Patterns: the Design Space of Incentives for Cooperation. Proceedings of the 2nd International Workshop on Agents and P2P Computing (AP2PC'03). Melbourne, Australia.

Omoto, A., & Snyder, M. 1995. Sustained helping without obligation: Motivation, longevity of service, and perceived attitude change among AIDS volunteers. Journal of Personality and Social Psychology, 68, 671-687.

Pew Internet Project: Internet Tracking report: More online, doing more (Pew, 2001)

Preece, J. 2000. Online Communities: Designing Usability, Supporting Sociability. Chichester, England: John Wiley & Sons.

Preece, J. 2001. Designing usability, supporting sociability: Questions participants ask about online communities. Paper presented at the Human-Computer Interaction INTERACT'01, Tokyo.

Preece, J. and Diane Maloney-Krichmar. 2003. Online Communities. In J. Jacko and A. Sears, A. (Eds.) Handbook of Human-Computer Interaction, Lawrence Erlbaum Associates Inc. Publishers. Mahwah: NJ. 596-620.

Pruitt, D. G. 1998. Social conflict. In D. T. Gilbert, S. T. Fiske, & G. Lindzey (Eds.), The handbook of social psychology (Vol. 2, pp. 470–503). New York: McGraw-Hill.

Ramaswamy, L., & Liu, L. 2002. Free riding: A new challenge to peer-to-peer file sharing systems. Proceedings of the 36th Hawaii International Conference on System Sciences.

Rawls, J. 1999. The Theory of Justice, rev. ed. Cambridge, MA: Belknap.

Rheingold, H. 2002. Smart mobs: The next social revolution. Cambridge: Perseus.

Rheingold, H. 2000. The Virtual Community, revised edition. Cambridge: The MIT Press.

Ridings S., C.M., Gefen, D. and Arinze, B. 2002. Some Antecedents and Effects of Trust in Virtual Communities, Journal of Strategic Information Systems (11:3-4), 2002, pp. 271-295.

Ripenau, M., Foster, I., & Iamnitchi, A. 2002. Mapping the Gnutella network: Properties of large scale peer-to-peer systems and implications for intelligent design. IEEE Internet Computing, 6(1).

Saijo, T., and H. Nakamura 1995, The Spite Dilemma in Voluntary Contribution Mechanism Experiments, Journal of Conflict Resolution 39, 535-560.

Sato, K. 1988. Trust and group size in a social dilemma. *Japanese Psychological Research, 30,* 88–93.

Snyder, M., & Omoto, A. M. 1992. Who helps and why? The psychology of AIDS volunteerism. In S. Spacapan & S. Oskamp (Eds.), Helping and being helped: Naturalistic studies (pp. 213-239). Newbury Park, CA: Sage.

Sproull, L. and S. Kiesler, Computers, Networks and Work, Scientific American. 265 (1991), 116-123.

Staples, D.D. and Jarvenpaa, S.L. Using Electronic Media for Information Sharing Activities: A Perception and Extension, in Proceedings of the 21st International Conference on Information Systems, 2000, pp. 117-133.

Stellin, S. 2001. Painting some pictures of the online shipper. The New York Times, pp. C4.

Subramanian, R., & Goodman, B.D. (2005). Peer-to-peer computing: The evolution of a disruptive technology. Hershey, PA: IDEA Group.

Sugden, Robert, 1982. "On the Economics of Philanthropy," Economic Journal, Royal Economic Society, vol. 92(366), pages 341-50

Taylor, S., & Todd, P. 1995. Decomposition and crossover effects in the theory of planned behavior: A study of consumer adoption intentions. International Journal of Research in Marketing, 12, 137–155.

Tanjev S. 2000. Mass media and the concept of interactivity: an exploratory study of online forums and reader email, Media, Culture & Society, Vol. 22, No. 2, 205-221 (2000)

Triandis, H.C. 1979. Values, attitudes, and interpersonal behavior. In Proceedings of Nebraska symposium on motivation: beliefs, attitudes, and values (pp. 195–259). Lincoln, NE: University of Nebraska Press.

Tiwana, A., & Bush, A. 2000. Peer-to-peer Valuation as a Mechanism for Reinforcing Active Learning in Virtual Communities: Actualizing Social Exchange Theory. Proceedings of the 33rd Hawaii Internatiotional Conference on System Sciences, IEEE.

Tweney D. 2006, Faboulous Freebies, The best things in life aren't just free-they're indispensable. Case in point: these outrageously useful downloads, sites, and services. Pcworld, May 2006.

Vassileva, J. (2004) Harnessing P2P Power in the Classroom. Proceedings Intelligent Tutoring Systems, ITS'2004

Venkatraman, N. 2000. Five steps to a dot-com strategy: How to find your footing on the Web. Sloan Management Review, 41(3), 15-27.

Wasko, M.M. 2003. Virtual commons or public goods? Applying theories of social dilemmas, collective action, and public goods to electronic networks of practice. Working paper, Florida State University.

Wasko, M.M. and Faraj, S. 2000. It is What One Does: Why People Participate and Help Others in Electronic Communities of Practice, Journal of Strategic Information Systems (9:2-3), pp. 155-173.

Weimann, Joachim. 1994. Individual Behavior in a Free Riding Experiment. Journal of Public Economics, 54(2), pp. 185-200.

Wellman, B., & Gulia, M. 1999. Net Surfers Don't Ride Alone. In B. Wellman (Ed.), Networks in the Global Village (pp. 331-366). Boulder: CO: Westview Press.

West, R. and Turner, L.H. 2001. Introducing Communication Theory: Analysis and Application, The McGraw-Hill Company.

Walton, R. E. 1989. Up and Running: Integrating Information Technology and the Organization, Harvard Business School Press, Boston, MA.

Whittaker, S., Issacs, E., & O'Day, V. 1997. Widening the net. Workshop report on the theory and practice of physical and network communities. SIGCHI Bulletin, 29(3), 27-30.

Wilcox, R. T. 2000. Experts and amateurs: the role of experience in internet auctions. Marketing Letters, 11 (4), 363– 374.

Wright, P. Marketplace metacognition and social intelligence. 2002. Journal of Consumer Research, 28, 4, 677–682.

Yamagishi, T. (1992). Group size and the provision of a sanctioning system in a social dilemma. In W. B. G. Liebrand, D. M. Messick, & H. A. M. Wilke (Eds.), *Social dilemmas* (pp. 267–287). Oxford, England: Pergamon.

Figure 1. Theoretical framework of antecedents of online sharing behavior

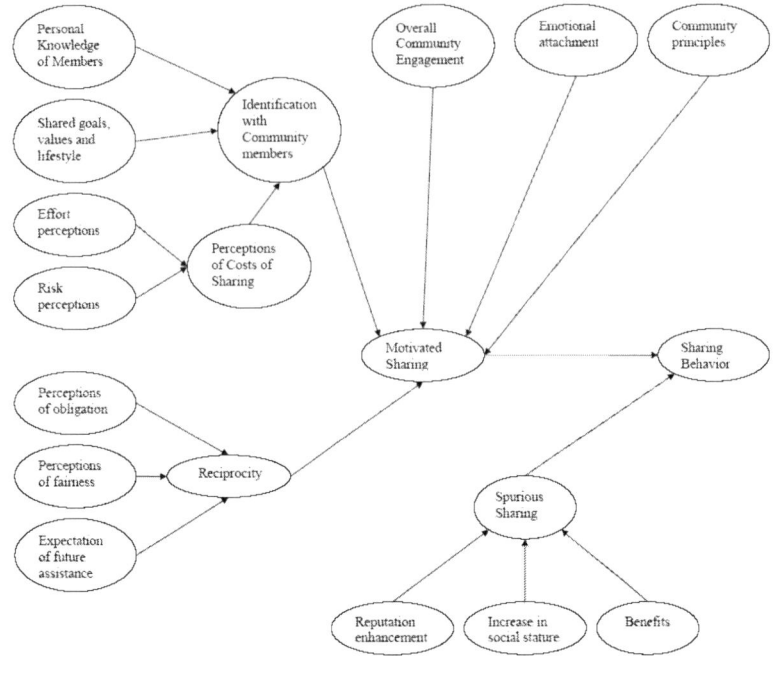

Figure 2. Free Riding Mitigating Mechanism

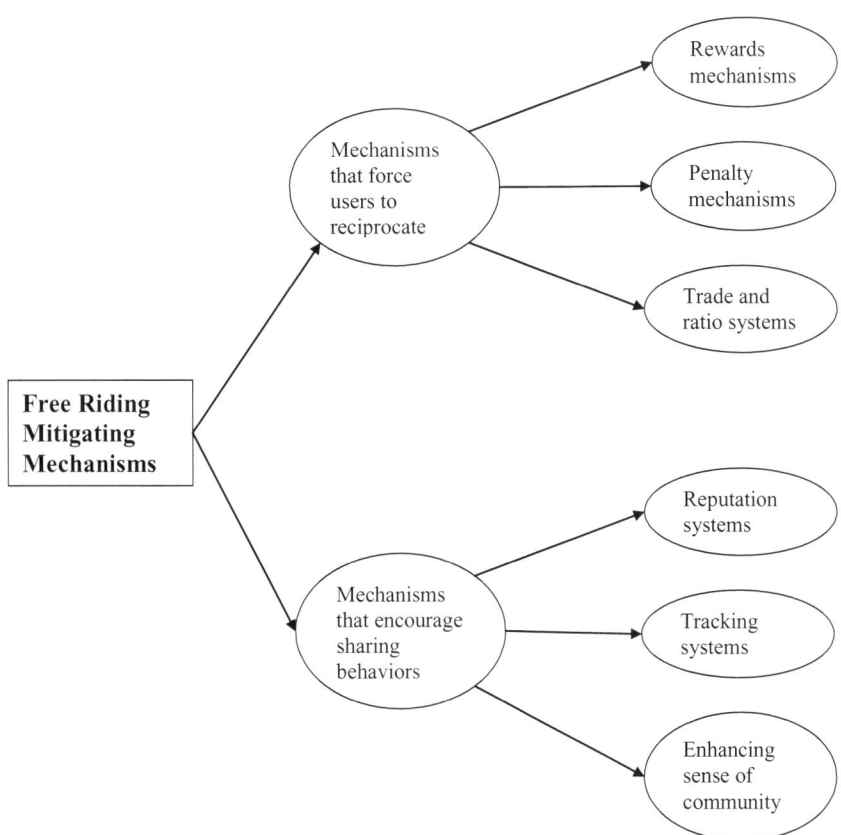

Chapter 4. A Study of Firm-Managed and Customer-Managed Brand Communities

Abstract

In the present research, we study firm-managed and customer-managed brand communities of many large firms, such as National Instruments and Microsoft. Our findings, derived using Netnographic methodology, in-depth interviews and online surveys, reveal among others, considerable overlap in membership across the firm- and the customer-managed communities. They also suggest that firm-managed communities are employed primarily for focused, instrumental purposes, whereas customer-managed communities allow more for broader "off-topic" social interactions among consumers not necessarily involving the firm's products and brands. Additionally, firms can play a meaningful role in customer-managed communities and firm-managed communities are more organized and comprehensive than customer managed communities. Furthermore, online brand communities participation, both in firm-managed and customer-managed, may influence positively brand loyalty. People seem to trust more the firm-managed community about technical issues. On the other hand, they seem to trust more the consumer-managed communities about product reviews and for honesty of participants, for example about product problems. We discuss the theoretical bases, the practical implications of our results and future research.

Key-words: Brand communities, consumer behavior, social influence, customer community marketing programs

1. Introduction: Defining the Brand Community Concept

Currently, consumers of a particular product or service can interact with one another in various online and offline forums, for a variety of reasons (e.g., Dholakia, Bagozzi, & Pearo, 2004; Kozinets, 2002). Coupled with the waning effectiveness of conventional marketing programs such as mass advertising, and the growing resistance of consumers to aggressive direct marketing campaigns (e.g., Dholakia, 2006), marketers have become more and more interested in organizing, nurturing, and monitoring such brand communities where their customers can interact with one another (Algesheimer, Dholakia, Herrmann, 2005; McAlexander, Schouten, Koenig, 2002; Muniz, O'Guinn, 2001). Brand communities are defined as "specialized, non-geographically bound community (ies), based on a structured set of social relationships among admirers of a brand" (Muniz and O'Guinn, 2001, p.412). The definition describes some key characteristics of brand communities where (1) specialized means that it is more specifically oriented, (2) non geographically bound that its members are not compelled to be located in the same physical area, and (3) the brand community gathers consumers attached to a particular brand or product. Amine and Sitz (2004, p.4) proposed a different definition of brand community as "a self-selected, hierarchical and non-geographically bound group of consumers that share values, norms and social representations and recognize a strong feeling of membership with other members and with the group as a whole on the basis of a common attachment to a particular brand." In this definition, they specify membership feeling exists on two levels: inter-individual and collective. Additionally, they point out hierarchy and duration of the brand community to exclude a temporary or non-durable group.

Examples of successful online brand communities include the Harley Davidson Motorcycles' Harley Owners Groups (HOGs; Bagozzi, Dholakia, 2006), Apple Computer's MacIntosh user groups (e.g., Belk, Tumbat, 2002), and Volkswagen drivers (Brown, Kozinets, Sherry, 2003). All these communities rely on consumption activities, which are distinctly geographically bound in nature. Other examples include Saturn

Homecomings, Siebel UserWeek Software conventions, Apple store events, and any other sort of 'brandfest', Green Bay Packers, Jeep, Oracle, DeWalt, and BMW.

Examples of blog brand communities are: Nike Blog, with The Art of Speed; Red Hat Blog [http://blogs.redhat.com/], road show and executive blogs; Channel 9 - Microsoft [http://channel9.msdn.com/], Microsoft employees and developers talking, learning, and listening globally; General Motors Blogs [http://smallblock.gmblogs.com/], community for small block enthusiasts; and Google Blog, Insight into the news, technology, and culture of Google.

Community is a distinct concept from society (Brint, 2001). In particular, "society" defines a social group built on a social contract, whereas "community" refers to a group of individuals gathered by emotional and organic links who share a common territory. In online brand communities they share a virtual territory, and have daily interactions with one another (Amine and Sitz, 2004). In this view, community is still intended as geographically marked, but due to the advance of the internet, the meeting of people from different places, cultures and backgrounds became easier (Kollock et Smith, 1999). The community is seen as a particular social network (Wellman and Gulia, 1999). It is not anymore geographically bounded and in need of spatial co-presence of the members since communities start growing correlatively with the development of the Internet (Costigan, 1999; Jones, 1995). Many virtual communities (Rheingold, 1993) or cyber communities (Ward, 1999) emerged and participation is based on a personal free will where members, and in online brand communities consumers, choose to take part of it since they share a common interest or passion for a product or a brand. This way consumption becomes the basis and the motivation for online interactions.

There are many different reasons why consumption may lead to online brand communities including:

1. Involvement in a product category or in a consumption activity (Kozinets, 2001; Thompson and Troester, 2002).

2. Rejection of the market ideology (Friedman, 1999; Kozinets, 2002a; Kozinets and Handelman, 1998).

3. Attachment to a particular brand (Schouten and McAlexander, 1995; Muniz and O'Guinn, 2001).

4. Nostalgic consumption (Belk and Costa, 1998; Peñaloza, 2001).

Furthermore, brand communities are different from subculture of consumption (Schouten and McAlexander, 1995), because there are different causes of members' interactions and because of different level of analysis.

A subculture of consumption refers to a group of consumers formed around a product category or a consumption category (involvement cause, aggregate level), whereas an online brand community would designate a group of consumers gathered on the internet around a particular brand (attachment cause, disaggregate level).

The online brand community concept has potentially important theoretical and empirical implications. Brand communities are often established not only by companies but also by customers. If they are established and managed by the company, they are called firm-managed brand communities; instead if they are established and managed by enthusiast costumers, they are called consumer-managed brand communities.

There are many reasons why these communities are important for companies. From a firm's perspective, organizing and orchestrating brand communities serves several useful purposes. First, these communities attract "devotees," self-determined customers who are intrinsically interested in the firm's products and services, and having higher degrees of attachment and loyalty to the firm's brand (Kozinets, 1999). Such customers are not only more likely to provide useful feedback to the firm as lead users (e.g., Franke, Shah, 2003), but they are also likely to serve as enthusiastic and influential opinion-mongers, disseminating brand-related information within the larger communities in which they live and work.

Second, the firm can employ its brand communities as credible evidence of its brand's success. It can encourage its new and/or occasional customers to participate in the community, and to be socialized by its engaged customers. Several studies have shown that such participation can have positive effects. For example, McAlexander, Schouten and Koenig (2002) found participation in a Jeep Brandfest event to significantly increase consumers' attachment to their vehicle as well as to the Jeep brand. Similarly, Muniz and O'Guinn (2001) reported that MacIntosh computer community members helped other members by sharing information regarding ways to enhance their computers' functioning.

Third, many brand communities such as those for firms selling software, technical and/or complex products, etc., serve as low cost, "always on" resources of product expertise. They supplement, and in some cases even replace, the firm's customer service and customer education functions. For example, in Microsoft's online communities (www.microsoft.com/ communities), new users can ask experienced consumers of a particular Microsoft product for help in installing, programming, or using the product. In most cases, they receive timely help.

2. Paper goals

Online community members are aware of the consuming nature of the society and their very nature of consumers (Featherstone, 1991), for this reason, they play with the cultural values linked to consumption (Holt, 2002). The development of the consumer society facilitates the emergence of online brand communities, both firm-managed and consumer managed. These communities bring together people sharing goals, passions, values, principles and representations emerging from consuming the same products and brands. As these brands go beyond the natural and national borders and become online, the communities of consumption are no longer national groups and gather people from around the world (Schouten and McAlexander, 1995).

Until recently, online communities formed around a particular brand, managed by companies or consumers, have been surprisingly ignored by the marketing literature, while potential consequences for the brand in which the community is interested may be attractive. We propose to explore the differences between the two categories of online brand communities. So far, surprisingly, very few studies have investigated and were interested in understanding the differences between the two categories and the way such communities could emerge, from firm or customer initiative. We noticed a gap in the literature on this issue, despite the importance of online communities is being increasingly recognized by contemporary marketers (see, e.g., Armstrong and Hagel, 1996; Bulik, 2000; Hagel and Armstrong, 1997; Kozinets 1999, Muniz and O'Guinn, 2001; White 1999). This gap gave us a strong motivation for this research. There are also only few researches dealing with online brand communities (McAlexander *et alii.*, 2002; Muniz and O'Guinn, 2001; Muniz and Shau, 2003).

For example, McAlexander *et alii.* (2002) studied the possibility for a brand to organize *brandfest* to reinforce relationships between customers, the brand and the marketers. However, these events do not guarantee that customers will continue to meet online after the event has ended to form a community. They studied how a company could build an online brand community by organizing brandfests. They looked at the communal state of the group formed during that particular event. They stated the group is not yet a brand community (or an online brand community), because it is not permanent and needs structure itself in a website after the brandfest to become an online brand community.

Muniz and O'Guinn (2001) show that online brand communities in fact exist, but do not try to show how such communities could emerge or what consequences they could have for the brand. They showed that consumers may organize into these customer-managed brand communities to share their experiences of a particular brand and to contribute to a better performance of the community. Brand community identify like-minded customers who identify with a brand and share significant traits. Furthermore, consumers in a virtual brand community represent an organized, interrelated and solid group that reflects the brand's values. In particular, "Brand communities represent a form of human association situated with a consumption context" Muniz and O'Guinn (2001, p.426) and are "affiliative groups whose online interactions are based upon shared enthusiasm for, and knowledge of, a specific consumption activity…" Kozinets (1999, p.3).

Some authors focus on the emergence process of a virtual brand community formed by consumers (Amine and Sitz, 2004). They studied the emergence of two online brand communities and compared their specific processes to extract the common factors and steps that contribute to form and structure these communities. This way they show how a brand community could emerge and be constructed by customers.

Consumers and a specific brand are no longer considered as dyadic relationships between a brand and an isolated consumer (Fournier, 1998), but rather as interactions overlapping associations and relationships among consumers within a specific group

(Gruen *et al.*, 2000). In particular, online consumer-managed brand community concept provides new ways for studying the word-of mouth by defining a specific group of consumers that diffuses information (Johnson-Brown and Reingen, 1987).

Thus, both types of virtual brand community present a special interest for marketers and brand managers, since they give new theoretical perspectives and because of their considerable, extensive and significant implications for marketing strategies.

In the present research, we study brand communities in online forums, such as user groups, bulletin boards, chats, newsgroups, and email lists. Many companies launching such communities recently for their customers have found that their customers have already established brand communities on their own initiative. For example, Algesheimer, Dholakia and Herrmann (2005) recount the example of National Instruments (NI) which launched the LabVIEW Zone, an online venue for the customers of its flagship software product LabVIEW three years ago, to interact and learn from each other. However, it found several thriving communities such as OpenG (www.openg.org) and LAVA (www.lavausergroup.org) that its customers had organized beforehand and were managing autonomously.

There are several important research issues here: under the circumstances that NI found itself in, what should it do? Should it go ahead with its plan of launching its own online community, perhaps competing with and alienating its loyal customers that already participate in OpenG and LAVA? Or should it seek to support these existing communities, thereby ceding a significant amount of control to its customers?

More broadly, although this issue has considerable practical significance, little research has examined differences between firm-managed and customer-managed brand communities. Some unanswered questions that we focus on are:

1. Do customers favor a particular type of community and are they entrenched within it?
2. Does company involvement reduce the enthusiasm of customers?
3. Which communities have a greater number of social interactions and are more effective in disseminating knowledge?
4. Do these communities favor different sorts of interactions?

Our goal is to create a comprehensive framework to compare customer participation and their consequences within firm-managed and customer-managed brand communities. To begin answering these questions, we compare and contrast brand communities supported by the firm and those organized by customers for two different branded products: NI's LabVIEW software and the Microsoft XBOX game console.

3. First Part: Qualitative Research Methodology

Our research focuses on recent online brand communities both firm managed and consumer managed that allow access to reliable data and lead to find out the key characteristics and factors explaining the community development, expansion, improvement and progress.

The initial portion of this research was exploratory, and employed netnographic observation and analysis: "Netnography extends the strengths of market-oriented ethnography by demonstrating how it can be efficaciously conducted online using existing online communities, often in an unobtrusive context" (Kozinets, 2002b, p. 62). Many anthropologists, sociologists and marketing researchers have perceived the need to specially adjust existing ethnographic research techniques to the communities that are emerging online (see, e.g., Escobar, 1994; Grossnickle and Raskin, 2000; Hakken, 1999; Jones, 1999; Kozinets, 1999; Miller and Slater, 2000).

We chose netnography since it provides researchers with a rigorous methodology adapted to the unique characteristics of virtual communities and this method was designed specifically to study "the language, motivations, consumption linkages, and symbols of consumption-oriented online communities" (Kozinets, 2002b, p. 70). As a marketing research technique, netnography uses information already available in online forums to "identify and understand the needs and decision influences of relevant online consumer groups" (Kozinets, 2002b, p.62). This methodology allows a systemic approach and understanding of the events in the online community and can be conducted in a completely unobtrusive manner, allowing continuing access to information in a particular online brand community. Netnography involves some limitations such as researcher interpretive skill, and the lack of informant identifiers present in the online context that implicate difficulty generalization of results to groups outside the online community taken in consideration. Researchers wishing to generalize results of a particular online group to other groups must consequently careful evaluate similarities and employ multiple methods for triangulation. On the other hand, similarly to ethnography, flexibility and adaptability are two of the greatest strengths (e.g., Fetterman 1989; Glaser and Strauss, 1967; Hammersley and Atkinson, 1995; Jorgensen 1989; Lincoln and Guba, 1985). In netnographic data collection and analysis, the researcher must follow conventional and rigorous procedures that the research is reasonable or "trustworthy". In most qualitative consumer research, the concept of "trustworthiness" is used rather than "validity," (see e.g. Wallendorf and Belk, 1989; Lincoln and Guba, 1985). Netnography is "based primarily upon the observation of textual discourse" (Kozinets, 2002b). To be trustworthy, the findings of a "netnography" should reflect the limitations of the online communication and the technique. Netnographers are professional "lurkers", who passively observes but does not actively participate in the exchange of the community. Four ethical research procedures are suggested using "netnography" and they were used during our research. First, the netnographer should disclose his/her presence, affiliations and intentions to online community users. Second, the netnographer should guarantee privacy and anonymity to informants. Third, the netnographer should search for and incorporate feedbacks from consumers of the online community being analyzed. Forth, the netnographer should contact community members and attain their consent to utilize any postings that are to be directly quoted in the research. Permission must also be obtained for using idiosyncratic stories (see: e.g. Sharf, 1999, p. 253-255).

Nethnographic method is made up of three major steps (Belk et Costa, 1998; Schouten et McAlexander, 1995; Werner et Schoepfle, 1987): familiarization with the culture of the studied group, data collection and interpretation of the data.

First, we observed the communities in a not systematic manner (i.e. lurking) to become familiar with the particular culture of the group (Kozinets, 2002b). Then, we became member of the community and participated more importantly in the exchanges and activities of the community. Later, we collected the data concerning the difference between the two categories of brand communities through in-depth interviews and triangulated them with data from other sites and/or interviews with the community founders via Internet. This allows us to have access to a large amount of information from different sources.

Choosing the right venue is important when doing Netnographic research. First, we conducted an extensive online research to identify brands that have both firm- and customer-managed communities. A list of communities we considered can be found in Appendix 2. We were seeking products that would evoke high involvement among consumers, and products involving professional and leisure applications. For our preliminary analysis and comparison, we chose NI's LabVIEW and the Microsoft XBOX. LabVIEW is a suite of graphical software applications that is used by engineers and scientists for test, measurement, and control purposes (More details at: http://www.ni.com/labview/). XBOX is a gaming console that Microsoft introduced in 2001. It has become the market leader in this product category world-wide, in part due to the ability of gamers to play online with others through the "XBOX Live" gaming service.

For LabVIEW, we studied the firm-managed community at http://forums.ni.com, and the two existing customer-managed communities, LAVA (http://forums.lavausergroup.org) and OpenG (http://openg.org). For XBOX, we studied the firm-managed community at http://www.XBOX.com/en-us/community, and two customer-managed communities, TeamXBox (http://www.teamxbox.com) and XBoxSolution (http://www.xboxsolution.com).

In communities that provided more than one kind of forum, we studied all of them. We wanted to learn as much as possible about the groups. As a starting point, we counted the number of interactions, then studied the topics discussed in-depth, the diversity of people who posted questions or comments, the size of the groups in which interactions occurred, and the number and types of events and activities outside the online environment provided by the community. In fact, as suggested by Kozinets (2002b), before initiating contact or data collection, the characteristics (e.g. group membership, market-oriented behaviors, interests, and language) of the online communities should be familiar to the marketing researcher.

The second part of data was collecting through in-depth interviews, one of the most common qualitative methods. Qualitative methods are particularly helpful for gaining knowledge of the rich symbolic world that underlies needs, desires, meaning and choice (see. e.g., Berg, 2004; Thompson, 1997; Denzin, Lincoln, 1994 and 2000; Miles, Huberman, 1984; Holbrook, 1995; Levy, 1959). These authors, among many others, point out that qualitative methodology provide many advantages. For example, it allows us to examine this complex phenomena to define the reality within, to explore and examine this topic in-depth. They are not limited to rigidly definable variables, and they allow us to redefine questions or reformulate them based on further data collection. Additionally, they allow us to search for negative case to disprove hypothesis and to probe for more information. They yield richest data, details, new insights, and they allow us to explain and help clarify questions, increasing the likelihood of useful responses, and allow us to be flexible in administering interview to particular individuals or circumstances.

This methodology permit us to include some additional questions in the questionnaire about topics we were involuntarily ignoring when we developed the first questionnaire. We became conscious we were missing some important issues after the first four interviews. In particular we added questions from 16 to 19 (see questionnaire in appendix 1).

As for Netnography methodology, it is necessary to mention that our findings are instructive, but they are not generalizable to the whole population.

Findings depend on research questions and available resources, e.g. number of online members willing to be interviewed, ability of online members to express themselves, time and researcher skill.

In depth interviews are very effective in giving a human face to research problems. Conducting and participating in interviews can be a rewarding experience for both participants and interviewers. For participants because in-depth interviews offer the opportunity to express their opinions in a way ordinary life rarely allow them. Many people find it gratifying, satisfying, and pleasing to discuss their ideas and experiences and to have someone listen with interest. Interviewers engaged in in-depth interviews are offered the privilege of having people who are virtually strangers entrust them with a glimpse into their personal lives. Our interviewing techniques were motivated by the desire to learn everything the consumer can share about brand community participation. In-depth interviews are appropriate for eliciting individual online experiences, opinions, feelings, knowledge, facts, familiarity, understanding, and expertise about both types of brand communities. The strength of this method is the possibility to extract in-depth responses, and to get at interpretive perspective, i.e., the connections and relationships a person sees between particular events, phenomena, and beliefs.

Messages were classified first as primarily on-topic or primarily off-topic, where the topic is the research question of interest. While including all the data in a first interpretation, marketing researchers will generally want to save their most intense analytical efforts for the primarily informational and primarily on topic messages (Kozinets, 2002b). As member checks (Arnould and Wallendorf 1994, p. 485; Hirschman 1986, p. 244; Lincoln and Guba 1985), a procedure whereby some or all of a final research report's results are presented to the consumers who have been studied to seek for their observations, after the interviews, we explained to the consumers some of our Netnographic findings. Member checks allowed us to obtain and elicit additional, and more specific insights into consumer meanings. In order to avoid influences on people responses during in-depth interviews, member checks were conducted after data collection and analysis had concluded, providing the chance for us to detect changing in consumer tastes, meanings and desires that generate important new marketing trends.

Summarizing, realizing that there are two different types of online brand communities, consumer managed and firm managed, our purpose was to study the differences. First, we needed to point out the main features of these communities that are social networks, even if they are computer mediated. Pointing out the relevant features through a nethnographic approach implies a series of different steps such as observation, lurking, become member and so on. When the main features were identifying, we were able to formulated some propositions and finally we tested them in SPPS with data collected through an online survey.

3.1. Data details

- In-depth interviews with customer community participants:

- 26 in Italy, 4 in Brazil
- Members of Nokia (2), Apple, Coke, Pepsi, Volkswagen, Toyota, BMW, iPaq and HP, Tiziano Ferro, Tampax, Play Station, rhinoceros 3d, Nintendo, Schermanet, Piero Pelu', Java, Emule, Limewire, Skype, DC++, Teddy, eBay, AC Milan, Oasis Band, Harley Davidson
- 45 minutes to 2 hours each interview

- Interviews and discussions with community and marketing managers, and community moderators/ content-providers of following firms:
  - *National Instruments* (USA)
  - *BMC software (USA)*
  - *eBay (Germany, Austria, Switzerland)*
  - *OpenBC (Germany)*
  - *Tilllate.com (Switzerland)*
  - *Hewlett Packard (USA, Netherlands)*
  - *Samsung FunClub (Netherlands)*
  - *Microsoft (Switzerland)*

- Interviews with organizers/ leaders/ moderators of following customer-managed communities:
  - *Nikonians* (USA, Mexico, Germany)
  - *Flickr groups (USA)*
  - *Lavausergroup (USA)*
  - *Southern Cruisers Riding Club (USA)*
  - *Several (BMW, Mini Cooper, Ford, etc.) car clubs (Germany, Austria, Switzerland)*

3.2. Findings from Netnography Observation: Elements Characterizing Online Brand Communities

Netnography, as online marketing research technique, gave us valuable information on the tastes, desires, representation, meanings, symbol system, decision making influence, and consumption patterns of online consumer groups. In particular, it gave us new insights about different elements characterizing online brand communities:

consciousness of kind, rituals and traditions, moral responsibility, heritage and brand history celebration, brand stories, exchange, sharing, produce and consume information. In this section we present each singular aspect in detail.

3.2.1 Consciousness of kind

The first and one of the most important elements of an online brand community is what Muniz and O'Guinn (2001) refers to as "consciousness of kind" or "shared consciousness". It is the intrinsic connection that members feel toward each other's, and the collective sense of difference from others belonging to different online brand communities. Consciousness of kind is shared consciousness, a way of thinking about things that is more than shared attitudes or perceived similarity. It is a shared knowing of belonging (Weber, 1978). We may call consciousness of kind, sense of community, or sense of belonging together, the acknowledgment that all other human beings are potential collaborators in the online brand communities, because they are capable of recognizing the mutual benefits of cooperation. In a hypothetical world in which the division of labor would not increase productivity, there would not be any online community. Consciousness of kind is a sense of "we-ness." For example, for Muniz and O'Guinn (2001) it is not important that the Mac community is mediated by mass media: magazines, books and the Internet. Even if members are spread all over the world, they simply believe they are alike because they imagine they share common values. It is like if they know each other at some level, even though they have never met.

3.2.2 Rituals and traditions

Members of brand communities engage in certain rituals and traditions. The second indicator of online brand community is the presence of these shared rituals and traditions that perpetuate the community's shared history, culture, and consciousness. Rituals serve to contain the drift of meanings and are conventions that set up visible public definitions (Douglas and Ishwerwood 1979, p65) and social solidarity (Durkheim,

1965). Traditions are sets of social practices that seek to celebrate and inculcate certain behavioral norms and values (Marshal, 1994, p. 537). For example, Saab drivers wave to each other as they pass on the road. Mac users often share stories about the brand such as the Mac's relative immunity to viruses. Additionally, there is the communal use of logos. Mac users prefer Apple stickers, T-shirts and Web banners (Muniz and O'Guinn, 2001).

3.2.3 Sense of moral responsibility

The third characteristic of a community is a sense of moral responsibility, which is a felt sense of duty or obligation to the community as a whole, and to its individual members (Szmigin, Canning, and Reppel, 2005). Sense of moral responsibility is that in which a consumer or the community deserves ethical evaluation for some acts or outcomes. It is noteworthy that it should not be confused with the causal sense of responsibility for some existing or past state of interactions. For example, when people say that "the storm was responsible for forty deaths," meaning that the weather caused these outcomes, we do not mean to attribute moral responsibility to the storm. Storms do not have moral responsibilities, and are neither responsible or irresponsible in the moral sense. In online consumer communities, this sense of moral responsibility is what produces, in times of threat to the community, collective action. Members have both a sense of moral responsibility to the community as a whole and to each other. People take care of each other, help and assist in repairing products, solve problems and share information, for example where to get the best deals. This sense of moral obligation to other members, as well as to the community as a whole, helps to motivate customers to act and to proceed accordingly (Murray, Habulin, 2007). Shared information is often more helpful than information provided by the marketer, because there is no self-interest (Muniz and O'Guinn, 2001).

3.2.4 Heritage and Brand History Celebration

Heritage is a brand attribute that provides sustainable competitive advantage.

192

Brand heritage is seen as employing marketing-mix variables that invoke the history of a particular brand, including all its personal and cultural associations (Aaker, 1996). An example is the rich historical associations of the Coca-Cola brand with Americana, patriotism, globalization, Santa Claus, and Christmas (Brown et al., 2003).

People know, buy, and experience brands that have a great heritage. For some of them, it is Mercedes, Philips or Disney, for others, it is McDonalds, Heineken, Prada or Gucci. A strong heritage makes these brands great; in facts, what they have in common is that they have had the time to build a meaningful and relevant past. Heritage is something nurtured over time. Consumers need time to use the brand, to make the brand a part of their lives, and to endow the brand from one generation to the next. Heritage speaks of a traditional way of life that is of value to present and future generations and speaks of status, character, social class, shared experience and a common history.

Many brands have an interesting heritage, but do not speak of it on their communities. They should know that heritage makes for interesting reading as well as enhances the brand's credibility. Additionally, it builds greater familiarity with the brand. If a brand can talk of its past, for example who started it, how it started and how it evolved over the years, then consumers get a sense of the brand's history and a more appreciative perspective of the brand.

Organizations should also document their corporate history and leverage anniversary celebrations as a marketing tool, good for public and community relations, brand reinforcement, nonprofit fund raising, employee and stakeholder relations, etc. Company's history is utilized for internal as well as external marketing purpose. Brand and corporate history makes up the corporate culture and affects how an organization and its brand are viewed. It also needs to be shared within the organization - through staff training materials, orientation, on the intranet, etc. - to make employees better and more knowledgeable and reinforce pride in their affiliation with their employer since sharing a company's history adds to employee loyalty. From a marketing point of view, it is profitable to celebrate upcoming corporate or brand milestone. It is easier to celebrate brand history with virtual communities either firm or consumer-managed, since they offer a different and additional tool to organize a successful celebration.

Some example of recently promoted milestones[27]

1. *Ford Motor Company* made effort to impress and to involve past and
   potential customers, as well as its employees, when it turned 100.
2. *Harley-Davidson,* drew 250,000 people to Milwaukee for the culmination
   of its 100th anniversary festivities.
3. New York's Mayor Bloomberg led the party to mark *Times Square's*
   centennial, as marketers from around the world bought space to promote
   the area's reputation as the pre-eminent location for outdoor advertising.

Companies not necessarily have to celebrate multiples of 25. In facts, for example
twenty years of history was the reason by *Domestications* to offer a marketing promotion
"20 percent savings on our 20 top picks". As other examples, *Southwest Airlines* offered
the special fare $33 one-way, to celebrate its 33rd birthday. For companies, using a
corporate or brand anniversary to market their organization it is very important and they
can choose which anniversary is significant for their brand since, if they take full
advantage of it, each anniversary could be a powerful marketing instrument.
Organizations have to be conscious that company's reputation is based upon its
accomplishments and they have an opportunity to focus attention on these
accomplishments when there is an anniversary coming up. Celebrate brand history is a
ready-made opportunity to demonstrate how company past has given a degree of strength
and expertise that is achievable only over time, and it can be the strongest criterion that
any stakeholder has to judge company future performance.

Through celebration, key audience may be reached to solidify and improve
brand's reputation and awareness as well as drive sales at the same time.

3.2.5 Employees' loyalty

Employees' loyalty is defined as a perceived alliance between the individual and
the company that is characterized by employee involvement, effort and commitment to

---

[27] http://www.kullbergconsultinggroup.com/news/BrandAnniversary.htm

the organization (Siguaw et al. 1994). Higher employee loyalty leads to better customer experience and represents an opportunity to increase revenue and profits. In facts, loyal employees may demonstrate commitment and focus on the customer. Employees play an important role in the service production process (e.g., Zeithaml and Bitner, 2003). There is substantial support that employee and customer satisfaction are positively related to each other (Koys, 2001; Tornow and Wiley, 1991).

Brand history celebration should also be used to create brand passion among company employees, since they represent one of the primary "media" in the majority of brand contacts. A Gallup survey says, "If your employees were 'fully engaged', your customers would be 70 more loyal, your turnover would drop by 70 percent, and your profits would jump 40 percent."[28] Company can use brand history celebration to create and strengthen the partnership between organization and employees, since they are one of the most important resource. They also might have a crucial significant role in online consumer-managed communities, as will emerge in this study. Brand anniversaries are an opportunity to build employee pride and passion, and to make them true brand advocates.

Furthermore, events and sponsorships allow companies to make personal contacts with the people who count, since they create bonds, both emotional and practical. They produce customer loyalty and employee involvement and dedication, with an opportunity to form a relevant connection with company's audiences, both internally and externally.

Online brand communities should include ideas about how a company will collaborate with customers and employees to grow and develop. It should be done in advance because, by significant advance planning, online communities can take advantage of marketing opportunities, since maybe competitors cannot match the same opportunities.

3.2.6 Shared brand stories

The story and meaning of a brand is one of its most valuable and irreplaceable asset. Stories capture consumers' imaginations, intrigue and engage them, and help give

---

[28] www.marketingprofs.com/2/hoover1.asp

their lives meaning. The stories that are told over and over again are those that reflect and enhance people lives. Every brand, large or small, has the potential to tell a unique and captivating story. Even though there may be parity products, there is no such thing as parity brands. Additionally, brand stories strengthen the brand image (Keller, 2003; Keller, 2002).

Each company should consider if its brand is telling a story that people want to hear, want to tell, and want to be a part of. In facts, brands should express and share their heritage in the form of a narrative, meaningful, and relevant brand story. Stories are entertaining, instructive, engaging and human; they connect people to people, and businesses to customers.

For example, Pepsi is not a soft drink, but a symbol of youth and vigor, Lord of the Rings is not a movie, but a fight between the evil and the good, and Harley Davidson, the road to unfettered freedom.[29] For most, a specific brand incarnates not only their actual lifestyle, but also a virtual expanded universe hosting an imaginary lifestyle of passions, feelings, and dreams.

These are only some examples of brand stories:

1. Nike's brand story is one of maximum performance, of challenging oneself to strive for their very best and calling that achievement perfection. "If you have a body, you are an athlete. And as long as there are athletes, there will be Nike." (www.nike.com/)

2. Disney's brand story is about the "ideal American community with clean streets, high moral values, happy families and a future where you never grow old, you never get sick, and you never die. Visiting a Disney theme park people experience the safety, security, and enjoyment of a small American town". (www.disney.go.com/)

3. Chanel's brand story is that of "the sensual, strong, and independent woman, who is seeking romance, spiritual love, and the experience of ecstasy" (www.chanel.com/)

---

[29] www.easyplanet.com/ep_value.pdf

4.   Marlboro's brand story embraces "nostalgia to exploit the myth of the stoic, solitary American cowboy: a place of wide-open spaces, and a time of simple choices, of good and evil, and of heroism".

5.   Toyota create an eco friendly car. At Toyota, they operate under a "global earth charter that promotes environmental responsibility throughout the entire company. They are leading the way in lowering emissions and improving fuel economy in gasoline powered vehicles. Not only they create the world's first mass-produced gas/electric hybrid car, but they are also at the forefront of developing tomorrow's fuel cell vehicles". (www.toyota.com/)

6.   MacDonald's have all of a sudden become health conscious. "MacDonald's also recognises the importance of a balanced diet and lifestyle and continues to seek quality new products that satisfy customer's expectations for taste and value" (www.mcdonalds.com/)

7.   BMW consistently delivers on "its four core values - technology, quality, performance and exclusivity and for over 25 years has kept to the same simple message, offering customers the ultimate driving machine" (www.bmw.com)

8.   Certain individuals become brands in their own times and they do this by associating themselves with the great stories of our common heritage that already live in our minds. For example, Muhammad Ali's brand story is to become the greatest. He seeks to become the source of ultimate strength. He wins the world boxing championship an unprecedented four times. Ali pays the price of his convictions when he refuses to fight in the Vietnam War because "the Black Man has no fight with the Yellow Man."

In essence, what these "superbrands" do is create an emotional link with its audience, balancing functional benefits with emotional ones. Emotional link is not just about appealing to a customer's values; a great brand must also be able to elicit an emotion that allows the consumer to identify easily the product. Nike create motivational slogans such as "just do it", and display a commitment to providing a service of human potential through powerful imagery and emotive commercials. They also use top athletes and sportsmen such as Michael Jordan to endorse their products which helps leverage the deep emotional connection that people have with sports and fitness making Nike both an inspirational and aspiration brand to obtain.

The Web is a multimedia communication venue; companies can use it effectively to deliver their marketing brand stories. In fact, marketing include also telling company stories in an effective way that embeds brand identity into the minds of target audience, connecting and communicating who the company is, what it does, and why the audience should be doing it with the company. Anyway, companies must be honest online to who they are, and what they really do.

3.2.7 Exchanging, sharing, producing and consuming information

This topic is strongly related and deeply discussed in paper number 2 of this dissertation. Also for online brand communities, exchange, sharing, producing and consuming information are important elements of community endurance.

3.3. Findings from in depth-interviews: propositions to be tested

After the Netnographic part of this research, we conducted in depth-interviews. They gave us new insights about trends in online consumer communities. From our in depth interviews, we were able to derive some propositions to better understand the online brand community phenomenon and the main similarities and differences between the two different types of virtual communities. Given the exploratory nature, these propositions needed further investigation and were confirmed and tested in a subsequent quantitative research. The structure of this section is as follows: propositions are presented in eight different paragraphs. Each paragraph will present an issue, a question or a problem in online consumer communities, both firm and customer-managed, deserving further investigation. Additional studies were needed both because the nature explorative of this study and because little research has been done so far for the particular topic of interest. This way, each proposition provides also future research possibilities on online brand communities. The propositions mainly concern about differences between the two types of online brand communities.

3.3.1 Brand and online community loyalty

For many reasons, such as stronger consumer price/quality awareness and increased emphasis on service and economic pressures, the companies need to develop new strategies geared towards achieving greater brand loyalty among customers. The importance of building and maintaining brand loyalty in electronic marketplaces has come into focus in marketing theory and practice in establishing sustainable competitive advantage.

Loyalty can be seen as an attitude where different feelings create an individual's overall attachment to a brand, a product, a service, an organization. On the other hand, loyalty can be seen as e-loyalty to an online community about a brand, a product, a service or an organization. These feelings define the individual's degree of loyalty and determine following behaviours. According to Kuttner (1998, p. 20), "The Internet is a nearly perfect market because information is instantaneous and buyers can compare the offerings of sellers worldwide. The result is fierce price competition and vanishing brand loyalty." Given the reduction in information asymmetries between sellers and buyers, there is a growing interest and attention in understanding the bases of customer loyalty in online environments. In particular if consumers can become not only brand loyal, but also online community loyal. E-loyalty is customer loyalty to a business that sells online or to a company with an online community, either firm-managed or customer-managed. Understanding if online communities can help companies gain a competitive advantage by devising strategies to increase e-loyalty is crucial for their business.

Brand loyalty can be considered an important goal in marketing (Reichheld and Sasser, 1990) and be demonstrated by repeated buying of a product or service or other positive behaviors such as word of mouth (Dick and Basu, 1994). However, brand loyalty is more than simple repurchasing, because customers may repurchase a brand due to situational constraints, a lack of viable alternatives, or out of convenience (Jones, Mothersbaugh, and Beatty, 2002). Instead, we might say that brand loyalty exists when customers have a high relative attitude toward the brand, which is then exhibited through repurchase behavior (Dick and Basu, 1994). The advantages for the company are for example that customers are willing to pay higher prices, they may cost less to serve, and can bring new customers to the firm (Reichheld and Sasser, 1990; Reichheld, 1993). Additionally, firms could have the capability to maintain premium pricing, they might have stronger bargaining power with channels of distribution, lower selling costs, a strong barrier to potential new entries into the same product/service category, and synergistic advantages of brand extensions to related product/service categories (Reichheld, 1996).

Despite the importance of e-loyalty to business success in online consumer brand communities, little research has been done so far in this field. Few researches have been restricted to practitioner-oriented suggestions on how to build loyalty to commercial websites (Smith, 2000; Reichfeld, Schefter, 2000).

About this topic, from our in-depth interviews, we got these answers when we asked: "How has participating in the online community influenced your relationship with the brand?":

"It makes it stronger because I understood many things about my mobile, many functionalities, some particular details and I start feeling an expert about NOKIA."

"Well, now I am definitely a real real Coke supporter, I could never buy PEPSI and betray the best brand. I go to every brand fest "COCA COLA live in tour. They did one just few days ago in Jesolo and it was so much fun, it was simply great"

"From when I started using APPLE, I always think there is no way for me to go back to other brands. The use of online APPLE community makes this feeling stronger, because I am able to realize even more product's limitations and strength".

"After two Volkswagen cars, I essentially decided do not own cars other than Volkswagen. Because Volkswagen is a lifestyle brand, automobiles are great and customers are always treating right."

"I think the iPaq community is a perfect example of people joining together for the common cause of helping others. It is sad many people are angry at the response they get because it's not what they want to hear but they always come back to get new information since they keep going using the brand."

"I love in the community I can communicate, chat and keep in touch 24/7 (24hour/7day a week) with other fans of Tiziano Ferro. Without the web this was impossible."

"I can't wait the new BMW model to be released. I don't want any other automotive brand."

"I drink only Diet Pepsi. No other cola is good for me! You cannot compare them"

"I only use Tampax, and cannot even think of using any other brand".

"This community is an invaluable source of information. I could answer to my questions just by browsing the forum topics. I can ask questions and receive immediately an answer. My own experience is useful to help other users experiencing the same problems. This kind of support is just amazing. This forum is the best resource available for Play Station users."

The loyalty topic is also discussed in many message boards in the online brand communities. As an example, in a virtual community we found this discussion. **Who is loyal to Sony?** [30]

1. "I'm Loyal. As you can see on my sig, I have firmware version 2.81 and I'm planning to update my PSP all the time. I have a PS2 and a PSP, but I also have a GBA SP. The only reason I have a GBA SP is because at the time I got it, Sony did not have a portable gaming console. I am not planning to get any consoles that are Nintendo or Microsoft. I am not getting a PS3 because I want to get accessories for my PSP and My PS2."

2. I will stick with Sony from now on; having 3 systems is too much to keep up with financially for me and I always update, i am not trying to brick my PSP with hacks. PS3 will have to drop its price before I buy it.

3. I Am loyal and always will be to Sony, I bought the PSP because I felt dirty after buying the XBOX. The PS3 will dominate, and maybe the Wii will also, only because Sony and Nintendo are older wiser companies. The XBOX 360 sucked, and that proves how Microsoft is a young hasty company rushing to get your money.

---

[30] http://boardsus.playstation.com/playstation/board/message?board.id=psp&message.id=2530240&page=3

Additionally, one of the most significant contemporary example of brand loyalty is the devotion of many Mac users to the Apple company and its products. Consumer behaviorist Tom O'Guinn thinks the key to Apple's loyalty is the Mac community itself. Apple users are not loyal to Apple per se. They are loyal to Apple and to each other. "It's not just about the relationship to the marketer," he said. "It's a triad between marketer, customer and customer." "You may get mad at the company, but the bond with the community means you don't really have a choice," he said. "You may complain, but you're not going to leave. In a cohesive community, the marketer can get away with all kinds of stuff because the cohesion is so strong." "This is about brands," the authors wrote. "This is the tie that binds."

For both LabVIEW and XBOX, we found considerable overlap in customer memberships across the firm- and customer-managed communities. Many of the most active participants tended to post and respond to messages actively in both community venues. Even moderators and organizers of one community tended to participate in other communities. This can be seen in the posts of one member participating in both the XBOX Solution and the Microsoft XBOX communities.

Based on the above discussion, we suggest that two propositions, needed further investigation, are the following:

Proposition 1a. Online brand communities participation, both in firm-managed and customer-managed, may influence positively brand loyalty.

Proposition 1b. Customers faithful to the brand could also be faithful to a particular online community.

3.3.2 Community's purposes

Defining the community's purpose is important so that new potential members know what to expect (Lazar and Preece, 1998). In fact, highly motivated customers may be prepared to browse web pages and messages, but most individuals want to find out immediately if the community is worth joining or not.

Online branding can be considered as attaching a company name to a new idea of value, owning that idea in a credible way and always delivering what company promises in everything they do and say (Schley and Nichols, 2005). But this is not enough, in fact for an online brand community, social interactions are important concepts that on firm-managed communities seems to receive less attention than they deserve. The reason for this apparent lack of interest may stem from an overly instrumental orientation that does not appeal to more socially oriented communities, such as consumer-managed. Three central criteria for an online brand community can be the effectiveness, efficiency and satisfaction with which users can achieve specified goals online, which seem to be restricted to goals related to an instrumental view on the use of communities. To broaden this view, we focus on how the concept of instrumental purpose can be understood and used within a social action context. How social goals are related to the effectiveness, efficiency and satisfaction criteria should be addressed specifically. It is argued that in order to improve online brand communities, organizers should consider both instrumental and social goals, since their combination constitute a fundamental part of the social action context in which online communities take place. It is important to make sure the home page always portrays the purpose of the community (Lazar et al., 2000).

A secondary function of online brand communities is providing for members a place to find friends from all over the world. Whether they are looking for brand information or a place to hang out and chat with people, they will find everything they need in consumer-managed communities. In the last years, brand communities helped people make friends, brought singles together in relationships than organizers cannot keep track of, they have had countless marriages of couples of all ages, and even "online babies". Brand communities are extending consumer networking capacity, enabling people to establish interaction across space with old and new friends who share their values, hobbies and interests.

About these topics, from our in-depth interviews, we got these answers (on brackets, the reader can find which community people were referring to and if it was a firm or a consumer managed community).

"You cannot talk about some topics in the company website, hormones are shut up there. If you want to talk about dating or sex you have to use dating websites such as…, if you use this community, you do because you want to have technical information". (Apple: firm-managed community)

"Well no..who cares about that? In this software technology website usually it really does not matter with who you are interacting with, it only matters suggestions are right and they work properly" (rhinoceros 3d: firm-managed community)

"In this community you can talk about everything you want, for example about psychology, medicine, literature and so on" (Schermanet: consumer-managed community).

"I met my ex-girlfriend in this community since we are both enthusiast of the same singer, this community is fantastic because you can meet many people with your same passion. We were together for 6 years" (Piero Pelu': consumer-managed community).

"In the official websites there are some rules you have to respect, otherwise administrators can banned you, instead in the unofficial websites rules are more relaxed and as long as you do not offend other people or voluntary provoke other members you can talk about everything you want"(Emule: comparison between official and unofficial communities).

"The unofficial site is more informative than its official rivals because it is not restricted by anything, and it possesses a limitless worldwide staff, the members, who capture information to share" (Limewire: comparison between official and unofficial communities).

"The official forum is used mostly to ask technical question about how to use the tampax, for example the first time for young girls and so on. Instead, the unofficial community is utilized mostly to talk about female problems, issues and interests. In the customer managed community you can meet many good people willing to help and listen to you." (Tampax: comparison between official and unofficial communities).

"I communicate my real personality within the community and i am respected by other members for it. A friendship in a fan community is different from a friendship in the official website because people tend to open up more to others when in a fan club. People get to know each other much more and tell each other what they think and so it creates this incredible bond with one another (Tiziano Ferro: consumer-managed community)"

"Using this community, I got the possibility to meet many people with my same passion. This gave me the opportunity to interact and participate together at brand events, and also the possibility to meet and have a personal contact and not just online friends (Coke: consumer-managed community)"

"If a person helped me many times, obviously I consider this member like a friend of mine, even though I have never met him personally" (DC++: consumer-managed community)

"Online friendships can be substantial because people are less superficial online. The removal of physical presence forces people to interact with each other with no prejudices and stereotypes than they would have in real life" (HP: consumer-managed community).

We consistently found that whether by design or evolution, the firm-sponsored communities tend to contain topics and discussion that primarily concern the firm's products and services. Virtually all the forums and topics in firm-sponsored communities were for specific product-related matters (e.g. doubts or technical questions about the product, how to get new releases, which hardware better perform with the software or game, comments and suggestions etc.), leading to exchanges that were instrumental and focused, like the following example:

(In the firm-managed community LabVIEW Zone)

Topic: LabView8 at NI

I've been using the LV8 evaluation version for a little while, and am slightly intrigued by the idea of shared variables…. My question is if I can use this to decouple the OPC communication from my actual LabVIEW application.

Answer by NI engineer

Your understanding of shared variables seems correct. For a network scoped shared variable, PSP (Publish and Subscribe Protocol) is used. This protocol is the new NI network protocol replacing the functionality of DataSocket, although it works in a similar way….It easiest just to think of it as writing and reading values to/from memory.

Kind Regards,

XXXX -ApplicationsEngineer National Instruments

In contrast, the customer-managed communities tended to have specific venues only for discussing "off topic" issues. In the LAVA community, for example, the LavaLounge has posts wishing members "happy birthday," proclaiming that "I'm a daddy," opining that "Niagara Fall is beautiful" etc. See the following post as an example:

(In the customer-managed community LAVA)

Topic: I'm a Daddy

"3-th October my sweet baby-girl was born!"

Answer from another member

"Little girl's age is the same with LabVIEW 8.0 Congratulations!!!"

As can be noticed from all these examples and witness statments, two propositions provide interesting new insights on the difference between the two types of online brand communities. The firm-managed communities tend to contain topics and discussion that primarily concern technical discussions about the firm's products and services. In particular:

Proposition 2a. Firm-managed communities seem to be employed primarily for focused instrumental purposes; customer-managed communities seem to allow more for broader "off-topic" social interactions.

Proposition 2b. Customer-managed members seem to engage in broader interactions, and form relationships more often.

3.3.3 Online community organization and comprehensiveness

Companies would like to have the ability to monitor systematically online conversations on their blogs, message boards and chat rooms to track opinions and perceptions around their brands, products or/and competitors. Firm-managed communities add the ability for marketers to create their own online brand communities, which act as an ongoing research panel. Companies want to find a method that works well for website visitors while still effectively optimizing for the search engines. The best way to organize an online brand community involves dividing products, services, and articles into categories. Each category has an individual page, each of which companies would optimize for a specific category. They provide chat rooms, a comprehensive search, quick mails, message boards, assistance and so on.

Online communities could also be classified based on the supporting software used by the community. Some online communities are supported using software such as Listservers, Usenet, Bulletin Boards, Internet Relay Chat, Chat Rooms, or combinations or more than one of these tools (Lazar and Preece, 1998). These software tools may differ in the type of interface (text-based, graphical, etc.), as well as the time lag (synchronous vs. asynchronous). For instance, listservers can deliver community messages directly to an individual's e-mail inbox, and provides asynchronous communication. A chat room might require special software, and is synchronous group communication. Additional features that add life to online brand communities are for example: Interactive Tours, Interactive Graphics, Flash, Dynamic HTML, Java Scripts and Applets, Animation, Guestbook, Slide Shows, Bulletin Boards, Forums, Message Boards, Web Site Pages Consumers Can Update Themselves, Multi-lingual Sites, E-Commerce Solutions.

From our in-depth interviews:

"Customer-managed communities usually are disorganized. It is difficult to search on previous discussions to find the topic a person is searching for" (Apple: consumer-managed community)

"Topics very often are not divided in sections. Unofficial websites are disorganized or they do not have animations, tutorials. They are not as good as the official communities" "I like for example when images change over time" (rhinoceros 3d: firm-managed community)

"I would like sometimes something new, for example a new graphics, a new function, and so on. Instead, this community is static. They rarely change their interface; website images are very important." (schermanet: consumer-managed community)

"There are too many white-washing attacks, that is too many people join the community with different nicknames, then they start a new conversation, they answer themselves in a polemic way with the other nick, they start new discussions with inappropriate terminology with the purpose of messing things up in the community. Only the network administrator can realize this because posts come from the same IP address. (Nokia: consumer-managed community)"

"Customer-managed communities stuck (go very slowly) when there are too many people connected (Piero Pelu': consumer-managed community)"

"I would like more functions and more interactions with others" (Tiziano Ferro: consumer-managed community)

"What I do not really like is that most of the time in the unofficial website I cannot find what I am searching for because sometimes they are messy and they provide too much content without a clear website organization" (Limewire: consumer-managed community)

"Sometimes the problem is that you get outdated information. People have to be very careful the material they read is recent and not related for example to old versions or models" (HP: consumer-managed community)

"Well, I do not like that even if I do not know why but some features of the unofficial community often may not work, but anyway there is much more stuff elsewhere". (Pepsi: consumer-managed community)

Generally speaking, all these witnesses gave us the opportunity to extrapolate the following proposition:

Proposition 3. Firm-managed communities seem to be more organized and comprehensive than customer managed communities.

3.3.4 Company role in consumer-managed communities

Members of online communities should be aware of the unreliable nature of Internet "information" spreading: if another member online in a firm-managed community telling you a product is a must-buy could be an objective and informed employee. On the other hand, in consumer-based community he could also be 9 years old. Companies should help consumer-managed communities to post reliable information.

Additionally, it seems that customer-managed communities may lack the organizing and/or financial resources necessary to orchestrate offline events. For this reason, members can feel consumer-based communities as less appealing.

The solution to a lot of problems on consumer-managed communities could be to give employees direct and continuous access to consumer-managed online communities, so they can learn, participate, listen and collaborate.

The ideas emerging from in depth interviews are controversial:

"How do you think Nokia can provide an official website like this one with all the mobiles tricks??? Are you crazy? Beh I know they exist because…well i am sorry but i am not an engeeneer for nothing ;-)

"……Well, this community organized by nokia (impossible thing btw)? it could be more accurate. For sure they give more accurate information without compromising your mobile or even worse without crash it completely (make it to die)."

"I think that if an employee reveals news about releases before the official company communication he/she is fucking the company, right? Because if everybody knows there is an imminent new version of one product everybody will wait that version and they won't buy what they are actually trying to sell and advertise right now."

"In Apple Customer Assistance point they do not really care about these unofficial communities because for example if you go there and you tell them that you got a certain type of information in an unofficial forum, they will answer you that there are all bullshit and that only them know really what to do and precise things about products and problems related".

"Employees (Apple) participate anonymously i think, because in the forum there are some sections about future development and they are always able to catch the latest news about future released, but if you think about it only someone who works for the company can have such an information"

"A synergistic collaboration between official sites and unofficial sites makes sense. And not only Skype can play a meaningful role in the unofficial forums, but it can also recruit people from the unofficial website to assist with the content of the official sites"(Skype).

"Firm can help the consumer-managed communities to improve them….For example the pages can be restructured and transferred to other web space, while new people and expert users willing to contribute can be added worldwide." (Java)

"Milan (forza Milan!!) could assist the fan clubs with monetary and financial helps. This way the unofficial communities would have more liquidity to organize events and to support more efficiently the team everywhere the team goes to play." (AC. Milan)

"In my opinion, the development of interactive programs between websites would improve both communities through an information exchange and stronger integration." (eBay)

"yes, of course online there are a lot of collaboration between websites. I guess, not sure though, they call it "affiliate programs". They represent the perfect way for the company to increases sales, improve content, and loyalty and an opportunity to register community members and traffic. They can all make more money and benefit by building business together." (Coke)

"Surely a collaboration between the communities would benefit both with a little investment in time and money, actually I really do not understand why do not they do that..any guess??" (schermanet).

As another example, NI was late in introducing online venues managed by itself and so its customers created venues like LAVA and OpenG for themselves. Yet, the company took a proactive approach, providing resources to these communities. For instance, NI employees answer questions in the LAVA community and the company provides resources for online meetings and places for physical meetings to OpenG members.

Even when the firm finds active incumbent customer-managed communities online, only it may be able to engage in certain types of community marketing programs. For example, we recorded the type and number of off-line events organized through the various LabVIEW communities. Every single one of these events such as work-shops, social get-togethers, and user group meetings in the next two months post- research was organized through the firm-sponsored communities. It seems that customer-managed communities may lack the organizing and/or financial resources necessary to orchestrate offline events. It is noteworthy that previous research has shown that face-to-face customer interactions encouraged through brand-centric events such as "Brandfests" are extremely effective in fostering brand communities (McAlexander et al., 2002).

It is important to test if a not invasive or disturbing firm participation in consumer-managed brand community will improve these communities' overall performances. In particular:

Proposition 4. Firms could play a meaningful role in customer-managed communities for what concerns financial help and/or information reliability.

3.3.5 Trust

The concept of social networking online relies heavily on honesty and establishing trust. Trust and security are important issues in any type of online community, because for consumers to communicate without restraint, they must feel that their privacy is protected (Preece, 2000).

There is a great deal of self-disclosure involved. Many communities ask users to list their income and religion on their profile page, even though they are not mandatory fields. The principle is that the more consumers share about them, the more people will be able to connect each other's. The reality, however, is that many people lie online. If people lie in normal conversations where they talk to another person face to face, of course they could do on the internet where the only witness is the keyboard. Even if people do not lie, they can of course exaggerate. When people are expected to use internet to create an impression to others, they have the opportunity to exaggerate their personality, presenting ourselves as somebody more interesting than they actually are in real life. As consumers try to manage the impression they make in person by wearing accoutrements or make-up, they do the same thing online, when for example they talk about something they do not know. The dynamics of a face-to-face setting are different from online interaction, where many constraints are dropped. Naturally, people can become more uninhibited online. There are things they do not normally tell their friends personally, but they can tell to unknown people online.

The growth of specialized online brand communities is expected to make social networking even more attractive to the internet crowd. Everyone should be careful what personal information is sharing with others and the reliability of information they can get online. There is control about technical issues in firm-managed communities since the company cannot provide unreliable information to their user. There is not such a control in consumer-managed communities where people can post information declaring they are expert about a topic, but without any warranty for what concerns information reliability. In fact, the main concern for participants in online communities is to get true information. For example, J. Ramón Palacios (jrp) and Bo Stahlbrandt (bgs) met online in a photography forum late 1999. A strong friendship develops. It grows from mutual respect, shared values and a common interest: Photography with a Nikon. They both reacted to the fact that many discussion forums "out there" were frequently pretty rude, with an impolite tone in the messages exchanged, and false. The main issues recurrently experienced at other sites and what they thought was wrong were:

- Lack of firm, consistent moderation in forums
- Low quality of content with false statements, no accountability, spreading of rumours and hearsay
- Unfriendly, rude and childish exchanges, lack of a code of honour for mature behaviour, "What brand is best" continuous flaming wars
- Parochial instead of international, never global
- Generic, not brand oriented
- A vacuum of Nikon specific up-to-date discussions
- Commercial in nature with questionable editorial credibility
- No real community spirit

So they decided to create their own. [31]

Generally speaking, only in the official firm website they assure to provide reliable information about technical problems. In the customer-managed communities members can get information to resolve their technical problems from other enthusiasms or experts without certification. During our interviews, we got these significant declarations from consumers:

"Your question does not make sense because you should absolutely divide "work" communities about a particular sector of the production from those with a vaster range of

---

[31] http://www.nikonians.org/html/about/genesis.html

users. Because in the communities we are talking about hormones are shut down. Instead in other types of communities they are very active and they change the attention and the focus of the discussion since psychology of people changes there. This website is organized by expert users and not by people paid by the software manufacturer. Cooperation is very very important…because many times these softwares do not use properly the ram and your laptop crash, understand? What I want to say is that for tech related issues is better you ask the producer directly but the cooperation is stronger in the unofficial forum. (but do you trust people in this forum?) yes of course I do, for example if there is a new version released we discuss which version is better and if the new version is worth enough…the company does not provide this information, they want you to buy the new version".

"Of course since they explain you what to do to fix a problem you have to be practical with electronics devices and fix the problem by yourself following their instructions. For example, you can never be able to do some of those things that is why i am an engineer and you are an economist!!!! ;-) I am kidding…"

"The difference is that Nokia could never write bullshit because this can create a customer revolution and attack toward the company (they can go to court and so on) in particular if suggestions are unrealizable or with catastrophic consequences"

"I think in this community (Apple) there are many people willing to help and they want to help if you have some tech mess to resolve. The problem is that they are not always right."

"Well the difference between official and unofficial? Mhm…in the unofficial they always tell you the truth because there are not economic interests to justify they cheat you, instead in the official website there are many interests involved. They tell you what they want about the product because they want you to buy as much as you can…."

"Well of course you can find accurate information, many people available and get an answer very quickly, just be careful though that they are not developers or employees, they are only enthusiasts or kind of experts; anyway you can be sure they will tell you everything they know and they will never give you voluntary erroneous information. No one wants to fuck you here…what is the point otherwise???"

"Organized by the company? Bah…I could feel maybe less comfortable, because they try to sell you what they want and they are often unreliable about product problems and imperfections."

"(do you consider it as a community?...) Well no…who cares about that? In a technology website usually it really does not matter with who you are interacting with, it only matters suggestions are right and they work properly."

"I think in this community there are many people willing to help and they want to help if you have some tech mess to resolve. The problem is that they are not always right."

"Well, this community organized by nokia (impossible thing btw)? it could be more accurate. For sure they give more accurate information without compromising your mobile or even worse without crash it completely (make it to die)."

"In Apple Customer Assistance point they do not really care about these unofficial communities because for example if you go there and you tell them that you got a certain type of information in an unofficial forum, they will answer you that there are all bullshit and that only them know really what to do and precise things about products and problems related".

Based on the above discussion, the following proposition needs further investigation:

Proposition 5. People seem to trust more the firm-managed community about technical issues. On the other hand, they seem to trust more the consumer-managed communities about product reviews and for honesty of participants, for example about product problems.

3.3.6 Competitors

An oppositional loyalty (Muniz and Hamer, 2001) might exist between opposite brands and competitors. In consumer-managed communities there are many extremely negative mails about the "enemy brand". These negative posts are normally not allowed by the "netiquette" (i.e. is a catch-all term for the conventions of politeness recognized on Usenet, in mailing lists, and on other electronic forums such as Internet message boards.

They are the usually accepted rules of the Internet). Negative posts are often called flames. They are hateful, rude or excessively critical comments. These flames are pretty common in the generalist forums concerning the product category.

Loyal customers to one brand might strongly reject the opposite brands. The opposition should not be considered to be as strong as it is presented in the messages exchanged within the community. The opposition to competitors is a symbolic representation that emerges between the members of a brand community. Even though this consumers' opposition to one particular brand considered as an enemy is not absolute, it establishes a common cultural reference and ties more strong links between the members of the online brand community, both consumer-managed and firm-managed. Examples from our interviews include:

"There is generally speaking more free speech in unofficial forum, because there is no control. In firm-managed communities there is more fear, since those communities have become less anonymous as companies use defamation suits to discover the identity of their online critics even though some members are starting to fight back. (Nokia: consumer-managed community)" .

"It is likely that the number of defamation claims will continue to rise online if there is no legal control, as in the case of consumer-managed community (Apple)"

"In this community it is normal people talk bad about other software because (probably they are company employees who post those comments) they can attract new customers by doing this (rhinoceros 3d)"

"In the official websites there are some rules you have to respect, otherwise administrators can banned you, instead in the unofficial websites rules are more relaxed and as long as you do not offend other people or voluntary provoke other members you can talk about everything you want"(Emule: comparison between official and unofficial communities).

A nice example of free speech in consumer-managed community is the following. On a forum managed by veteran flight attendant Kevin M. Griffin, several anonymous employees urged co-workers to stage sickouts, even though they are outlawed by federal labor statutes. The purpose was to force Northwest to cancel flights during the Christmas season. One post said "sickout en masse is one way the company will be convinced we are serious.... Let's not talk about it. JUST DO IT!". After a flood of sick calls forced the cancellation of 317 flights from Dec. 30 to Jan. 2, Northwest Airlines Corp. struck back. On Jan. 5, it sued the flight attendants' union and several others for staging an illegal strike.[32]

Based on this discussion, future researches should further investigate the reasons why on online brand communities seems that:

Proposition 6. In customer-managed communities people feel more freedom in talking bad about brand competitors and brand itself than in firm-managed brand communities.

3.3.7 Sensitive corporate information and new product launch

The consumer-managed communities provide additional content, compared to firm managed communities, consumers would not otherwise have. People not only are looking for unbiased and objective opinions on products as recommendations, but they also search for hidden information online, such as information the companies do not want to disclosure about their products. For example, if a product reveals some problems, consumers want to know this information, but it is rarely provided by the company.

Additionally, employers have considerable worries as to how employees handle their electronic communications by way of blogging and instant messaging (IM), camera phones and even iPods. There are many forms of electronic communication available to employees, and they can use them for potential violation of trade secrets and other corporate information.

The posting of corporate information in online brand communities may pose the risk of being liable for trade secret dissemination. The posting of this trade secret information can destroy its status as a trade secret, because the material will not longer be undisclosed. Cases involving the posting of this confidential information on the Internet have long raised legal implications in the Internet age. For example, "Following the recent departure of employees from our asset-backed and mortgage-backed business, we discovered that intellectual property and other proprietary business information belonging

---

[32] http://www.businessweek.com/2000/00_09/b3670155.htm

to the Bank had been wrongfully taken," said the spokesman of a Major U.S. bank involved in a trade secret dispute.[33] *(National Post Online - April 18, 2002).*

As another example, Apple won trade secrets legal dispute. Apple sued 25 employees who allegedly leaked confidential product information to three Web publishers. It sued several unnamed individuals, called "Does," who leaked specifications about a product code-named "Asteroid" to Monish Bhatia, Jason O'Grady and another person who writes under the pseudonym Kasper Jade. Their articles appeared in the online publications Apple Insider and PowerPage. "Apple is using this case as a desperate attempt to silence the masses of bloggers and online journalists that it cannot control but feels it can intimidate," Jade, who has been writing about Apple for more than eight years, wrote in an e-mail. The case has been widely watched in the fast-growing world of Web logs — or blogs, Web sites that contain articles or diary entries and that recently have propelled stories into the mainstream. (Konrad, 2005).

In several recent cases, companies have struggled to learn the identity of anonymous individuals who have posted company trade secrets on Web logs and message boards, sometimes in violation of company confidentiality agreements.

Companies who are injured stress the need for courts to identify the guilty parties and hold them accountable for theft of trade secrets or breach of confidentiality agreements. Defendant Web posters who wish to conceal their identities cite the First Amendment as granting them a constitutional right to free speech and privacy. Decisions in such cases have raised the issue of whether, and in what circumstances, companies have a right to sue information connected to these Web logs and message boards in order to identify the anonymous authors, or whether the bloggers can anonymously reveal trade secrets on the Internet. Anonymous Web posters are protected by a "qualified immunity," however, this protection must be balanced against a company's right to protect its trade secrets and enforce its confidentiality agreements (Wentzel, 2006).

"Trade secrets" is the legal term for confidential business information: a secret belonging to a business that allows the company to compete effectively. Examples of trade secrets include: customer identities and preferences, vendors, product pricing,

---

[33] http://www.wipo.int/sme/en/documents/wipo_magazine/05_2002.pdf

marketing strategies, company finances, manufacturing processes and other competitively valuable information.

The information must not be "generally known or readily ascertainable" through proper means. The information must have "independent economic value due to its secrecy." And finally, the trade secret holder must use "reasonable measures under the circumstances to protect" the secrecy of the information. Failure to adequately protect company's proprietary information may allow competitors and ex-employees to reduce company's profits.

If a top employee leaves the company, the employee had learned every major area of the company. S/he was an invaluable asset to the company. This employee can spread online secret information with a fake identity. It is rarely done in firm-managed communities since it might be easier to be caught by the company.

People we talked to, provide the following comments:

"I joined because I wanted to enrich my knowledge such as tricks and software about a particular type of NOKIA mobile phone".

"How do you think Nokia can provide an official website like this one with all the mobiles tricks??? Are you crazy? Beh I know they exist because…well i am sorry but i am not an engineer for nothing ;-)"

"Wait, first of all NOKIA would never organize such a community because they will never disclosure themselves all their tricks since they have consumer assistance service where you have to pay A LOT for every single stupid thing you ask them…."

"What sort of things do you talk about in the Apple community with others? Tech tricks and deceits such as unlock secret code for software, cracks, code to format and so on"

"Organized by the company??? Noooooooo..this is insane… we can talk about cracks to get many materials for free and how to make it works…the official company can never do such a thing"

"It is very nice that in the unofficial community you can ask people where to get tickets that you might not otherwise have." (AC. Milan)

"Limewire provides every day a new tip about how to improve program performance, but still if you use the forum you can get many new undisclosed hints"

"In the emule board I can find tricks about how to download efficiently. For example, there is a special session called: small trick to speed up emule and windows"

Based on the above, we expect:

Proposition 7a. Members use the consumer-managed community to get hidden information, such as tricks or deceits about a product or company rumors.

Additionally, once a product is developed, effectively product launch becomes the critical step to its success. The product launch process must address all the steps necessary to start volume production, plan and execute marketing activities, develop needed documentation, train sales and support personnel (internal and external), fill channels, and prepare to install and support the product. An improved product launch process results in faster time-to-market and time-to-profit. Activities are better planned and coordinated and more tightly integrated. System data requirements are better understood, and systems may be better integrated. The result is better production ramp-up, more effective marketing, a sales force better prepared to begin selling the new product, and a service and support group better able to service and support the new product, leading to greater customer acceptance.

Advertising is an effective way to launch company's latest new product regardless of whether company plan to market the new product on a local, national or international scale. Anyway, it is critical to carefully plan and execute product launch using a strategic approach. Companies sometimes make mistakes when developing new product launch campaigns. Avoiding these pitfalls greatly increase their odds of success. For example, a potential mistake is if companies do not plan the launch until right before the release date. Companies need a launch strategy to persuade consumers to buy their new product. That is not something they can create overnight, so start their launch campaign planning early is a good strategy. If possible, they should begin launch planning when the product gets the "go" sign from management. That way, companies have the same amount of time to plan and execute product launch as the production team has to manufacture the product.

A problem might arise when the employees know about the new product launch. Companies should not educate the employees until after the news breaks elsewhere. Because even though employees are the most important word-of-mouth brand ambassadors, educate them about the launch plan and prepare them to talk about the product with their family and friends, it is not always a good strategy. In fact, many times, unsatisfied employees may reveal online in consumer-based communities, with fake identities, secret corporate information about new product releases, creating the so called "cannibalization" phenomenon. In marketing, cannibalization refers to a reduction in the sales volume, sales revenue, or market share of one product as a result of the introduction of a new product by the same producer. Cannibalization can happen also before the new launch if people know there is a new product or version ready to enter the market. In fact, some experts claim that a pre-announcement for a new product can cannibalize the sales of an old product in a prior period. Online the cannibalization is a common phenomenon. For example, Pet Smart, like Barnes and Noble and Toys 'R' Us before, launched an online venture as a separate company. With this launch, they cannibalized sales at their brick and mortar stores, in some cases pricing online goods lower than those in their stores. Other retailers are following similar strategies with Web-based versions of their retail stores. Bank One launched a completely virtual bank, Wingspan Bank.com, with more attractive rates than Bank One.[34] It is important to enrol "passionate" in companies launch strategy so they can reinforce what is going to be said when the product is introduced in the trade, business and consumer press, but this must be done carefully in order to avoid cannibalisation. This information is not available in firm-managed communities, but they might be available in consumer-managed communities. Some comments from our in-depth interviews:

"I think that if an employee reveals news about releases before the official company communication he/she is fucking the company, right? Because if everybody knows there is an imminent new version of one product everybody will wait that version and they won't buy what they are actually trying to sell and advertise right now."

"Employees participate anonymously i think, because in the forum there are some sections about future development and they are always able to catch the latest news about future releases, but if you think about it only someone who works for the company can have such an information"

---

[34] http://www.referenceforbusiness.com/small/Bo-Co/Cannibalization.html

" Well, of course in the community you can get information about new songs or album released." (Tiziano Ferro)

"I can't wait the new BMW model to be released. I don't want any other automotive brand….i definitely try to get information about new product release in the community".

Specifically, we suppose:

Proposition 7b. Members use the consumer-managed community to know when the company will launch a new product.

3.3.8 Communities' target

Managers and firm-managed brand community organizers sometimes erroneously consider that once their companies determine their target market, everything else will fall into place. Some brands might miss their potential target market with their marketing communication. Companies that identify online underserved segments can outperform the competition by developing uniquely appealing products, services and online communities.

Customer segmentation in online communities is most effective when a company adapts offerings to segments that are the most profitable and serves them with distinct competitive advantages. This prioritization can help companies develop marketing campaigns and pricing strategies to extract maximum value from both high- and low-profit customers. A company can use customer segmentation as the principal basis for allocating resources to product development, marketing, service and delivery programs.

In the XBOX communities we studied, the firm-managed community appeared to be designed for, and populated by the primary XBOX target segment: "hardcore gamers" between the ages of 15 and 28. In contrast, we found the Team XBOX core participants to be much older and "non-traditional". This was evidenced through conversations discussing articles regarding Hurricane Katrina from the New Republic magazine, sharing a first-person account of a Presidential speech, and arguing the politics of banning violent games. One practical implication of this finding is that customer-managed communities may provide valuable information regarding overlooked segments.

221

We hypothesize there might exist the following difference between the two types of online brand communities:

Proposition 8. Firm-managed communities are targeted toward specific, well-defined segments; customer-managed communities may have customer groups overlooked by firms. Customer-managed communities are more diverse, and have the opportunity to diffuse the product to other non-targeted segments.

4. Second Part: Quantitative Research Methodology

We collected a large survey of online consumer community members, included consumer managed brand community users and firm managed brand community users, to test some of the proposed propositions. In particular, the following table is a summary of the propositions we tested and it indicates which variables in our survey tested them.

Proposition 1a. Online brand communities participation, both in firm-managed and customer-managed, may influence positively brand loyalty.	Brand Loyalty and Community partecipation
Proposition 2a. Firm-managed communities seem to be employed primarily for focused instrumental purposes; customer-managed communities seem to allow more for broader "off-topic" social interactions. Proposition 2b. Customer-managed members seem to engage in broader interactions, and form relationships more often.	Instrumental Purposes and Social Purposes
Proposition 3. Firm-managed communities seem to be more organized and comprehensive than customer managed communities.	Community Organization and Offline Event Organization
Proposition 4. Firms could play a meaningful role in customer-managed communities for what concerns financial help and/or information	Community Organization and Offline Event Organization

reliability.	
Proposition 5. People seem to trust more the firm-managed community about technical issues. On the other hand, they seem to trust more the consumer-managed communities about product reviews and for honesty of participants, for example about product problems.	Technological and Social trust
Proposition 6. In customer-managed communities people feel more freedom in talking bad about brand competitors and brand itself than in firm-managed brand communities.	Fredoom of speech and Brand Competitors Discussions
Proposition 7a. Members use the consumer-managed community to get hidden information, such as tricks or deceits about a product or company rumors.	Hidden/Rare Information
Proposition 7b. Members use the consumer-managed community to know when the company will launch a new product.	Hidden/Rare Information
Proposition 1b. Customers faithful to the brand could also be faithful to a particular online community.	Future research
Proposition 8. Firm-managed communities are targeted toward specific, well-defined segments; customer-managed communities may have customer groups overlooked by firms. Customer-managed communities are more diverse, and have the opportunity to diffuse the product to other non-targeted segments.	Future research

A total of 102 active virtual community members participated in this research. For "active", we consider currently direct participation on a regular basis in one of the 2 types of communities. We used the screening condition that respondents had to engage in participation in an internet- based group such as a consumer managed or firm managed brand community. Data were collected by conducting an internet-based survey, which was publicized by contacting people online in different communities.

The study was introduced as an "Opinion Survey-Brand Community on the Internet". First, participants selected the name and type of Brand Community that they most frequently engage in. In the rest of the survey, they were asked questions pertaining to the one type of group interaction that they chose.

Details of the measures are provided in Appendix 3.

In the following table we summarize the descriptive statistics for the two different samples.

Table 1

Descriptive statistics for samples from the two brand community type

Brand Community Type	Sample Size	% Female Respondents	% Male Respondents	Average Age
Consumers	50	45,8	54,2	26,58
Firms	52	8,2	91,8	25,63

Table 2 summarizes the number of measures, the means, standard deviations, and Cronbach alpha reliabilities of the constructs. The reliabilities were adequate in all cases.

Table 2

Means, Standard Deviations, and Reliabilities of Construct Measures

Scale	# of Items	Mean	Std. Dev.	Reliability
Tech Trust	5	20.76	9.30	.946
People Trust	5	23.83	6.30	.860
Community Organization	7	29.80	11.17	.939

Freedom of Speech	3	15.21	4.25	.882
Brand Competitors Discussion	2	9.32	3.41	.749
Get something for free	2	9.53	3.27	.638
Offline Event Organization	3	12.38	5.40	.866
Instrumental Purpose	13	64.65	11.28	.845
Social Purpose	19	92.88	16.43	.867

Results

ANOVA analyses

We conducted One-way Analysis of Variance (ANOVA) on our dependent variables as described by measures to test our hypotheses.

One-way ANOVA tests allow a researcher to determine if one given independent variable, such as interactivity and engagement, has a significant effect on user offline and online behavior across *any* of the groups under study. A significant p-value resulting from a one-way ANOVA test would indicate that a dependent variable is differentially expressed in at least one of the groups analyzed. ANOVA analysis test main effects.

There are two assumptions underlying the ANOVA technique. First, it is assumed that within each group to be compared the data follow a Normal distribution. Second, it is assumed that these Normal distributions share a common standard deviation (SD). Nevertheless, ANOVA is robust against violations of these assumptions, at least where all groups are of roughly equal size as in our study (Tabachnick et al., 1983). ANOVA is performed in two stages. First stage is an analysis to see if any differences exist. If it seems there may be differences, the second stage is to identify the nature of the differences. The null hypothesis tested by ANOVA is that the group means are equal:

Null hypothesis H0: $\mu_1 = \mu_2 = ... = \mu_N$

A t-test is also appropriate to test differences in means with only two groups.

We consider Brand Community Type and point out similarities and differences between firm-managed and consumer-managed brand communities. We conducted these analyses to verify and to better understand specific effects and differences across these two groups. We analyzed these measures by comparing statistical differences between members of firm and consumer managed brand communities. These analyses were done by running a one way (firm, consumer) ANOVA with the reported change in level of the *Instrumental Purpose, Social Purpose, Offline Event Organization, Technological Trust, People Product/Service Reviews' Trust, Community Organization, Freedom of Speech, Brand Competitors Discussion, Get something for free, Hidden Information* as dependent variables. ANOVA analyses were used to compare the groups on effects of online social interactions, as well as to uncover offline behavior related differences.

Table 3 provides a summary of results of any hypothesis test, besides hypothesis 1, since the first hypothesis does not test a difference between the two online community types and it is discussed separately. The analysis generally supports the research hypotheses.

Table 3

Hypothesis number	Variable name	Firm Managed Brand Community means	Consumer Managed Brand Community means	Significance level
2a	*Instrumental Purpose*	5,14	4,82	F (1, 94) =3,194*
2b	*Social Purpose*	4,6	5,14	F (1, 92) =10,189**
2	*Get something for free*	3,54	5,94	F (1, 96) =113,891**
3	*Community Organization*	5,33	3,05	F (1, 92) =95,663***
4	*Offline Event Organization*	5,67	2,68	F (1, 94) =213,168**
5	*Technological Trust*	5,62	2,61	F (1, 95)=182,18***
5	*People*	3,94	5,58	F (1, 95) =70,362***

	Product/Service Reviews' Trust			
6	*Freedom of Speech*	4,49	5,65	F (1, 96) =19,433***
6	*Brand Competitors Discussion*	3,3	5,97	F (1, 97) =153,418***
7	*Hidden company information*	3,87	5,16	F (1, 97) =18,802***

As expected, there are many significance differences between the two types of online brand community. Results are divided by hypothesis tested.

Hypothesis 1. Online brand communities participation, both in firm-managed and customer-managed, may influence positively brand loyalty.

Our results show that 71,1 % of people feel that participating to the brand community has increased their knowledge about the brand products and services.

Additionally, 62,9 % feel that participating to this brand community has increased their willingness to buy brand products and 58,8% feel that participating to this brand community has increased their inclination to buy the brand.

Furthermore, 66,7 % feel that participating to the brand community has increased their commitment to the brand and 69,1 % feel that participating to this brand community has increased their willingness to pay a higher price for this brand over other brands.

Moreover, 69,1% feel that participating to this brand community has increased their willingness to recommend this brand to others.

Additionally, to test this hypothesis we ran in SPSS a linear regression. We used brand loyalty as dependent variable and online brand community participation as independent variable.

Linear Regression estimates the coefficients of the linear equation, involving independent variables, that best predict the value of the dependent variable. Linear regression is used to model the value of our dependent scale variable, brand loyalty, based on its linear relationship to our predictor, community participation.

The linear regression model assumes that there is a linear relationship between the dependent variable and each predictor. This relationship is described in the following formula.

$$y_i = b_0 + b_1 x_{i1} + \ldots + b_p x_{ip} + e_i$$

where:

y_i: is the value of the ith case of the dependent scale variable

p: is the number of predictors

b_j: is the value of the jth coefficient, $j=0,\ldots,p$

x_{ij}: is the value of the ith case of the jth predictor

e_i: is the error in the observed value for the ith case

The model is linear because increasing the value of the jth predictor by 1 unit increases the value of the dependent by bj units.

The measures of the independent variables were indicated by the answers we got in a 7-Likert scale from:

-How many times do you visit this brand community?

-How many times do you purchase something on this brand community?

-How many times do you post your own thoughts and comments about the brand on a web site bulletin board, in a chat room or on an email listserv?

-How many times do you read others' thoughts and comments about the brand on the web site bulletin board, in the chat room or on the email listserv?

This table shows the coefficients of the regression line.

Coefficients[a]

Model		Unstandardized Coefficients		Standardized Coefficients	t	Sig.
		B	Std. Error	Beta		
1	(Constant)	8,213	2,075		3,957	,000
	commpart	,999	,385	,217	2,598	,011
	p2	1,447	,408	,309	3,548	,001
	p3	,714	,358	,167	1,992	,049
	p4	1,140	,315	,296	3,623	,000

a. Dependent Variable: brand_loyalty

The coefficients of the regression line show statistically significant results. It implies that community participation positively influence brand loyalty. The model fit looks positive, the first section of the coefficients table shows that all the predictors in the model are significant, indicating that these variables contribute to the model. To determine the relative importance of the significant predictors, we looked at the standardized coefficients. P2 (number of time people buy something in the online community) is the variable that contributes more to the model because it has a larger absolute standardized coefficient.

In particular if community participation increases, brand loyalty will increase as well.

The ANOVA table tests the acceptability of the model from a statistical perspective.

ANOVA[b]

Model		Sum of Squares	df	Mean Square	F	Sig.
1	Regression	1899,816	4	474,954	30,385	,000[a]
	Residual	1422,424	91	15,631		
	Total	3322,240	95			

a. Predictors: (Constant), p4, p2, commpart, p3
b. Dependent Variable: brand_loyalty

The regression row displays information about the variation accounted for by the model. The residual row displays information about the variation that is not accounted for by the model. The regression sum of squares is greater that the residual sum of square, which indicates that more than half of the variation in brand loyalty is explained by the model.

The significance value of the F statistic is less than 0.05, which means that the variation explained by the model is not due to chance.

While the ANOVA table is a useful test of the model's ability to explain any variation in the dependent variable, it does not directly address the strength of that relationship.

Model Summary[b]

Model	R	R Square	Adjusted R Square	Std. Error of the Estimate
1	,756[a]	,572	,553	3,95361

a. Predictors: (Constant), p4, p2, commpart, p3
b. Dependent Variable: brand_loyalty

The model summary table reports the strength of the relationship between the model and the dependent variable. R, the multiple correlation coefficient, is the linear correlation between the observed and model-predicted values of the dependent variable. Its large value indicates a strong relationship. R Square, the coefficient of determination, is the squared value of the multiple correlation coefficient. It shows that more than half the variation in brand loyalty is explained by the model. With the linear regression model, the error of our estimate is considerably lower, about 3,95.

We also checked for multi-collinearity . When the tolerances are close to 0, there is high multi-collinearity and the standard error of the regression coefficients will be inflated. A variance inflation factor greater than 2 is usually considered problematic, and the greatest VIF in the SPSS table was 1,6. The collinearity diagnostics confirm that there are no problems with multicollinearity. Eigenvalues are not close to 0, indicating that the predictors are not intercorrelated and that small changes in the data values may not lead to large changes in the estimates of the coefficients. The condition indices were computed as the square roots of the ratios of the largest eigenvalue to each successive eigenvalue. Values greater than 15 indicate a possible problem with collinearity; greater than 30, a serious problem. No indices were larger than 15, suggesting we have no problems with collinearity.

All these results confirm our hypothesis that online brand communities participation, both in firm-managed and customer-managed, may influence positively brand loyalty.

Hypothesis 2: Firm-managed communities seem to be employed primarily for focused instrumental purposes; customer-managed communities seem to allow more for broader "off-topic" social interactions. Customer-managed members seem to engage in broader interactions, and form relationships more often.

About instrumental and social purpose, as expected, results are on the opposite direction. In particular, people prefer to use firm brand communities for instrumental purpose and consumer managed communities for social purpose. This result is supported since differences in means for the groups are significant: 5,14 for the firm managed brand community versus 4,82 for the consumer managed brand community for instrumental purpose; 4,6 for the firm managed brand community versus 5,14 for the consumer managed brand community for social purpose.

Additionally, people search mostly to get something for free from other people in consumer brand communities. This result is supported since differences in means for the groups are significant: 3,54 for the firm managed brand community versus 5,94 for the consumer managed brand community.

Hypothesis 3. Firm-managed communities are more organized and comprehensive than customer managed communities.

People prefer how online communities are organized by firms compared to the other group. They argue that firm managed communities are organized into small functional units such as small groups and different sections and by topics. Generally speaking are better organized, easily and intuitive to use and allow them to find what they need. This result is supported since differences in means for the groups are significant: 5,33 for the firm managed brand community versus 3,05 for the consumer managed brand community.

Hypothesis 4. Firms could play a meaningful role in customer-managed communities for what concerns financial help and/or information reliability.

One-way ANOVA results indicate that individuals prefer to use firm managed brand communities for offline brand event organization. Consumer managed brand communities lack financial availability to organize such events. This result is supported since differences in means for the groups are significant: 5,67 for the firm managed brand community versus 2,68 for the consumer managed brand community.

Hypothesis 5. People seem to trust more the firm-managed community about technical issues. On the other hand, they seem to trust more the consumer-managed communities about product reviews and for honesty of participants, for example about product problems.

Results show that if people need to ask a technological question they prefer to use firm managed communities since they can get a reliable answer, but if they have to ask a product review they prefer to use consumer managed brand communities. This result is supported since differences in means for the groups are significant: 5,62 for the firm managed brand community for technological trust versus 2,61 for the consumer managed brand community for technological trust; 3,94 for the firm managed brand community versus 5,58 for the consumer managed brand community for people Product/Service Reviews' trust.

Hypothesis 6. In customer-managed communities people feel more freedom in talking bad about brand competitors and brand itself than in firm-managed brand communities.

We expected that people feel free to discuss different topics on consumer managed brand communities and they feel less freedom on the correspondent firm community. This expectation is supported by our results. In facts, in the consumer brand communities they feel more free to express their opinions and they feel more free to get involved in discussions related to other brands. This result is supported since differences in means for the groups are significant: 4,49 for the firm managed brand community versus 5,65 for the consumer managed brand community for freedom of speech; 3,3 for the firm managed brand community versus 5,97 for the consumer managed brand community for brand competitors discussion.

Hypothesis 7. Members use the consumer-managed community to get hidden information.

Results show that members use the consumer-managed community for example to know when the company will launch a new product or to get tricks or deceits about a product or company rumors. This result is supported since differences in means for the groups are significant: 3,87 for the firm managed brand community versus 5,16 for the consumer managed brand community.

6. Conclusions

Overall, our propositions warn that there is the chance that customer-managed communities exert more and multi-faceted influence on its members than comparable firm-managed communities.

Summarizing, although consumer marketing firms have embraced customer community marketing programs, many of them are maybe failing to create cohesive and influential customer communities. They are missing out to dynamic customer enthusiasts and savvy third-party entrepreneurs who have been more successful in creating influential and engaging customer-managed communities.

Through netnography and in-depth interviews, we were able to extrapolate 8 different propositions identifying new potential online trends. Since the explorative nature of this research, we did additionally research through online surveys to confirm what we suggested. In particular, online brand communities participation is a great tool to increase brand loyalty since customers are faithful to the brand and can become loyal to the particular online community as well. However, in customer-managed communities, members seem to engage in broader interactions, and form relationships more than in the corresponding firm-managed community.

Another possible restraint of firm-managed communities is that they are targeted toward specific, well-defined segments; instead customer-managed communities may have customer groups overlooked by firms. Since customer-managed communities are more diverse, they have the opportunity to diffuse the product to other non-targeted segments with positive implications for firms.

Firms could play a meaningful role in customer-managed communities, if their presence is not "disturbing" for consumers. For example, about technical issues, people seem to trust more the firm-managed communities, but they seem to trust more the consumer-managed communities about other topics for people they interact with. A synergistic collaboration between official sites and unofficial sites could be beneficial for both. Companies should help them, for example by financing them, since we discover firm-managed communities are more organized and comprehensive than customer managed communities and they have greater opportunities to organize off-line events. We expect a healthy partnership is possible.

Companies should also be careful of information spreading, since members declare to use the consumer-managed community to get hidden information, such as tricks or deceits about a product, and to know when the company will launch a new product.

A quote is a significant depiction of our propositions: "The best brands are not owned by the manufacturers, the producers, the businesses. Rather, they are owned by the people who love them."[35]

7. Future research

By serving both types of online brand communities with useful and enlightening content delivered regularly, companies could employ them to get positive benefits. In particular, future researches should focus on verifying the following points, identifying potential benefits that companies could get through online brand communities.

1. Articulate the brand message in a way that customers can transmit to new prospects and recruiting new members. Online brand community members can become brand best promoters, because they broadcast the brand message and their passion for it into the market. They can also act as the channel for feedbacks from the market.

2. Reduce advertising and promotions costs with programs that build upon each another. People in facts can find many news, photos, videos, and discussion boards devoted to their favorite brands with just quickly scan of the Web. This implies a lot of free advertising for the firm. For example, Coca-Cola, Harley-Davidson, and LEGO have in common that all are highly dependent on online brand communities. These three brands developed such potent spirit that their core audiences accept them almost as personal brands. Consumers assume ownership of the brand and do most of the communication work for the company as part of a brand community. As other examples, Harry Potter,

---

[35] Kevin Roberts, in Lovemarks: The Future Beyond Brands. http://www.inc.com/magazine/20040801/schlitz.html

Pokémon, and Teenage Mutant Ninja Turtles are brands where the product is irrelevant. As long as the brand name is attached, a product will sell on the name's strength. Four Harry Potter books have been published to date, yet over 3,000 related products have been released! [36]

3.   Develop customized marketing programs. Both types of online brand communities may represent an organized cohesive, solid and interconnected group. Marketers could treat online customers like subscribers or members and develop membership-oriented programs that strengthen, intensify and expand customer relationships and customer loyalty. An online membership-oriented program promotes integrated communications that include websites and blogs, email newsletters, chat, e-books, live events, message boards and other media components. Customer-managed communities should work on this aspect since we discovered they lack of some components and potentials. Each component provides branding and promotional opportunities, occasions to interact, chance to improve the brand and by combining them, marketers can increase their effectiveness and success while lowering costs.

4.   Provide an interactive communication and research channel that tracks members' interests over time and use feedbacks from the online brand communities, both firm and consumer-managed communities, to decide strategic moves in the market. Online brand community members can become the source of valuable customer research data about their needs, interests, curiosities, and so on. Online brand communities collect considerable customer data and can use them to build their own membership-oriented marketing communications programs. For example, a large international banking client created a branded site for its best "global citizen" clients, ones that had banked with them in multiple countries and had a high net worth. The community site it created offers users a place to share trials and tribulations of world travel, moving abroad, and other similar issues common among the group. The bank uses feedback from the message boards and online polls to decide what content to offer, and in turn learns more about this important target audience. Companies should move from ad-hoc projects to a continuous

---

[36] http://www.clickz.com/showPage.html?page=1557431

communication with its key consumers. "We'll be in a position to let consumers tell us what products or messaging we should be developing, as opposed to the other way around, which is happening today," Amoroso told ClickZ. "We're very excited about this new opportunity and truly believe this will help us get smarter about understanding our consumers' needs and motivations."[37] Strategic moves in the market might include: determine appropriate product pricing, choose specific product features, design an optimal distribution strategy; support ongoing promotions, e.g., for new products, and events.

5.   Through online brand communities, companies have the opportunity to keep their brand identity in a customized world. For example, first was Nike iD, a customization concept that permits consumers to design their own pair of Nike shoes. Jones Soda offered a customization platform: bottles became vehicles for consumers' customized labels, and the fans' bottles were distributed in stores. Build-A-Bear Workshop broke new ground in the teddy bear game, inviting kids to construct their own bears. The Lego Factory enables kids to design their own Lego sets; Mercedes-Benz's has the build-your-own-car option and hundreds of clothing Web sites that offer consumers the chance to design their ideal apparel. In online brand communities, the concept of customization is important. Once consumers have had the chance to pick and choose, to decide their own brand universes, product functions, and designs, there might be no turning back. Through online brand communities in the future, people will be able to customize every item they use. For the brand is important to remain instantly recognizable, even without a logo because the growth in customization, in particular online, requires brands to expand and preserve more coherent, stronger brand identities that originate from all the product and service components, not just from a logo. The brand should be perceptible, distinctly perceivable, to justify the consumer's choice of it for her customized product.[38]

6.   Brand communities give the opportunity to increase the time consumers spend enjoying a brand through online participation and strengthen brand stories. In

---

[37] http://www.clickz.com/showPage.html?page=3623081
[38] http://www.clickz.com/showPage.html?page=3622934

an online brand community, the graphics are important and so are other factors such as distribution, product design and product quality. Anyways, customers should be linked emotionally and intellectually with the product and for this purpose they need a brand story. Companies should share their stories on the online community, reveal them, strengthen them, and allow them to define the brand's identity and encourage customers to share their stories about company product. Branding is creating an emotional network around the product. In facts, the more sophisticated the network of values, the more compatibly they match the core values of the brand, the better the brand is armed against competitors.[39]

7.   Establish appropriate service options to stick customers to the brand. Sticky branding is when customers are hooked on the brand as much for the emotional attachment as for its features, making it difficult to try another. People use Microsoft Word or PowerPoint instead of Persuasion or WordPerfect not because they love Microsoft products. The point is that if people install new software their files would be incompatible with almost every other office computer. Word and PowerPoint are global to the rest of the business world, they guarantee anyone can open the documents. There is no rational or emotional argument that could persuade people to change. Sticky branding can be so oppressive the consumer finds it difficult to become unstuck. An example is Nokia phones. Nokia's universal charging plug is one of its many sticky brand components. If the batteries die, chances are people find a colleague with a charger they can hook up to or at the hotel reception desk probably has a spare one for just such an occasion. Additionally, Nokia's navigation is so intuitive and remains so consistent that once a consumer is used to it, change would be particularly disconcerting. Another example is Apple computers. Since the iPod hits the market, distribution was not anymore Apple's weak link. Sticky branding is a combination of human habit, strong distribution, and consistent navigation as a technique in which a consumer finds it hard to switch. Very few brands truly succeed in making it happen.

8.   Online brand communities perform several other important functions on behalf of the brand such as perpetuating the history and culture of the brand, providing free

---

[39] http://www.clickz.com/showPage.html?page=3599361

help and information, and exert a lot of pressure on members to remain loyal. They give consumers a greater voice, provide an important information resource and grant wider social benefits through communal interaction.

References

Aaker, D. (1996), Building Strong Brands. New York: The Free Press.

Algesheimer, R., Dholakia, U.M., Herrmann, A. (2005). The social influence of brand community: Evidence from German car clubs. Journal of Marketing, 69 (3), 19-34.

Amine A., Sitz L. (2004) Marketing: Where Science Meets Practice, Esomar Conference, Warsaw. http://www.univ-paris12.fr/irg/cahiers/AmineSitzSept2004.pdf

Armstrong, A., Hagel, John, III (1996). The Real Value of On-Line Communities, Harvard Business Review, May-June, 134-141.

Bagozzi, R.P., Dholakia, U.M. (2006). Antecedents and purchase consequences of customer participation in small group brand communities. International Journal of Research in Marketing, forthcoming.

Bearden, W. O., Etzel, M. J. (1982). Reference Group Influence on Product and Brand Purchase Decisions, Journal of Consumer Research, Vol. 9, pp. 183–194.

Belk, R. W., Costa J. A. (1998). The Mountain Man Myth: A Contemporary Consuming Fantasy, Journal of Consumer Research, 25, 218-140.

Belk, R.W., Tumbat, G. (2002). The Cult of MacIntosh. Salt Lake City, UT: Odyssey Films.

Berg, B. L. (2004). Qualitative Research Methods for the Social Sciences. Fifth edition. Boston: Pearson Education, Inc.

Brint, S. (2001). Gemeinschaft Revisited: A Critique and Reconstruction of the Community Concept, Sociological Theory, 19:1, 1-23.

Brown, S., Kozinets, R.V., Sherry, J.F. Jr. (2003). Teaching old brands new tricks: Retro branding and the revival of brand meaning, Journal of Marketing, 67 , 19-33.

Bulik, B. S. (2000), The Brand Police, Business 2.0, November 28, 144-155.

Costigan J. T. (1999), Introduction. Forest, Trees, and Internet Research", in Steven Jones (ed.), Doing Internet Research. Critical Issues and Methods for Examining the Net, Sage Publications, Thousand Oaks, xvii-xxiv.

Cliff D'Arcy "Free Online Books And Music" August 31, (2006) http://www.fool.co.uk/news/comment/2006/c060831b.htm?ref=foolwatch

Denzin, N.K., Lincoln, Y.S. (eds. 1994). Handbook of Qualitative Research, Sage, Thousand Oaks.

Denzin, N.K., Y. S. Lincoln, (eds. 2000). Handbook of Qualitative Research. Second edition. Thousand Oaks, CA: Sage.

Dholakia, U.M. (2006). How customer self-determination influences relational marketing outcomes: Evidence from longitudinal field studies. Journal of Marketing Research, forthcoming.

Dholakia, U.M., Bagozzi, R.P., Pearo, L. (2004). A social influence model of consumer participation in network- and small-group-based virtual communities. International Journal of Research in Marketing, 21 (3), 241-263.

Dick, A. S., Kunal Basu (1994). Customer Loyalty: Toward an Integrated Conceptual Framework, Journal of the Academy of Marketing Science, 22 (2), 99-113.

Douglas, M., Isherwood, B. (1979). The World of Goods. New York: Basic

Durkheim, E. (1965).The Elementary Forms of the Religious Life. New York: Free Press.

Englis B. G., M. R. Solomon. (1994). The Big Picture: Product Complementarity and Integrated Communications. Journal of Advertising Research, Vol. 34.

Escobar, A. (1994). Welcome To Cyberia: Notes on the Anthropology of Cyberculture, Current Anthropology, 35, 211-231.

Featherstone M. (1991 [2002]), Consumer Culture and Postmodernism, Sage Publications, London.

Fetterman, D. M. (1989). Ethnography: Step by Step, Vol. 17, Applied Research Methods Series. Newbury Park, CA: Sage.

Fournier S. (1998). Consumers and Their Brands: Developing Relationship Theory in Consumer Research, Journal of Consumer Research, 24, 343-373.

Franke, N., Shah, S.K. (2003). How communities support innovative activities: An exploration of assistance and sharing among end-users. Research Policy, 32, 157-178.

Friedman M. (1999). Consumer boycotts: Effecting change through the marketplace and the media, Routledge, New-York.

Glaser, B. G. and A. L. Strauss (1967). The Discovery of Grounded Theory, Chicago: Aldine.

Grossnickle, J., O. Raskin (2000). The Handbook of Online Marketing Research: Knowing Your Customer Using the Net, New York: McGraw-Hill.

Gruen T. W., S. John O., A. Frank (2000). Relationship Marketing Activities, Commitment, and Membership Behaviors in Professional Associations, Journal of Marketing, 63 (July), 34-49.

Hagel, J. and A. G. Armstrong (1997). Net Gain: Expanding Markets Through Virtual Communities, Boston, MA: Harvard Business School.

Hakken, D. (1999). Cyborgs@Cyberspace?: An Ethnographer Looks to the Future, New York: Routledge.

Hammersley, M. and P. Atkinson (1995). Ethnography: Principles in Practice, 2nd Edition, New York: Routledge.

Holbrook, M., (1995). Consumer Research: Introspective Essays on the Study of Consuption, Sage London.

Holt D. (2002), Why Do Brands Cause Trouble? A Dialectical Theory of Consumer Culture and Branding, Journal of Consumer Research, 29, 70-90.

Johnson B. J., Reingen P. H. (1987). Social Ties and Word-of-Mouth Referral Behavior, Journal of Consumer Research, 14 (December), 350-362.

Jones, Michael A., David L. Mothersbaugh, and Sharon E. Beatty (2002). Why Customers Stay: Measuring the Underlying Dimensions of Services Switching Costs and Managing Their Differential Strategic Outcomes, Journal of Business Research, 55, 441-50.

Jones S. G. (1999). Doing Internet Research: Critical Issues and Methods for Examining the Net, Thousand Oaks, CA: Sage.

Jones S. G. (1995). Understanding Community in the Information Age, in Cybersociety: Computer-mediated Communication and Community, edited by Stephen G. Jones, Thousand Oaks, CA: Sage, 10-35.

Jorgensen, Danny L. (1989). Participant-Observation: A Methodology for Human Studies, Vol. 15, Applied Research Methods Series. Newbury Park, CA: Sage.

Kalman, D.M. (2005). Brand Communities, Marketing, and Media 2005 Terrella Media.

Keller, K. L. (2003). Brand Synthesis: The Multidimensionality of Brand Knowledge. Journal of Consumer Research, 29 (4), 595-600.

Keller, K. L. (2002). Strategic Brand Management (2 ed.). Upper Saddle River, NJ: Prentice-Hall.

Kollock P. and Smith Marc (1999). Communities in Cyberspace, in Marc A. Smith and Peter Kollock (eds.), Communities in Cyberspace, Routledge, London, 3-25.

Konrad R., AP Technology Writer Friday, March 11, 2005.
http://www.sfgate.com/cgi-bin/article.cgi?f=/news/archive/2005/03/11/financial/f122955S64.DTL

Koys, D. J. (2001). The Effects of Employee Satisfaction, Organizational Citizenship Behavior, and Turnover on Organizational Effectiveness: A Unit-Level, Longitudinal Study, Personnel Psychology, 54 (1), 101-114.

Kozinets, R. V. (2001), Utopian Enterprise: Articulating the Meanings of Star Trek's Culture of Consumption, Journal of Consumer Research, 28, 67-88.

Kozinets, R. V. (2002a), Can Consumers Escape the Market? Emancipatory Illuminations from Burning Man, Journal of Consumer Research, 29, 20-38.

Kozinets, R.V. (2002b). The field behind the screen: Using netnography for marketing research in online communities. Journal of Marketing Research, 39(1), 61-72.

Kozinets, R.V. (1999). E-tribalized marketing? The strategic implications of virtual communities of Consumption. European Management Journal, 17 (3), 252-264.

Kuttner, Robert (1998). The net: a market too perfect for profits, BusinessWeek, 3577 (May 11), 20.

Kozinets, R. K. and Handelman Jay (1998). Ensouling Consumption: A Netnographic Exploration of the Meaning of Boycotting Behavior, Advances in Consumer Research, 25, 475-480.

Lazar, J., Preece, J. (1998). Classification schema for online communities. Proceedings of the 1998 Association for Information Systems Americas Conference, 84-86, Baltimore, Maryland, August 1998, Hoadley, E., and Benbasat, I, editors. Atlanta, 42, Georgia: Association for Information Systems.

Lazar, J., Hanst, E., Buchwalter, J., Preece, J. (2000). Collecting User Requirements in a Virtual Population: A Case Study. WebNet Journal: Internet Internet Technologies, Applications, and Issues, 2(4), 20-27.

Levy, S. J. (1959), Symbols for Sale, Harvard Business Review, 37 (July-August), 117-124.

Lincoln, Y. S. and E. G. Guba (1985), Naturalistic Inquiry, Beverly Hills, CA: Sage.

Marshall, G. (1994). The Concise Oxford Dictionary of Sociology. Oxford: Oxford University Press.

McAlexander, J.H., Schouten J.W., Koenig, H.F. (2002). Building brand community, Journal of Marketing, 66, 38-54.

Miles, M.B., Huberman, A.M. (1984). Qualitative Data Analysis: A Sourcebook of New Methods, Sage Publications, Newbury Park, CA.

Miller, D., Don Slater (2000). The Internet: An Ethnographic Approach, Oxford: Berg.

Muniz, Jr., A.M., O'Guinn, T.C. (2001). Brand community, Journal of Consumer Research, 27, 412-432.

Muniz A. M., Hamer Lawrence O. (2001), Us versus Them: Oppositional Brand Loyalty and the Cola Wars, Advances in Consumer Research, 28, 355-361.

Muniz A. M., Schau Hope Jensen (2003), Power and Resistahce in the Brand Community for a Discontinued Product, Advances in Consumer Research, Special Session Summary, 30, 193-194.

Murray, K. B., Habulin, C. M. (2007). A community facilitation model for e-government: A case study in monitoring water quality. In Hakim, L. (Ed.), Global e-government: Theory, applications and benchmarking (pp. 114-126). Hersey, PA: Idea Group. Forthcoming.

Peñaloza, L. (2001). Consuming the American West: Animating Cultural Meaning and Memory at a Stock Show and Rodeo, Journal of Consumer Research, 28 (December), 369-398.

Preece, J. (2000). Online Communities: Designing Usability , Supporting Sociability. New York: John Wiley & Sons.

Reichheld, F. (1996). The Loyalty Effect. Boston: Harvard Business School Press.

Reichheld, F. (1993), Loyalty-Based Management, Harvard Business Review, 71 (2), 64-73.

Reichheld, F., W. Earl Jr. Sasser (1990), Zero Defections: Quality Comes to Services, Harvard Business Review (September-October), 105-11.

Reichheld, F., Schefter, P. (2000). E-Loyalty, Harvard Business Review, 78 (4): 105-114.

S. Rempel Aug. 29, 2006Gimme, gimme gets They've got it, you want it, here's how to

get it all for free. TORONTO STAR
http://www.thestar.com/NASApp/cs/ContentServer?pagename=thestar/Layout/Ar
ticle_Type1&c=Article&cid=1156758429189&call_pageid=968332188492

Rheingold H. (1993 [2000]), The Virtual Community. Homesteading on the Electronic Frontier, MIT Press Edition, Cambridge.

B. Schley, C. Nichols Jr (2005). Why Johnny Can't Brand: Rediscovering the Lost Art of the Big Idea. Portfolio Hardcover.

Schouten, J.W., McAlexander, J.H. (1995). Subcultures of consumption: An ethnography of the new bikers, Journal of Consumer Research, 22, 43-61.

Sharf, B. F. (1999). Beyond Netiquette: The Ethics of Doing Naturalistic Discourse Research on the Internet, in Jones, Steve, ed. Doing Internet Research: Critical Issues and Methods for Examining the Net, Thousand Oaks, CA: Sage, 243-256.

Siguaw, J. A., Brown, G., Widing, R. E. (1994). The influence of the market orientation of the firm on sales force behavior and attitudes. Journal of Marketing Research, (February), 106-116.

Smith, E. R. (2000) E-Loyalty. New York: Harper Collins.

Szmigin, I.; Canning, L.; Reppel, A. E. (2005). Online community: enhancing the relationship marketing concept through customer bonding. International Journal of Service Industry Management, Volume 16, Number 5, pp. 480-496(17).

Thompson C. J., Troester Maura (2002). Consumer Value Systems in the Age of Postmodern Fragmentation: The Case of the Natural Health Microculture, Journal of Consumer Research, 28 (March), 550-571.

Thompson, C. J. (1997). Interpreting Consumers: A Hermeneutical Framework for Deriving Marketing Insights from the Texts of Consumers' Consumption Stories, Journal of Marketing Research, 34 (November), 438-455.

Tornow, W. W., J. W. Wiley (1991). Service Quality and Management Practices: A Look at Employee Attitudes, Customer Satisfaction, and Bottom-Line Consequences, Human Resource Planning, 14 (2), 105-15.

Wallendorf, M., R. W. Belk (1989). Assessing Trustworthiness in Naturalistic Consumer Research, in Interpretive Consumer Research, ed. Elizabeth C. Hirschman, Provo, UT: Association for Consumer Research, 69-84.

244

Ward K. J. (1999). The Cyber-Ethnographic (Re)Construction of Two Feminist Online Communities, Sociological Research Online, 4 (1), http://www.socresonline.org.uk/socresonline/4/1/ward.html

Weber, M. (1978). Economy and Society. An Outline of Interpretative Society. University of California Press. Berkeley.

Wellman B., Gulia Milena (1999), Virtual Communities as Communities, Net Surfers Don't Ride Alone, in Marc A. Smith and Peter Kollock (ed.), Communities in Cyberspace, Routledge, London, 167-194.

Wells, W., D. Tigert (1971). Activities, Interests and Opinions, Journal of Advertising Research, 11: 27-35.

Wentzel K. E. (2006). United States: Northern California Court To Decide Whether Employees Can Anonymously Reveal Company Trade Secrets In Web Postings. 30 August http://www.mondaq.com/article.asp?articleid=42480&searchresults=1

Werner, O., G.M. Schoepfle. (1987). Systematic fieldwork: Ethnographic analysis and data management. Sage Publications, Newbury Park, California.

White, Erin (1999). Chatting' a Singer Up the Pop Charts: How Music Marketers Used The Web to Generate Buzz Before an Album Debuted, Wall Street Journal, October 5, B1, B4.

Zeithaml, Valarie A., and Mary J. Bitner (2003), Services Marketing: Integrating Customer Focus across the Firm. (3rd ed.). New York: McGraw-Hill Irwin.

Appendix 1.

Brand Community Questionnaire

Dear Respondent, I came across your postings on [Community Name]. I am a doctoral student at XXX University, and I am conducting research studying customer participation in online communities. Since you are a regular user of this online community, I would be very grateful if you could take some time to discuss your experiences and opinions regarding this community. Please note that I am not trying to sell you anything, nor am I going to collect any personal information from you. My goal is only to conduct academic research, which has no commercial purposes.

Do you have any questions?

I will now ask you a number of questions regarding this community

1. When did you first join this customer community?

2. Why did you join it?

3. Do you really think of this group as a "community"? [Probe and ask for details behind their response]

4. How did you discover this community?

5. What do you like most about this community? [Probe and ask for details behind their response]

6. What don't you like about it? [Probe and ask for details behind their response]

7. What sort of things do you talk about in the community with others? [Probe and ask for details behind their response]

8. How is your relationship with other members of the community? (For example, would you consider any of them to be friends)? [Probe and ask for details behind their response]

9. Do you consider all community members to be similar to each other? [Probe and ask for details behind their response]

Next, I will now ask you a few questions regarding [company name]'s role in the community

10. If this community were organized by the company, would you do anything differently? If yes, what?

11.   Would you feel less or more comfortable if this community was organized by [company name]? [Probe and ask the reasons for their response]

12.   Do you think [company name] employees should participate in this community? [Probe and ask the reasons for their response]

13.   In your opinion, does [company name] value all members that belong to this community to the same extent? [Probe and ask the reasons for their response]

14.   How has participating in the community influenced your relationship with [brand name]? [Probe and ask the reasons for their response]

15.   How has participating in this community influenced your relationship with competing brands? [Probe and ask the reasons for their response]

16.   Do you use the community to get hidden information such as tricks or deceits about a product? [Probe and ask for details behind their response]

17.   Do you use the community to know when the company will launch a new product or release a new version? [Probe and ask for details behind their response]

18.   Do you use the "unofficial" community to get something for free such as gadgets or information that in the "official" community you have to pay? [Probe and ask for details behind their response]

19.   Do you trust more information you get in the "official"or "unofficial"community? [Probe and ask for details behind their response] (Probe and ask for details…for example…In particular, which one do you trust more about technical problems you need to resolve? And which one about product reviews? Which one about people you interact with? Which one about product reliability and potentials? And so on ...it depends on the type of company and product they sell)

Appendix 2.

1	Coca cola	http://www.cocacola.com/usa/flashIndex1.html	http://www.topix.net/forum/com/ko
2	Star wars	http://www.starwars.com/community/	http://www.starwarz.com/ http://bbs.furryconflict.com/
3	Limewire	http://www.limewire.org/forum/	http://www.zeropaid.com/limewire/
4	Simpson	http://www.thesimpsons.com/index.html	http://forum.thesimpson.it/ (italian, http://www.ioffer.com/clubs/Simpsons-Fan-Club-91
5	eBay	http://hub.ebay.com/community	http://www.theebayforum.com/forum/ http://myebayforum.com/
6	Ferrari	http://www.ferrariworld.com/FWorld/fw/community/communityHome.jsp?language=en	http://www.ferrarilife.com/
7	Hp	http://forums1.itrc.hp.com/service/forums/bizsupport/home.do?forumId=2	http://www.hpsoftwareforum.com/ Miami/index.cfm (co-produced by Hewlett Packard Company and OpenView Forum, the independent users group) http://www.topix.net/forum/computers/hp
8	Emule	http://forum.emule-project.net/	http://www.big-

			boards.com/highlight/866/1/
			http://www.big-boards.com/kw/emule/f/
			http://www.zeropaid.com/emule/
9	sKype	http://forum.skype.com/ http://share.skype.com/forum_links/	http://www.skypeforum.co.uk/
10	Zippo lighter	http://www.zippoclick.com/	http://community.auctionsniper.com/eve/forums/a/tpc/f/295608021/m/161609121 http://www.student.virginia.edu/~programs/phpBB2/viewtopic.php?t=284&
11	Nokia	http://www.forum.nokia.com/main.html http://discussion.forum.nokia.com/forum/	http://rodrigo.typepad.com/nokia7710/2005/03/welcome_to_a_ne.html http://www.phonescoop.com/phones/m_forum.php?m=7 http://www.gsmhosting.com/vbb/forumdisplay.php?f=3
12	Rolex	http://www.vintagerolexforum.com/	http://www.newturfers.com/ http://www.watchuseek.com/rolexforum/
13	Tiziano ferro	http://www.tizianoferro.com/community/index.php?f=2	http://tznferro.altervista.org/frmspc_.html (italian) http://cgi.walhello.info/readmes?tiz

			iano+ferro
			http://eil.com/shop/artistlist.asp?ar *tistname=tiziano-ferro*
14	*Martini*	*http://www.martiniforums.com/*	*http://p088.ezboard.com/fzigysmar* *iniloungefrm2* *http://www.themartini.net/martinis* *message-board.aspx*
15	*Toyota*	*http://www.toyotanation.com/*	*http://www.carsmart.com/content/r* *esearch/forums/index.cfm/action/F* *orums/fid/44* *http://www.big-* *boards.com/kw/toyota/* *http://www.automotiveforums.com* *message_board/*
16	*Nintendo*	*http://www.nintendo.com/community* *http://forums.nintendo.com/nintendo*	*http://world-of-nintendo.com/* *http://www.the-* *magicbox.com/forums/forumdispla* *y.php?f=2* *http://www.big-* *boards.com/highlight/472/* *http://www.gamearena.com.au/mes* *sageboards/nintendo/index.php*
17	*Harry potter*	*http://harrypotter.warnerbros.com/*	*http://217.155.74.1/hpforums/inde* *.php?act=home*

			http://www.hpana.com/forums/ *http://www.hp-lexicon.org/forum/forum.html*
18	*Milan*	*http://www.acmilan.com/en/InfoPage.aspx?id=13131*	*http://forum.acmilan-online.com/* *http://www.milanmania.com/forums/index.php* *http://www.soccer-corner.com/Clubs.Italy.Serie-A.AC-Milan.htm*
19	*Marvel*	*http://www.marvel.com/universe/Main_Page*	*http://www.sketchyorigins.com/comics/forumdisplay.php?f=55* *http://forums.comicbookresources.com/forumdisplay.php?f=10* *http://www.icq.com/groups/group_details.php?gid=11991873*
20	*Play station*	*http://boardsus.playstation.com/playstation*	*http://www.psxforum.com/* *http://www.pstation.co.uk/*
21	*Nestle*	*http://www.forum.nestle.com/forum/*	http://www.forumcommunity.net/?t=1386569 (italian) http://www.mouthshut.com/Search/search.php?category=0&data=nestl%E8&stype=product

			http://www.reviewcentre.com/Nest e__21.htm
22	*Movies and Sony*	*http://www.sonypictures.com/movies/*	http://www.flixster.com/
			http://www.topix.net/forum/com/tv x
			http://moviething.com/cgi-bin/onepagedirectory.cgi
23	*Tampax*	*http://www.beinggirl.com/en_US/page s/expressyourself.jsp*	http://tampax123.tripod.com/
24	*Hellboy*	*http://www.sonypictures.com/movies/ hellboy/site/index_flash.html*	http://hellboyboards.proboards44.c om/
		http://boards.sonypictures.com/hellbo y/	
25	*Bioware corp*	*http://forums.bioware.com/forums/ind ex.html*	http://www.big-boards.com/highlight/30/1/
			http://www.gamebanshee.com/foru ms/forumdisplay.php?forumid=12
			http://www.big-boards.com/kw/neverwinter-nights/f/
26	*Southwest*	*http://www.blogsouthwest.com/*	http://www.epinions.com/trvl-Airlines-US_Canada-Southwest_Airlines/display_~revi ws
			http://www.my3cents.com/search.

			gi?criteria=Southwest%20Airlines
			http://www.rateitall.com/i-6999-southwest-airlines.aspx
27	*Rolling Stone*	http://www.rollingstone.com/community/account/login	http://www.keno.org/Home.html
			http://www.stickyfingersjournal.com/
28	*Adobe*	http://www.adobe.com/communities/	http://www.photoshopsupport.com/resources/forums.html
			http://www.tek-tips.com/threadminder.cfm?pid=229
29	*Java*	http://java.sun.com/community/	http://www.codecomments.com/Java_Forum/
		http://forum.java.sun.com/index.jspa	http://java.about.com/mpboards.htm
			http://www.apl.jhu.edu/~hall/java/Java-Forums.html
			http://www.gidforums.com/f-54.html
30	*Oracle*	http://www.oracle.com/technology/community/index.html	http://dba.ipbhost.com/index.php?showforum=2

			http://www.experts-exchange.com/Databases/Oracle/
			http://www.digitalpoint.com/lists/oracle.html
31	*Python*	http://www.python.org/community/	http://www.tek-tips.com/threadminder.cfm?pid=278
			http://forums.belution.com/en/python/
			http://web.gat.com/forums/python/
			http://python-forum.org/py/index.php
32	*Roxen*	http://community.roxen.com/	http://source.riverweb.com/discuss.index.html?forum=3
33	*Mozilla*	http://www.mozilla.org/community/developer-forums.html	http://forums.mozillazine.org/index.php
			http://sillydog.org/forum/viewforum.php?f=1
			http://ilias.ca/mozilla/forums/
			http://www.nabble.com/Mozilla-f6640.html
34	*Netscape*	http://browser.netscape.com/ns8/community/default.jsp	http://sillydog.org/forum/viewtopic.php?t=9584

			http://ilias.ca/netscape/forums/
35	Boston Red Sox	http://www.forums.mlb.com/ml-redsox	http://www.baseball-fever.com/forumdisplay.php?forumid=15 http://www.masslive.com/forums/redsox/
36	Apple	http://discussions.apple.com/forum.jspa?forumID=1107 http://discussions.apple.com/index.jspa	http://www.big-boards.com/kw/apple/f/ http://www.macassist.co.uk/forums/ http://forums.macnn.com/
37	LabVIEW	http://forums.ni.com	http://forums.lavausergroup.org http://openg.org
38	XBOX	http://www.XBOX.com/en-us/community	http://www.teamxbox.com http://www.xboxsolution.com

Appendix 3. Measures Details

1. Please indicate to what degree your goals overlap with goals of others brand community members, as you perceive it. On a scale of 1-7 (1=Strongly Disagree to 7=Strongly Agree), rate these statements.

	1. Strongly Disagree	2.	3.	4. Neither agree nor disagree	5.	6.	7. Strongly Agree
My goal of sharing information overlaps with those of other brand community members	1	2	3	4	5	6	7
My goal of getting information overlaps with those of other brand community members	1	2	3	4	5	6	7
My goal of getting something for free overlaps with those of other brand community members	1	2	3	4	5	6	7
My goal of getting something I want overlaps with those of other brand community members	1	2	3	4	5	6	7
My goal of meeting new people overlaps with those of other brand community members	1	2	3	4	5	6	7
My goal of participating in	1	2	3	4	5	6	7

offline brand events overlaps with those of other brand community members							
My goals of talking bad about brand competitors overlaps with those of other brand community members	1	2	3	4	5	6	7

2. Please express your extent of agreement or disagreement with the following statements. Chose number corresponding to your reaction. On a scale of 1-7 (1=Strongly Disagree to 7=Strongly Agree), rate these statements:

	1. Strongly Disagree	2.	3.	4. Neither agree nor disagree	5.	6.	7. Strongly Agree
I use functions, such as chat room, or instant messaging, to contact other brand community members	1	2	3	4	5	6	7
I answer a question only if someone asks me for it in a chat or instant messaging	1	2	3	4	5	6	7
I have personal relations with other members, such as regular contacts or online friends	1	2	3	4	5	6	7
I have no relations with other members	1	2	3	4	5	6	7
I communicate a lot with other brand community members	1	2	3	4	5	6	7

I have met people on this brand community who I now consider to be friends	1	2	3	4	5	6	7

4. Please express your extent of agreement or disagreement with the following statements (chose number corresponding to your reaction to these statements):

	1. Strongly Disagree	2.	3.	4. Neither agree nor disagree	5.	6.	7. Strongly Agree
If I need something, I am sure other brand community members will assist me to solve my problems	1	2	3	4	5	6	7
I feel I have to help brand community members if they ask me for it	1	2	3	4	5	6	7
I expect to receive future assistance from brand community members	1	2	3	4	5	6	7
I consider this online brand community to be an important source of support	1	2	3	4	5	6	7
I find the information on this brand community to be personally helpful	1	2	3	4	5	6	7

5. Please express your answer to the following questions (chose the number corresponding to your reaction to these questions):

	1. Strongly Disagree	2.	3.	4. Neither agree nor disagree	5.	6.	7. Strongly Agree
I am attached to	1	2	3	4	5	6	7

the brand community							
I have positive feelings toward the brand community	1	2	3	4	5	6	7
I have strong feelings of belongingness toward the brand community	1	2	3	4	5	6	7
I feel I am a valuable member of the brand community	1	2	3	4	5	6	7
I feel I am an important member of the brand community	1	2	3	4	5	6	7

6. Please express your extent of agreement or disagreement with the following statements (chose number corresponding to your reaction to these statements).

I partecipate within the brand community for the following purpose:

	1. Strongly Disagree	2.	3.	4. Neither agree nor disagree	5.	6.	7. Strongly Agree
I partecipate within the brand community for the following purpose: To get information	1	2	3	4	5	6	7
To get practical advice	1	2	3	4	5	6	7
To get hidden information	1	2	3	4	5	6	7
To know about new product release	1	2	3	4	5	6	7
To get easily what you search for	1	2	3	4	5	6	7
To be entertained	1	2	3	4	5	6	7
To get to know	1	2	3	4	5	6	7

others							
To get something for free	1	2	3	4	5	6	7
To learn how to do things	1	2	3	4	5	6	7
To provide others with information	1	2	3	4	5	6	7
To talk bad about brand competitors	1	2	3	4	5	6	7
To participate in off-line brand events	1	2	3	4	5	6	7
To get someone to do something for you	1	2	3	4	5	6	7
To solve problems	1	2	3	4	5	6	7
To play	1	2	3	4	5	6	7
To stay in touch	1	2	3	4	5	6	7
To relax	1	2	3	4	5	6	7
To make decisions	1	2	3	4	5	6	7
To contribute to a pool of information	1	2	3	4	5	6	7
To pass the time away when bored	1	2	3	4	5	6	7
To feel less lonely	1	2	3	4	5	6	7
To feel important	1	2	3	4	5	6	7
To get information about brand off-line events	1	2	3	4	5	6	7

7. Please express your extent of agreement or disagreement with the following statements. Chose number corresponding to your reaction. On a scale of 1-7 (1=Strongly Disagree to 7=Strongly Agree), rate these statements:

	1. Strongly Disagree	2.	3.	4. Neither agree nor disagree	5.	6.	7. Strongly Agree
I trust technical information provided in the brand community	1	2	3	4	5	6	7

I feel confident I get reliable technical information in the brand community	1	2	3	4	5	6	7
I feel the technical service provided by experts is dependable	1	2	3	4	5	6	7
I find the information on this brand community to be accurate	1	2	3	4	5	6	7
I only trust information on this brand community which is posted by the site's authors	1	2	3	4	5	6	7
I trust the information on this brand community which is posted by other users, such as experts	1	2	3	4	5	6	7

8. Please express your extent of agreement or disagreement with the following statements. Chose number corresponding to your reaction. On a scale of 1-7 (1=Strongly Disagree to 7=Strongly Agree), rate these statements:

	1. Strongly Disagree	2.	3.	4. Neither agree nor disagree	5.	6.	7. Strongly Agree
Generally speaking, I would say that most people on this online brand community can be trusted	1	2	3	4	5	6	7
I believe that other people reviews are honest	1	2	3	4	5	6	7
I cannot be too careful in dealing	1	2	3	4	5	6	7

with people on this community							
I believe that other people reviews will not harm or deceive me	1	2	3	4	5	6	7
I feel safe posting my thoughts and feelings on this site	1	2	3	4	5	6	7
Since visiting this brand community, I feel comfortable talking to people on this site about brand products	1	2	3	4	5	6	7

9. Please express your extent of agreement or disagreement with the following statements. Chose number corresponding to your reaction. On a scale of 1-7 (1=Strongly Disagree to 7=Strongly Agree), rate these statements:

	1. Strongly Disagree	2.	3.	4. Neither agree nor disagree	5.	6.	7. Strongly Agree
The brand community is organized into small functional units such as small groups	1	2	3	4	5	6	7
The brand community is organized in different sections	1	2	3	4	5	6	7
The brand community is organized by topics	1	2	3	4	5	6	7
The brand community is very well organized	1	2	3	4	5	6	7
The brand community is easy and intuitive	1	2	3	4	5	6	7

to use							
The brand community is organized by category and each category has subcategories	1	2	3	4	5	6	7
The brand community allows me to find what I need	1	2	3	4	5	6	7

10. Please express your extent of agreement or disagreement with the following statements. Chose number corresponding to your reaction. On a scale of 1-7 (1=Strongly Disagree to 7=Strongly Agree), rate these statements:

	1. Strongly Disagree	2.	3.	4. Neither agree nor disagree	5.	6.	7. Strongly Agree
I feel free to express my opinions in the Brand Community	1	2	3	4	5	6	7
I feel free to get involved in discussions related to other brands	1	2	3	4	5	6	7
The Internet is a world wide network that should not be regulated or censored by any one country	1	2	3	4	5	6	7

11. Please express your extent of agreement or disagreement with the following statements. Chose number corresponding to your reaction. On a scale of 1-7 (1=Strongly Disagree to 7=Strongly Agree), rate these statements:

	1. Never	2. Rarely	3. Sometimes	4. Often	5. Very often	6. Almost every day	7. Every day
How many times do you visit this brand	1	2	3	4	5	6	7

community?							
How many times do you purchase something on this brand community?	1	2	3	4	5	6	7
How many times do you post your own thoughts and comments about the brand on a web site bulletin board, in a chat room or on an email listserv?	1	2	3	4	5	6	7
How many times do you read others' thoughts and comments about the brand on the web site bulletin board, in the chat room or on the email listserv?	1	2	3	4	5	6	7

12. Please express your extent of agreement or disagreement with the following statements. Chose number corresponding to your reaction. On a scale of 1-7 (1=Strongly Disagree to 7=Strongly Agree), rate these statements:

	1. Strongly Disagree	2.	3.	4. Neither agree nor disagree	5.	6.	7. Strongly Agree
I feel that participating to this brand community has increased my knowledge about the brand products and services	1	2	3	4	5	6	7
I feel that participating to	1	2	3	4	5	6	7

this brand community has increased my willingness to buy brand products							
I feel that participating to this brand community has increased my inclination to buy this brand	1	2	3	4	5	6	7
I feel that participating to this brand community has increased my commitment to this brand	1	2	3	4	5	6	7
I feel that participating to this brand community has increased my willingness to pay a higher price for this brand over other brands	1	2	3	4	5	6	7
I feel that participating to this brand community has increased my willingness to recommend this brand to others	1	2	3	4	5	6	7

Chapter 5. Summary, Strengths, Limitations and Conclusions

The goal of the first research was to contribute to the growing interest, attention, curiosity and comprehension concerning online group interactions in developing countries. First, from our sample, we were able to better comprehend how involving in online social interactions in 7 different venues relates to the member's online and offline social behavior. Second, we pointed out similarities and differences in participant's online and offline social behavior if interactions occur in high or low interactivity venues. Third, we identified similarities and differences in consumer's online and offline social behavior if there is high engagement with the group or low engagement. Through the study of specific differences between online group participants, the contribution was to the promising literature on the effects of internet use for group interactions (e.g., Bagozzi, Dholakia, & Pearo, 2005; Dholakia & Bagozzi, 2004; Flanagin & Metzger, 2001; Kraut et al., 2002; Shah et al., 2001; The UCLA Internet Report, 2003). Forth, many interesting key interactions emerge and were discussed. Many positive effects emerge from group engagement and group interactivity.

Findings have theoretical and practical value. Contrarily to expectations, group engagement and high interactivity are a positive factor in everyday life. The empirical survey based-study found overall support for our proposed sets of hypotheses.

Results show many significant differences in members' behavior online and offline. Additionally, significantly gender differences allow us to obtain a user profiling to have better understand participants' online characteristics.

Many interesting differences between high- and low- interactivity groups and high- and low- engagement groups were uncovered. The following different effects were found in both set of results: mutual behaviors, such as mutual accommodation, support, commitment, agreement and liking, positive and negative anticipated emotions, past and current participation behavior, use of communication media, use of Email and Web, we-intentions, social identity, purposive value, self-discovery value, maintaining interpersonal interconnectivity, social enhancement value, entertainment value, subjective norms, positive attitude, perceived behavioral control.

Many interesting key interactions emerged, were discussed, and showed that the monitoring and management of online communities is best viewed as an ongoing task by their organizers. The most significance of them were deeply and further discussed in the other two papers of the dissertation.

Future researches examining these interactivity and engagement key group differences in a structural equation model may favorably help our understanding of participants' online and offline behaviors.

Assuming the cooperation distinction proposed in Bagozzi et al. (2006), and in Bagozzi and Lee (2002) between fully cooperative, partially cooperative and minimally cooperative group action, other two potential research opportunities emerged about cooperative and non-cooperative social interactions.

First, since we assume high interactivity and high engagement in-group participation, another interesting research opportunity was to study sharing behavior or cooperative behavior in consumer communities. This topic may give a theoretical and practical contribution to the social psychology and marketing literatures, as well as significant managerial implications.

Second, a research should study free riding or non- cooperative mechanism in consumer communities to provide an actionable framework to marketers, organizers of communities, copyright holders and consumers through which to encourage or discourage free- riding behavior in all types of consumer networks. Free rider is defined as an individual who consume resources of the social group interaction without contributing (McKenna and Bargh, 1999). Both these two issues were studied in this dissertation, both from theoretical and managerial point of view, in the second paper.

Another research opportunity required theoretical and practical attention. More developments are needed into understanding offline behaviors modifications in other activities not included in this study. It is noteworthy to explain why high engagements in online social participation lead somehow to more offline activities. Is social group participation decreasing the minimum time to perform some tasks? Or is the web in general decreasing the minimum amount of time to get information, make decisions and perform other tasks? Assuming a positive answer to the two previous questions, they may lead us to include our findings in a more comprehensive framework and model.

For example, can we conclude that both online social group and the web decrease time spending on learning during high-school and college? Can we also conclude that group venues members are more proficient in their education because of online social interactions? Or do they have time for doing other activities because interaction in collaborative venues decreases time to complete other tasks? In conclusion, do we need to assume there are some other antecedents, moderators, and variables not predicted yet that we should include in a model? Following these directions, more developments and studies are needed about this topic, including other potential significant variables in both online and offline behavior.

Moreover, many interactions emerge from the first study. The first topic is consumer sharing behavior. It was studied in the second paper of the dissertation, where we seek to better understand why consumers contribute content, and share their resources in customer communities. It is noteworthy that online sharing behaviour has not been systematically analyzed in the literature. The digital-content and related industries have to further understand the consumers who share files, information, material and so on.

Designing incentives to ensure that online communities are sustainable is one of the most challenging and important problems for these consumer communities. As a result of our structural equation model, we proposed many mechanisms that take into account the needs of the online consumer community (e.g. more new contributions) and the user's personal style of contributing (e.g. fewer but higher-quality contributions versus many mediocre ones). We are confident that the use of these mechanisms can improve the quality and quantity of contributions because, for example, they encourage the members who have a good reputation for sharing high quality resources to share more and inhibit the contributions from the user, who does not have a good reputation. To ensure sustainability, the incentive mechanism needs to: reward participation, discourage excessive useless participation, guarantee a way to evaluate the quality of contributions, encourage timely contributions (when most needed by the online consumer community) and high-quality contributions (from people who tend to have higher standards), make the consumer aware of the rewards for different actions at any given time.

The second topic is online brand communities. It was analyzed in the third paper of the dissertation, where we study firm-managed and customer-managed brand communities of many large firms such as National Instruments and Microsoft. Marketers have become more and more interested in organizing, nurturing, and monitoring such brand communities where their customers can interact with one another. The online brand community, both firm and consumer managed, concept has potentially important theoretical and empirical implications. So far, very few studies were interested in understanding the difference between the two categories and the way such communities could emerge, from firm or customer initiative.

In facts, brand communities are often created not only by companies but also by customers. For this reason, we proposed to explore the difference between the two categories of online brand communities. Both types of virtual brand community present a special interest for marketers and brand managers, since they give new theoretical perspectives and because of considerable, extensive and significant implications for marketing strategies.

Until recently, online communities formed around a particular brand, managed by companies or consumers, have been surprisingly ignored by the marketing literature, while potential consequences for the brand in which the community is interested may be interesting.

In this study, we found that customer-managed communities exert more and multi-faceted influence on its members than comparable firm-managed communities.

Summarizing, although consumer marketing firms have embraced customer community marketing programs, many of them are maybe failing to create cohesive and influential customer communities. They are missing out to dynamic customer enthusiasts and savvy third-party entrepreneurs who have been more successful in creating influential and engaging customer-managed communities.

Online brand communities participation is a great tool to increase brand loyalty, since customers seem to be faithful to the brand and can become loyal to the particular online community as well. However, in customer-managed communities, members engage in broader interactions, and form relationships more than in the corresponding firm-managed community.

Another restraint of firm-managed communities is that they are targeted toward specific, well-defined segments; instead customer-managed communities may have customer groups overlooked by firms. Since customer-managed communities are more diverse, they have the opportunity to diffuse the product to other non-targeted segments with positive implications for firms.

Firms can play a meaningful role in customer-managed communities, because for example about technical issues or brand information people might trust more the firm-managed communities, but they might trust more the consumer-managed communities for people they interact with and about product reviews and for honesty of participants. A synergistic collaboration between official sites and fan sites may be crucial. For their own interest, companies could participate more in the customer-managed community. They should also help them to get their collaboration, for example by financing them, since we discover firm-managed communities are more organized and comprehensive than customer managed communities. A healthy partnership seems possible.

Companies should also be careful of information spreading, since members use the consumer-managed community to get hidden information, such as tricks or deceits about a product or rumours, and to know when the company will launch a new product.

1. Dissertation Strengths

Overall, the dissertation present various strengths.

PhD dissertations are usually written basically for a small community, researchers with the same scientific background as the writer. Some scientific marketing literature being published as dissertations, journal articles and conference papers fail of being comprehensible by marketing practitioners, community organizers and the general public. In this dissertation, I have tried to write papers that satisfies both the scientific community's requirements in method and writing, but also allows people in companies and other organizations to understand and use its content and results. I use a simple, descriptive language and the structure is kept in a way that makes reading as easy as possible in order to allow different types of reader to be able to understand my results.

I believe a strength of my dissertation lies in the quantitative and qualitative analysis that has yielded significant and positive results. In facts, I found significant results in all the three different studies. The thesis results contribute to knowledge, understanding and comprehension on online consumer communities. The methodology I chose seems to be appropriate and rigorous to design the studies I wanted to deal with. The methodology also seems to fit the research questions. I used two statistical software, SPSS and LISREL to analyze my data, since they are usually employed for their flexibility and their ability to manipulate large amounts of data for business applications. Another positive characteristic is the breadth of the array of information I used for my analysis; I do not only used new data and recent data, I also investigated and explore through nethnographic observation into historical archives in many different websites to assess, for example, the impact of the online consumer community in its members.

Additionally, another strength of the dissertation lies in the solid challenge of many preconceived ideas, together with new proposals put forth to replace them, and lies in the way in which I have approached my subject and my willingness to strengthen some parts with further quantitative analysis.

The topic of the dissertation is interesting and I present a thick, broad, and extensive description of the online consumer community process in developed country, an empirical case study approach to them that is under-represented in the literature. For many reasons, the subject treated in this dissertation is very important, as I explained in the introduction. In facts, the topic was chosen because of: my existing knowledge of online consumer communities and the strength of my desire to learn more about it; its perceived relevance to the academic departments in which I studied during the dissertation developments; my ability to employ the proposed methods of data gathering (such as interviews, questionnaires and observations) and data analysis (such as statistical analysis); the feasibility of completing the studies within the time and resources available and constraints.

I have also tried to explain how my dissertation relates to existing theory on each topic. The literature review is not merely a descriptive list of a number of research projects related to the topic; but it shows in each paper my capable of thinking critically and with insight about the issues raised by previous research. I used the literature review for many functions, such as to indicate what researchers in the area already know about the subject matter; to provide background information for the non-specialist reader seeking to obtain an overview of the topic to indicate major issues, questions, problems in the field; to indicate what those in the field do not yet know about the topic in each paper, that is the 'gaps' in the literature for that particular argument; to ensure that new researcher avoids the errors of some earlier researches.

Furthermore, I reported the online trends that will face managers and online community organizers in the future. An important feature of the online consumer communities is their ability to learn from one another, share new ideas, and deliver positive changes in their own organization and community. It is crucial for their success that managers and organizers know the new trends and possible updates.

2. Limitations

Every study in the published literature has its limitations. In my case, the choice of methodology for data gathering and for data analysis was determined by time constraints imposed by the PhD program, in particular for the third paper. It could be improved by developing and empirically testing a structural equation model and identify moderators (which firms are better or worse at tacking the problem of firm managed community myopia).

In qualitative research, subjectivity leads to procedural problems and replicability is very difficult. Additionally, research bias is built and unavoidable and qualitative research is not understood and appreciate well by "classical" researchers. Findings are of course instructive but not generalizable to the whole population. Another limitations is that qualitative researchers cannot rigorously scrutinize the detailed structures underlying multifaceted natural interaction. On the other hand, quantitative researchers can be unsuccessful, because they can neither adequately identify nor accurately measure enough of the variable to understand complex natural interactions. Many researchers conclude that quantitative and qualitative methodologies are simply different ways of looking at phenomena and I used them both in my dissertation.

In the second paper and in the third paper, data were collected by conducting an internet-based survey, which was publicized by posting a message in many message boards, blogs, chats related to the particular type of community and encourage people to participate. The use of an internet-based survey does not permit me to assess response rates, since I cannot determine how many potential respondents were reached through my posts. Thus, the nature and extent of response bias are unknown. Nevertheless, as the number of specific instances of groups from each venue and the total sample are large, I think that the convenience sample is relevant for testing hypotheses, although I cannot make any conclusions as to generalizability. Anyways, the sample size can be increased, and surveying methods may move away from the on-line survey, which may account for a disproportionately tech-savvy sample. In fact, additionally, data were collected at Cà Foscari (Venice) and ESE (New York). Students were encouraged to participate in class and by posting a message in the university's message board. My findings for the second paper are specific to the particular social-cultural context I considered since I stick to an Italian sample. It will be interesting a cross-cultural study to test my sharing behavior structural equation model in another social-cultural context.

About internal validity of my findings, it equates to credibility. To be credible, the right setting and informants must be considered. Furthermore, accurate reflection of situation and informant perceptions are needed. Finally, it is requested that multiple approaches lead to similar results and multiple researchers yield similar interpretations. Further studies could confirmed or disconfirmed the internal validity of my results.

About external validity, it equates to transferability of my results. I need to point out that transferability is responsibility of readers and not of researchers, each reader should decide if my results are transferable or not to other situations or the whole population. External validity should be tested.

What I did in my three studies to seek validity, both internal and external, was to listen and observe carefully, and to record accurately every observation. Furthermore, I used all data for my final report, and I looked for feedback and balance.

About reliability of my findings, it equates to dependability: it happens when different researchers reach similar interpretations, repeated examinations produce similar observations and multiple researchers produce similar interpretations of the same data. My studies should be replicate to test reliability as well.

For internal, external validity and reliability, in the third paper I used triangulation technique of the data to give strongest evidence for credibility, dependability and transferability. Triangulation offers the opportunity to get multiple perspectives of the same observation. The ratio is that the more angles are known of the same phenomena, the more accurate will be the unknown.

3. Conclusions

My findings suggest that marketers and online community organizers should focus on providing the right conditions for consumers to get together and meet often enough for online consumer communities to form, and then naturally exert their influence on participating. More research is needed to determine all of the benefits these communities can provide since the optimism expressed by scholars on this regard. These communities are likely to grow in importance and influence.

In conclusion, I strongly expect this subject to be a vibrant area of research activity, as online communities become more persistent, durable, and appreciated by more and more consumers, as consumers become more comfortable and acclimatized with these environments, and as marketers and organizers learn how to forecast, monitor, and design their communication programs to take advantage of such opportunities. They deserve continued and increasing attention from both practitioners and academicians.

5613961R00158

Printed in Great Britain
by Amazon.co.uk, Ltd.,
Marston Gate.